DoD SECURITY CLEARANCES AND CONTRACTS GUIDEBOOK

WHAT CLEARED CONTRACTORS NEED TO KNOW ABOUT THEIR NEED TO KNOW

DoD SECURITY CLEARANCES AND CONTRACTS GUIDEBOOK

WHAT CLEARED CONTRACTORS NEED TO KNOW ABOUT THEIR NEED TO KNOW

Jeffrey W. Bennett, SAPPC, ISP

DoD Security Clearances And Contracts Guidebook-What Cleared
Contractors Need to Know About Their Need To Know

Published by: Red Bike Publishing

Library of Congress Control Number: 2011923509
ISBN 13: 9781936800995
ISBN 10: 1936800993

ABOUT THE AUTHOR

Jeffrey W. Bennett, SAPPC, ISP has a combined 25 years of security experience and is board certified to protect classified information. He is a former Army officer who has served in military intelligence, logistics and speaks three languages. He has an MBA from Columbia College and a Masters Degree in Acquisitions and Procurement Management from Webster University. Jeff is a featured speaker in many venues including a presenter at the University of Alabama in Huntsville.

To find out more about the author, visit: www.redbikepublishing.com

ABOUT RED BIKE PUBLISHING...

Mission:
Red Bike Publishing exists to create value for our partners, shareholders and customers by building a business to last. This is what we are dedicated to. As the foremost niche publishing organization, we offer what other publishers cannot; focused delivery of industry publications to enhance the professional's skill levels. We do this by writing and publishing superior fiction, nonfiction, traditional and eBooks and providing empowering training resources at affordable prices.

Vision:
Red Bike Publishing will be valued for its one of a kind niche publishing and ability to positively impact our customers.

See more at www.redbikepublishing.com

NOTE TO THE READER

The defense industry is booming and cleared contractors are benefiting. Those who know how to execute classified contracts are in demand. Additionally, the Departments of Defense, Department of Energy, the Nuclear Regulatory Commission, Central Intelligence Agency and their many supporting contractors are in great need of experienced and qualified security specialists, managers and Facility Security Officers. As the industry becomes more demanding and positions more competitive, today's security specialists need to be on top of their game.

This book goes beyond the Presidential Executive Orders and the National Industrial Security Program Operating Manual. Being technically proficient is great, but building an award winning security program gets you noticed. This book will help make the move from being an administrator to becoming the "go to" security manager. Additionally, business owners and smaller defense contractors will understand what it takes to get security clearances and move to the next step of protecting classified information.

Uncleared contractors-for those who desire to perform on classified contracts, this book will show you how to do so. It unravels the web of requirements to lead you to a smooth transition to that of a cleared defense contractor.

Small organizations-cleared employees wear many hats. In small companies the roles are many. Responsibilities and positions traditionallay held by a single employee focused on one mission are instead reversed with one employee performing many tasks. This book can show you how to assign and share critical taskes and keep classified contracts.

DEDICATION

This book is dedicated to the men and women of all vocations and walks of life who defend our country and protect our Nation's secrets.

ACKNOWLEDGEMENTS

None of this would have been possible without the loving support of my family. You have so willingly provided encouragement while understanding my need to write this book. The time involved in writing and editing meant burning a lot of midnight oil. Kathleen, Patrick, Claire and Molly, I love you all.

Appreciation to Joe Farkas, Stan Koryta and countless other Facility Security Officers (FSO) who choose to remain nameless, but have provided excellent technical editing for this project.

DISCLAIMER

This book is designed to give defense contractors insight into the National Industrial Security Program. Our intention is to help defense contractors understand what is required of them should they become cleared facilities working on classified contracts. Any security and compliance related issues that an organization may face should be pursued with the Cognizant Security Agency (CSA), Government Contracting Activity (GCA) or other Federal agencies and legal activities.

This book is meant to compliment the federal regulations and executive orders bringing about the National Industrial Security Program. It is also designed to help the reader draw from experience and suggests ways to improve security programs. Those who are new to the field can use this as a guide, but should consult their CSA. We have made every effort to make this book as accurate and complete as possible. It has been written by an author board certified by the DoD to protect classified information. It has been reviewed and edited by some of the most experienced Facility Security Officers , defense contractors and ISP's in the business. It is reviewed often and revised to keep current.

Not every defense contractor is the same. Classified contracts further differentiate requirements. Each contractor may have a unique mission based on skill sets and core competencies. Each contract has unique requirements based on product and service needs. Defense contractors working on classified contracts will have further defined roles based on requirements listed in the Contract Security Classification Specification (DD Form 254) and contract clauses and language. Specifically, cleared contractors have unique security requirements based on the DD Form 254 identifying the clearance level and classified storage level. The following are two examples out of many possible scenarios:

Example 1: A defense contractor is required to have a Facility Security Clearance (FCL) of TOP SECRET while having a classified storage level of TOP SECRET. In this case they can expect to have employees with TOP SECRET security clearances supporting contracts on site with TOP SECRET work and TOP SECRET information. In the course of their work they will store tens of thousands of classified items. Their security requirements are complex depending on the amount of classified items, level of classified information, amount of international contracts, and etc.

Example 2: In another example a contractor has a SECRET FCL and no authorization to store or perform classified work on site. They require the SECRET FCL for the sole purpose of providing employees with security clearances to perform work off site at a customer location. They will have no requirement for security containers or in-depth security to protect classified information on site.

The purpose of this book is not to provide exact solutions for each of thousands of possible scenarios. There are too many variables to be contained in any one book. It is written to inform and provide resources that the defense contractor can use to either seek additional expert help from the CSA, GCA, Prime Contractor or competent consultant. This book is written to reflect guidance from the National Industrial Security Program Operating Manual (NISPOM), but is not written to be used instead of the NISPOM. Additionally, there is guidance in the NISPOM not covered in this book. This book is written to familiarize and inform defense contractors of NISPOM requirements. The NISPOM is the manual cleared contractors should use to build their security programs to protect classified information.

This book covers general areas most cleared contractors may encounter. It is meant to help the reader determine which parts of NISPOM apply, direct the reader to available resources and suggest general ways of implementing the NISPOM. The reader should always consult NISPOM, GCA, Prime Contractor and the CSO concerning policy and contract requirements.

Table of Contents

CHAPTER 1 WHY THIS BOOK — 19

Introduction — 19

A National Level View of Protecting the Nation's Secrets — 20

Original Classification Authority (OCA) — 21

Facility Security Officer (FSO) — 21

Threat to National Security — 23

Executive Order 12829 — 23

The NISPOM — 25

How the US Government Oversees Classification Management — 27

Executive Order 13526 — 27

Classification — 27

How The Government Assigns Classification — 28

The OCA Six Step Process — 33

Security Classification Guide (SCG) — 36

Classification Markings — 36

Classification Limits — 36

Compilation — 37

Challenges to Classification — 37

Derivative Classification — 38

Protection of Classified Information — 38

Summary — 39

Problems — 40

Resources — 41

CHAPTER 2 THE FACILITY SECURITY OFFICER — 43

Introduction — 43

The Facility Security Officer and Security Clearances — 43

Creating a Security Conscious enterprise — 45

Reporting Structure — 47

DD Form 254 — 49

Managing Classified Information — 49

How to Conduct the Risk Assessment — 50

Identifying what needs to be protected — 51

Identifying the Risk to Classified Information — 51

Assessing Probability of Occurrence — 52

Assessing Impact of Threat to Classified Information — 53

Make a Determination 54

Focused Effort Based on NISPOM Structure 55

Summary 57

Problems 58

Resources **58**

CHAPTER 3 SECURITY CLEARANCES **59**

Introduction 59

Facility Security Clearances 59

How Uncleared Facilities can Win Classified Contracts 59

Requirements for obtaining an FCL **60**

The Investigation Process 61

Oversight **62**

Required Government Forms 62

Granting FCLs 64

Personnel Security Clearances (PCL) 65

The Continuous Evaluation Process 72

The Adjudicative Process 72

Summary 74

Problems 75

Resources 75

Helpful Websites: 76

CHAPTER 4 CONTRACTING PROCEDURES **77**

Introduction 77

Identifying Customer Requirements 77

Interpreting Requirements in the DD Form 254 and NISPOM 80

Interpreting the DD Form 254 81

Summary 96

Problems 96

Resources 97

Helpful Websites 98

CHAPTER 5 RECEIVING CLASSIFIED MATERIAL **99**

Introduction 99

The Information Management System (IMS) 99

Centralized Classified Information Processing 100

Reporting Security Violations 101

Train Cleared Employees How to Introduce Classified Information 101

Restrict Flow of Visitor Traffic   102

Inspecting Classified Information Deliveries   102

Reporting Requirements   106

Safeguarding the Classified Information   107

Summary   111

Problems   111

Resources   112

CHAPTER 6 MARKING CLASSIFIED MATERIAL   **113**

Introduction   113

Guidance for Marking Classified Material   113

Downgrade and Declassification   115

Marking a Sample Classified Document   117

Special Handling   118

Marking Classified Information   118

Caution   119

Reminders   120

Simple Solutions   120

Types of Classification Markings   120

Identification Marking   121

Page Marking   122

Component Marking   122

Portion Marking   122

Derivative Marking   124

Previous Classification Guidance   127

When to apply classification markings   128

Alternative Marking Methods   129

Transmittal Papers   130

Compilation   131

Training Aids   131

Declassifying Information   131

Upgrading Information   133

Challenging Classified Material   134

Summary   135

Problems   135

Resources   137

CHAPTER 7 CLASSIFIED INFORMATION   **139**

Introduction   139
Protect Oral Transmission   139
Meetings and Visits   140
End of day security checks   140
Non-possessing Facilities   140

Possessing Facilities   141
Magnets and Reminders   142
Other Inspection   142
Develop emergency procedures to protect classified information   143
Classified Information Accountability Process   144
Information Management Systems (IMS)   146
Working Papers   146
Classified Material Storage   147
Classified Reproduction   147
Restricted Areas   149
Closed Areas   151
Vaults   152
Security Containers, Locks and Combinations   152
Key and Combination Control   153
Keyed Locks   156
Access to Classified Information   157
Security Awareness Training   157
Threat Awareness   158
Defensive Security Briefing   158
Reporting   159
Task Oriented   159
Summary   160
Problems   160
References   161

CHAPTER 8 CLASSIFIED COMPUTER SECURITY   **163**

Introduction   163
Government Certifications and Approvals   163
Required Audits   164
Accreditation   165
Certification   166

The ISSM   167
Designated IS Users   168
Security and Protection Requirements   168
Cleaning and Sanitization   169
Inspections   171
Identification and Authentication   171
Audits   172
How to Use Identification and Authentication   172
Passwords   173
Maintenance of IS   173
Personnel and Physical Security Measures   174
Configuration Management   174
Protection Levels   175
Audit capability   177
Data Backup   178
Data Transmission   178
Access Controls   179
Identification and Authentication (I&A)   180
Resource Controls   181
Session Controls   181
Security Documentation   182
Separation of Function   183
System Recovery   183
System Assurance   183
Security Testing   183
Summary   184
Questions   185
Resources   186
Helpful Websites   189
CHAPTER 9 REMOVING CLASSIFIED MATERIAL   **191**
Introduction   191
Accountability   192
Classified Information Dissemination Process   192
Classified Material Preparation for Shipment   193
Alternate wrappings   196
Transmitting material by classification level within the U.S. and Territories-

Overview   198
TOP SECRET   198
SECRET   198
CONFIDENTIAL   198
Transmitting material within the U.S. and Territories In Detail   199
TOP SECRET   199
SECRET   200
CONFIDENTIAL   202
Destruction of Classified Material   210
Approved Destruction Methods   211
Summary   211
Review Questions   211
Resources   212
CHAPTER 10 TRAINING AND REPORTING   **215**
Introduction   215
Briefings   219
Initial Security Briefings   219
Annual Refresher Training   **223**
Reporting Security Violations   228
Security Through Walking Around   232
Investigating Security Violations   234
Summary   236
Problems   237
References   238
Helpful Websites   238
CHAPTER 11 INTERNATIONAL OPERATIONS   **239**
Introduction   239
Determining Export Jurisdiction   240
State Department Jurisdiction   242
Commerce Department Jurisdiction   244
Plan Ahead   244
What is a US Person?   **246**
Technology Transfer   247

Foreign Travel   248
Classified Information Disclosure   249

When Classified Transfer is Authorized 250

Approved classified gatherings 251

Visits by Non-US Persons 251

Temporary Exports 251

Commercial Arrangements 252

Subcontracting 252

International Transfer 253

Foreign Government Information 255

Classified Visits 257

Summary 260

Problems 260

Resources 261

Helpful Websites 263

CHAPTER 12 PUTTING IT ALL TOGETHER **265**

Introduction 265

FSO Qualities 265

Appointing The Wrong FSO 266

Appointing the Right FSO 267

Corporate Culture 269

Metrics 270

Convergence 280

Preparing for Growth 284

Summary 286

Problems **286**

References 287

Helpful Websites: 287

CHAPTER 13 CAREER ADVANCEMENT **289**

Introduction 289

Potential for Security Clearance Required Jobs 290

Becoming A Cleared Contractor 290

Becoming a Cleared Security Professionals 291

Industry Sponsored Certification 300

Industrial Security Professional Certification (ISP) 301

Other certification 303

Certified Protection Professional 304

Certified Professional Investigator 304

Physical Security Professional   305
Certified Information Systems Security Professional   305
OPSEC Professionals Society   306
Summary   306
Resources   307
Helpful Websites   307

APPENDIX A   HOW TO PREPARE FOR A DEFENSE SECURITY SERVICES (DSS) INSPECTION   **309**

APPENDIX B DEFINITIONS   **313**

APPENDIX C ACRONYMS   **319**

INDEX   **321**

ABOUT RED BIKE PUBLISHING   **331**

CHAPTER 1 WHY THIS BOOK

INTRODUCTION

D
efense contractors who desire to perform on classified contracts do not always know where to go to find information on
what might be expected of them. Some might purposefully
bid for classified contracts while others find that contracts beginning
as unclassified may become classified at a later time, leaving them with
a steep learning curve. The leadership of companies not experienced in
working with classified contracts may not know where to look for information or gain access to training or possible expenses until after the
Government grants their facility and personnel security clearances.

There are numerous training opportunities within the industrial
security community, government services, and professional organizations. However, other than government regulations, there are few published books addressing the subject. This book is intended to provide
answers that help those who would like to know more about what it
takes to get a clearance and prepare for work on classified contracts.
It will assist the college student studying security, upstart companies
looking for classified work, and new industrial security employees with
understanding the fundamental demands of a new career. The following chapters will teach about Original Classification Authorities
(OCA), the qualifications and reasons for classification, how to get security clearances and how to protect classified information.

A defense contractor is a business entity that has registered to bid
on government contracts. A cleared contractor is a defense contractor
that has been granted a facility security clearance, authorizing them

to perform on classified contracts. This book's purpose is to equip the defense contractor with some knowledge of what it takes to work on classified contracts and protect classified material. The reader will also learn about resources available to help them protect our nation's secrets and become value added employees in their organizations. The cleared contractor's designated Facility Security Officer (FSO) is the front line in any enterprise working with classified materials and is responsible for security awareness training and prevention of unauthorized disclosure of Government secrets.

A National Level View of Protecting the Nation's Secrets

Under the National Industrial Security Program (NISP), the Department of Defense, Department of Energy, Director of National Intelligence, the Nuclear Regulatory Commission and their cleared contractors are charged with protecting classified information. Classified information is US Government material, documents, software, hardware, or any other official information in any other format that requires protection from unauthorized disclosure. Unauthorized disclosure could cause damage to national security.

Each of the above mentioned government agencies are also known as Cognizant Security Agencies (CSA) and each has established guidelines for protecting classified information and ensuring compliance. Though each agency has its own written guidelines, the NISP ensures that each follows a national standard. The CSAs have Cognizant Security Offices (CSO) that take care of administrative functions. The CSAs are identified with their CSOs as follows:

- CSA: Department of Defense
  - CSO: Defense Security Services (DSS)
- CSA: Department of Energy
  - CSO: Department of Energy Field Offices Safeguards and Security Divisions
- CSA: Central Intelligence Agency
  - CSO: Contract Officer's Security Representative (COSR)

- CSA: Nuclear Regulatory Commission
  - CSO: US Nuclear Regulatory Commission

This book addresses protection of classified information in the Department of Defense (DoD) and their contractors. The DoD is a CSA and DSS is the CSO. Guidelines for protecting classified information are found in the National Industrial Security Program Operating Manual (NISPOM). The NISPOM provides oversight and inspection guidelines to ensure classified information is not disclosed in an unauthorized manner. It is provided under Presidential Executive Order 12829 and under the authority of Department of Defense Directive 5220.22, National Industrial Security Program. The NISPOM provides guidance for protecting classified information and ensures that holders of classified information should be able to produce the classified information within a reasonable amount of time [1]. The loss, compromise or suspected compromise of classified information should be investigated and reported. Loss, compromise or suspected compromise could occur without proper control, accountability, and documentation of classified information.

Original Classification Authority (OCA)

An original classification authority (OCA) follows a six step process that determines sensitivity, demonstrates the level of damage to national security and communicates that classification level. The OCA assigns classification to qualifying equipment, documents, tools, pictures, software, and other items that need protection against unauthorized disclosure. For the purposes of this book, we will refer to classified items of all configurations and media as classified information.

Facility Security Officer (FSO)

Because this book is about performing on classified projects, the emphasis is on the FSO. Why all the emphasis an FSO while addressing the NISP? Because FSOs are a large part of the process at cleared defense contractors. The appointment of an FSO is required for the establishment of a Facility Security Clearance (FCL). Classified contract awards are dependent upon the FSO. Defense contractor organizations trying to get or are in the process of obtaining an FCL and Personnel Security Clearance (PCL), or are currently performing on classified contracts, appoint a cleared employee to perform. Employees who need a clearance rely on the FSO to initiate the clearance, answer questions about security clearances and lead the continuous evaluation process. The FSO is going to make or break the cleared contractor's security clearance eligibility. Security clearances and FSOs go hand in hand; one does not go without the other.

Cleared contractors falling under the NISPOM are required to appoint a FSO to design and implement a security program to protect classified information. DSS provides mandatory training and offers other helpful topical training for the FSO. Training punctuates the serious implications of losing accountability. In cases of security incidents involving classified information, FSOs initiate a targeted preliminary inquiry to determine whether or not a loss, compromise or suspected compromise occurred. When loss, compromise or suspected compromise cannot be ruled out, the FSO reports it to DSS. Loss, compromise or suspected compromise of classified information can cause damage to national security, lead to reduced company profits or loss of the contract and or criminal penalties.

Someone in the cleared contractor must be appointed as the FSO. The FSO must complete mandatory training either designed for working in possessing or non-possessing facilities. A possessing facility is approved for storing classified information on site. A non possessing facility is not authorized to store or classified information on site and work is usually performed at other approved locations. In either case, the FSO establishes and continuously ensures classified information is protected by properly identifying, handling, transmitting, and destroying it. Additional training includes: personnel security, safeguarding classified material, risk management, international security operations and much more.

This book addresses situations where designated FSOs are full time security employees or are designated responsibilities in addition to their regular job description. In many cases human resources personnel, executive assistants, engineers, business developers, owners, presidents, contracts managers or other cleared employees perform FSO functions as an additional duty. They may not have the luxury of dedicating as much time to managing classified information as does a full time FSO.

Threat to National Security

For over 18 years John A. Walker, Jr. had sold secrets during and after his career in the Navy. Though entrusted with a security clearance and a "need-to-know", he began to violate the trustworthiness his thorough background investigation deemed him worthy. He took advantage of his position and responsibilities to smuggle classified information to his Russian connections.

During the investigation into his arrest, authorities discovered a complex spy ring consisting of family members and other recruited operatives. Walker had influenced some family members to help commit one of the most notorious of all espionage cases. As a result of his crimes, he received a two life terms plus 10 year, his son received 25 years and the damage to the US national security was tremendous [2.]

The ignored indicators of espionage activities as in the case of Walker and others are enlightening. Properly trained and alert cleared employees should be part of the countermeasures implemented to help identify attempts of espionage. The safeguarding procedures, security awareness training and documentation required by the NISP should be applied to protect assets and recognize and prevent future instances of costly espionage.

Executive Order 12829

The US Government awards contracts, grants and licenses to defense contractors in the course of providing a product or service. The contracts, grants and licenses may be classified in nature. The NISP is designed to protect classified government information that is released to cleared contractors. The result is a partnership between the government and the cleared contractor to protect the classified information at the level the government has determined it to be.

On Friday January 6, 1993, the President of the United States signed Executive Order (EO) 12829, establishing the NISP. The NISP gives guidance, training and directives that those in industrial security should use to better protect classified materials. It also creates agencies that have oversight of contractors performing on classified contracts.

The NISP's purpose is to safeguard classified information that has been or may be released to "...current, prospective, or former contractors, licensees, or grantees of United States agencies". It is also designed to provide for the protection of classified material as outlined in EO 12356 and the Atomic Energy Act of 1954, as Amended [3].

The implementing and monitoring of the NISP is granted to the Director of the Information Security Oversight Office (ISOO), under the guidance of the National Security Council (NSC). While the NSC provides policy and direction, the ISOO is the operations unit. As such, the Director of ISOO provides guidelines to industry for how classified information is designated and proper classification markings.

EO 12829 also provides guidance for safeguarding classified information, required security education topics and training programs. The ISOO monitors NISP compliance and gives contractors guidance for self-inspection programs. The director has many other responsibilities while working with other agencies to develop directives for implementation; reviewing and modifying regulations; overseeing compliance; inspecting and conducting on-site review of cleared contractors who have access to or store classified information; reporting violations to heads of agencies or the senior official designated; addressing issues and complaints concerning the NISP and report annually to the President through the NSC [4].

The NISP also establishes the National Industrial Security Program Policy Advisory Committee (NISPPAC). This NISPPAC is designed to represent the departments and agencies affected by the NISP and is chaired by the Director of ISOO. Together they work to advise departments and the President on matters concerning the NISP, recommend changes to policies identified in the executive orders and discuss policy issues in dispute.

The NISPOM

The members of the NISPPAC are both government and contractor representatives. The Administrator of General Services supports the committee with resources to include facilities and staff. The EO requires that the Secretary of Defense work with the Secretary of Energy, the Nuclear Regulatory Commission and the Director of Central Intelligence to issue and maintain the NISPOM [5.]

The agencies have sections included in the NISPOM. For example, the Secretary of Energy and the Nuclear Regulatory Commission (NRC) will have the lead in detailing requirements for protecting classified information identified in the Atomic Energy Act of 1954. The Director of National Intelligence (DNI) will provide a section for intelligence sources and methods, to include Sensitive Compartmented Information (SCI). However, in this coordination each agency maintains its authority.

The NISPOM applies to authorized users of classified information and equips those working on classified contracts with critical instruction on how to implement the NISP within their organizations. It is up to the cleared contractor and DSS to work together in providing accurate interpretation of the NISPOM to the specific classified contract requirements. It is this interpretation that DSS will use while conducting annual security reviews.

Defense contractors should apply the concept of risk management while implementing the NISPOM. There are three factors necessary in determining risk. The first is the damage to national security that could be reasonably expected to result from unauthorized disclosure of classified material. This book will discuss later the levels of classification that are used to designate and recognize the severity of damage. At this point it is important to know that the NISPOM provides explicit guidance to users on how to identify and protect classified items at all levels.

The second factor is the existing or anticipated threat to disclosure of information. The third factor is the short and long term costs of the requirements, restrictions, and other safeguards. The second and third factors aren't spelled out in the NISPOM, but are recognized as legitimate concerns that the FSO and DSS should be prepared to address.

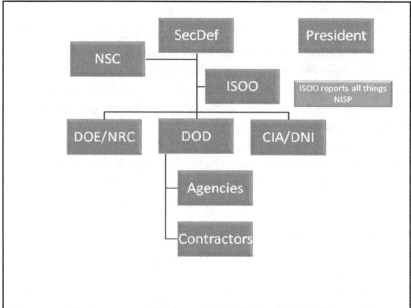

Figure 1-1 - The Secretary of Defense, DoE/NRC and CIA/DNI provide input to and issue the National Industrial Security Program Operating Manual.

The Secretary of Defense inspects, monitors, and determines who has access to classified material. The Director of Central Intelligence serves the same purpose for matters of intelligence and has oversight. The Secretary of Energy and the NRC have similar oversight roles concerning energy. The Director of Central Intelligence, the Secretary of Energy and the NRC can enter into written agreements giving the Secretary of Defense authorization to inspect or monitor programs or facilities (Figure 1-1) [5]. Otherwise the areas are carved out and not inspected or monitored by the Secretary of Defense.

As the executive agent, the Secretary of Defense can work with the other agencies to standardize procedures to help promote and implement the NISP. Without this standardization, the implementation of the NISP would prove difficult. EO 12829 directs the Secretary of Defense and agencies involved to document and account for all costs associate with the program. These costs will be reported through the Director of Information Security Oversight Office to the President.

How the US Government Oversees Classification Management

How do classified items receive their designations? Who is responsible for assigning classification levels? What recourse do security managers have after discovering a classification error? Can anything be assigned a classification level by anyone? These are questions that may be asked by those new to the NISP. Although there is guidance to demonstrate proper control, accountability, documentation, storage, dissemination and destruction of classified material, new industrial security specialists and FSOs may not understand the fundamentals. Executive order 12958, As Amended provides guidance until a new NISPOM is published. Then the new Executive Order 13526 will apply providing the history, disposition and future status of classified information. This book will make future reference to the new EO 13526.

Executive Order 13526

The President signed the latest executive order defining Classified National Security Information in December of 2009. The new EO defines a cohesive method for classification designation, protecting and declassifying national security information.

Classification

The Government has designed policy to ensure that classified material is protected at the level designated to prevent unauthorized disclosure. The President has designated the authority to assign a classification level. EO 13526 defines an accountability process to ensure classification is assigned at the appropriate level and protection is adequate. The person holding the appointed position of OCA has both the duty and responsibility to classify information properly.

Classified information is marked with CONFIDENTIAL, SECRET or TOP SECRET and must be afforded protection at the appropriate level. TOP SECRET has more restrictions than SECRET and SECRET has more restrictions than CONFIDENTIAL. Each must be protected according to the classification markings. For example, unauthorized disclosure of CONFIDENTIAL information could reasonably be expected cause damage; SECRET could reasonably be expected to cause serious damage; and TOP SECRET could reasonably be expected to cause exceptionally grave damage to national security.

When the classification level is determined, the OCA places the proper markings. The markings indicate the level of classification, identify the exact information to be protected, provide guidance on downgrading and declassification, give reasons for classification and sources of classification, and warn of special access, control or safeguarding requirements. According to a report from the Chairman of the House National Security Subcommittee, 10% of secrets should have never been classified and that nearly 90% of classified information has been assigned a classification level higher than required. For example, classified information marked as TOP SECRET should have been marked CONFIDENTIAL or SECRET. In another report provided by DSS in 2003, nearly $6.5 billion was spent to classify information [6.]

How The Government Assigns Classification

To prevent system abuse, EO 13526 provides guidance to train and prevent OCAs from arbitrarily assigned a classification level. The information has to meet certain criteria before the level can be designated. The EO also ensures that delegation of OCA is not haphazardly assigned. Specific job positions are reserved for the responsibility. The OCA attends extensive training in preparation of the responsibilities ahead of them.

As over-classification results in unnecessary costs, under-classification can lead to possible compromise of classified information. In cases where items may be assigned an original classification, four conditions must be met [7]:

- A designated OCA is applying the classification level
- The information is owned by, produced for, or is controlled by the US Government
- Information meets one of eight categories
- The OCA determines unauthorized disclosure could cause

damage to national security to include transnational terrorism and they can identify or describe the damage. National security is the defense of our nation or foreign relations of the United States.

1. Original Classification Authority (OCA)

How is information classified or who designates the level of classification? A review of EO 13526 provides the answer. Original classification authority is practiced by designated officials. These individuals are selected to assign a classification level based on specific guidelines and whether or not the information meets certain criteria. These safeguards are in place for many reasons, including preventing unnecessary classification which may become a burden to the NISP.

The President and in certain circumstances the Vice President, agency heads designated by the President in the Federal Register, and appointed US Government Officials can serve as OCA [7.] Agency heads are responsible for ensuring that only the minimum amount of subordinate officials are delegated original classification authority. It is these Government checks and balances that ensure responsibility and accountability. Classified information should be identified and protected accordingly throughout its existence.

The President, Vice President, agency heads, and officials designated by the President can delegate TOP SECRET original classification authority. SECRET and CONFIDENTIAL OCA also may be given to senior agency officials who are designated by agency heads in writing. The authority may not be automatically re-delegated [7.]

The OCAs attend annual training covering how to identify classified information, how to determine classification level, proper safeguarding of classified information and the criminal, civil, and administrative penalties charged against those who fail to protect it from unauthorized disclosure.

In some cases a non OCA could produce information that they believe should be classified. As such, they should protect the information as if it is classified at the level they believe it to be. The discoverer should transfer the information (with proper protection) to the agency having knowledge and classification authority for a determination. Less complicated situations can be handled at a lower level. Typically, this involves the defense contractor notifying the government program manager or the GCA of the issue or coordinating through DSS.

2. The Information is Owned by, Produced for or Under the Control of the US Government

An OCA cannot assign a classification level to anything that is not owned by, produced for or under the control of the US Government. The work is based on a legitimate US Government requirement. For example, a government agency contracts a company to make a product that should be protected according to the NISP. As part of the contract, the government requires that the company construct and assemble items that must be safeguarded at the SECRET level of classification. The government agency will also provide direction and means for production and security. The contractor then agrees to protect the classified information in the course of the contract.

3. Information meets one of eight categories

Classification levels are assigned to classified materials and information only if they fall into one of eight categories designated in EO paragraph 1.4.

3a. Military plans, weapons systems or operations

The US Government provides instructions for protecting weapons and plans. If plans and operations were released to the wrong hands, the information could damage national security and adversely affect the nation's ability to defend itself. Cleared contractors with responsibility of providing for the construction, modification, repair or other service of weapons is charged with protecting these items at the highest level required.

3b. Foreign government information

An example of foreign government information includes classified documents, products or other information provided by a foreign country government in fulfillment of a Government to Government contract or as collaboration. It is worth mentioning that in many instances and depending on the contract, a company may find itself safeguarding Foreign Government Information (FGI) or information classified by a foreign country. This information has been entrusted to the United States Government and is expected to be protected at the indicated equivalent level or higher. Appropriate agencies describe procedures for companies possessing FGI to include, but are not limited to separate storage and documentation.

3c. Intelligence activities, sources, or methods or cryptology

Sources of classified information must be protected. One can imagine what damage could take place if any intelligence gathering sources, methods or activities were compromised. The suspecting adversary could become aware of the threat and cease their activity or design countermeasures designed to thwart future collection efforts.

3d. Foreign relations or activities of the United States including confidential sources

This information includes US foreign policy activities and sources friendly to US efforts and US organizations. Such is protected to ensure the safety of the relations and success of the activities. Compromise of any sources could cause damage to National Security.

3e. Scientific, technological, or economic matters relating to national security, including defense against transnational terrorism

Unauthorized access to national security related US scientific, technological, and economic data could compromise plans, production, and strategies and leave certain vulnerabilities. Furthermore, foreign adversaries could gain the advantages of expensive US research and development without sacrifice.

A more realistic example concerns Noshir S. Gowadia; an Indian-born engineer was indicted on 21 counts of exports violations, espionage and other charges. While working in Hawaii he had allegedly provided information to a Chinese agent and missile technicians. Through covert email messages he gave information for the purpose of building a radar evading cruise missile. This information gave the Chinese the capability to build a missile to evade anti-missile technology [8.]

3f. US programs for safeguarding nuclear materials or facilities

Risk managers assess their material and facilities. They then identify threats, how to prevent the threats, the impact of the threat and how to reduce that impact. Good security managers work with their companies and government customers to provide operations security (OPSEC) and support strategies to protect nuclear materials or facilities. Vulnerabilities and strengths are assessed to ensure the best possible measures are in place to protect these items. Plans, strategies and programs are only effective if enforced and access is limited. An adversary could use the programs to gain advantage, steal, damage, or destroy nuclear materials or facilities.

3g. Vulnerabilities of systems, installations, infrastructures, projects, plans or protection services related to national security including terrorism

Government and civilian organizations develop procedures for safeguarding classified information. The systems are tough and well thought out. However, the people the system is designed to protect and help are often the biggest threat. Industrial security professionals may agree that the insider provides the greatest threat and the damages are great as the following event illustrates:

In 2001, the Federal Bureau of Investigation (FBI) arrested FBI Agent Robert Phillip Hanssen on charges of espionage. From 1985 until 2001, Agent Hanssen had worked closely with the Russians, providing highly classified intelligence information. Some of his charges included revealing information about intelligence collection efforts, double agents and critical research on the KGB [9]. This information revealed weaknesses in security that had since caused considerable and irreparable damage to national security. Aside from national security, the damages also resulted in prison sentences and execution for Russian citizens abroad. In 2007 Hollywood turned this famous case into the movie *Breech*. The case also provides a training model for many security awareness programs and counter-intelligence lessons.

3h. Weapons of Mass Destruction

Information fitting this category is classified to prevent unauthorized disclosure. Such unauthorized disclosure could make the US vulnerable to adversaries. Looking back in history, we can learn from the events leading to the bombing of Japan using Nuclear weapons. The development of such technical data had been kept secret throughout the lifecycle. Many of the nation's top scientists worked in absolute secrecy in the construction and testing phases. The US was in a race to produce the first nuclear bomb. If technical and classified information had not been appropriately protected, the US citizens could quite have possibly been on the receiving end of a nuclear strike.

4. Unauthorized disclosure could cause damage to national security to include transnational terrorism and they can identify or describe the damage

This is the fourth and final requirement that must be met before an original classification authority can assign a classification level. Classification levels are designed to implement the proper level of protection. It is part of the risk management component of security. The consequence of losing information is part of the categorization process.

The OCA Six Step Process

To determine whether or not information is classified, the OCA goes through a six step process. As a review, the OCA is an appointed position. The person holding that position may not actually conduct this review. More likely, it will be conducted by government employees responsible for the program. If classification is determined, the program will produce a security classification guide (SCG) for the OCA's approval.

1. Determine if the information is official government information

The US Government must own, have an interest or control the information. During the review, the OCA determines not only whether or not the information should be classified, but also whether or not the information has already been classified by another agency. If so, then the prior determination is used.

2. Determine if the information is eligible to be classified

This determination is made based on guidance provided in EO 13526. The EO lists the four conditions that must be met prior to classifying information.

3. Determine if there is potential for damage to national security if unauthorized release occurs

The OCA should be able to determine whether or not the unauthorized release of information will cause damage to national security and be able to describe the damage.

4. Assign a level of classification

The impact of disclosure is categorized from reasonably causing "damage" for CONFIDENTIAL information, "serious damage" for SECRET information and "seriously grave damage" for TOP SECRET information. The impact of loss or compromise of the information must be at one of the three defined levels in order to be assigned a classification. Also, the classifier should be able to describe or identify the damage to national security. This measure informs the user that the information is to be safeguarded at a necessary level and also to prevent the original classification authority from assigning a classification level needlessly.

5. Make a decision about the duration of classification

Once the classification authority assigns a classification level; they still have another task to fulfill; assigning a duration or time period. After the end date, the information should be automatically declassification based on the sensitivity level. This assists in the control of the classified information as well as ensuring items do not maintain an unnecessary classification.

The OCA's are trained to declassify information when classification is no longer necessary. Anyone who has extensive experience in the NISP may remember a time when duration was not always assigned a specific date or event. In many cases classified information had been labeled "Decl: OADR" or declassify on originating agency determination required. This practice may have created a large number of records and documents that needed costly maintenance and control. The EO 13526 designed parameters to ensure that information is only classified as necessary and for only as long as needed.

The OCAs should assign a date or event for declassification based on the national security sensitivity, but should not exceed 25 years. When the OCA is unable to determine an earlier date or event then they will assign a declassification date for 10 years from the original decision date (date of classification). When national security sensitivity requires more time, this date can be set not to exceed 25 years from the date of the decision [10]. Unless specifically identified as exempt from declassification, classified records that are over 25 years old should be automatically declassified by the 31st of December of the 25th year. Information that no longer meets the requirements for classification under EO 13526 or has reached the threshold of the declassification date should be declassified immediately. The defense contractor should contact the OCA or GCA before declassifying or downgrading.

6. *Communicate the decision*

The OCA communicates the classification level through a security classification guide and classification markings.

Security Classification Guide (SCG)

The security classification guide communicates classification instructions issued by the OCA. FSOs should ensure that an FSO is on site for each classified contract or as determined in the DD Form 254.

Classification Markings

Classified information should be conspicuously marked and immediately apparent. These important markings serve to alert holders to the presence of classified information, identify the exact information to be protected and the level of protection required, provide guidance on information sharing, warn holders of special access, dissemination control, or safeguarding requirements and provide guidance on downgrading and declassification for classified information.

Classified information should display markings conspicuously based on the type of media (compact disk, cassette, book, map and etc.). The proper display of classified markings will be covered in later chapters, but this introduction is necessary to demonstrate how material is identified and labeled. All classified information should be properly marked and protected.

Classified information should be marked to identify the classification level, the classification authority, the agency and office of classification authority, declassification instructions, and a specific reason for the classification. Furthermore, the classification should identify which pages, paragraphs and portions are classified and unclassified. There can be no doubt of which part of the media is or is not classified as it will notify the user of how to derive data for inclusion into new media.

Classification Limits

There are restrictions in determining classification levels. For example, a classification authority cannot assign a classification for personal or political gain. It is only to be designed to further national security and offer the proper protection. A classification cannot be assigned to hide legal violations, inefficiencies or mistakes. Nor can the OCAs assign a classification just to prevent embarrassment, prevent or restrict competition or delay the release of information that hasn't previously required such a level of protection [11.]

Compilation

A cleared contractor may find that while working with unclassified information they create a classified product after the introduction or compilation of new unclassified information. In the course of work requirements, they may assemble individually unclassified product into a collection. This collection of independently (or individually) unclassified information may become a classified product per the associated SCG. This is not a random event, as there are tools to help the user identify the probability of such events occurring.

Challenges to Classification

Holders of classified information could discover that the assigned classification level may be inappropriate or unnecessary. These holders have a duty to report their findings. The NISPOM requires the reporting of such discovery to the ISOO. However, such reports can be handled with the agency authorities and reviewed for a decision. Typically such challenges are handled through the government program channels. In other words, the defense contractor can notify their government program manager or comparable technical point of contact.

For example, two similar contract efforts might have different levels of classification. One government contract might be unclassified while the other is SECRET. The contractor could challenge the classification effort through their program manager or government industrial security specialist. The agency heads or senior officials are required to ensure there is no retribution for the report as well as notifying the individuals that they have a right to appeal the agency decisions to the

Interagency Security Classification Appeals Panel [12.]

Derivative Classification

Unless assigned as an OCA, holders and users of classified material do not have original classification authority. Original classification authority is delegated to a select few necessary to effectively and responsibly assign a classification level. However, holders of classified material may be contractually authorized to copy, quote, extract, summarize classified information or label classified material according to source material or the security classification guide.

Creating classified material as compilation or derived from other classified information requires the user to act responsibly by following OCA classification designations. Derivative classification markings also include the transfer of the declassification requirements identified on the original classified information source that possesses the longest duration of classification and a listing of the original sources.

For example, a user is creating a report from two different classified sources. The first source is classified as CONFIDENTIAL and has a declassification date of 31 December 2027. The second source is classified CONFIDENTIAL and has a declassification date 31 December 2019. The new compilation will have a derivative classification of CONFIDENTIAL with a declassification date of 31 December 2027.

Protection of Classified Information

Access to classified information requires authorization based on a security clearance and need to know of the information. Security clearances are awarded based on favorable information gathered from a properly executed investigation. This process can take over 12 months to complete. After the access is granted and prior to gaining access to the classified information, the individual signs a Classified Information Non Disclosure Agreement (SF 312). Cleared employees with access to classified information are trained on at a minimum, proper safeguarding procedures and sanctions imposed on those who fail to protect it from unauthorized disclosure.

Classified information should remain under the control of the originating agency. If classified information is necessary at another agency, then written authority is required from the originating agency. Classified information cannot be automatically transferred interagency without the proper approval. Each originating agency provides instructions on the proper protection, use, storage, transmission and destruction of the information. One important implied task for users of classified information is to properly document its status, manage receipts, and anything else necessary to allow retrieval of the classified information within a reasonable amount of time. In future chapters we will demonstrate how to properly document and catalog not only classified information, but the associated receipts that transmission, reproduction, and destruction require. Learning how to protect, document and account for classified information will help identify and prevent instance espionage, theft and other events of unauthorized disclosure.

This book will demonstrate how to properly protect classified information throughout its lifecycle and provide more specific examples of the proper methods of protecting, documenting and accounting for classified material. This chapter has provided a glimpse into the national level policy of how information is designated with a level of classification and the protection expected by the OCA. Future chapters will help determine how cleared contractors and employee operate under the standards of the NISP.

Summary

Executive Order 12829 created the NISP. The purpose of the program is to protect Government classified information at cleared defense contractor facilities from unauthorized disclosure. The NISPOM was created to provide guidance on protecting classified information. Presidential Executive Order 13526 provides classified national security protection information. It delivers a cohesive method for the assignment of a classification, protecting and declassifying national security information. The executive order describes the authority to classify information and provides strict requirements.

Classified information should always be marked to indicate the classification level. These markings notify the user how to protect the information from unauthorized disclosure. If information has been found to be classified improperly, the person discovering the error should challenge the classification through the government program. Users of classified material may compile classified information into a new document in a process called derivative classification.

Before employees access classification they must possess a security clearance, have a need to know and sign the SF312. Security clearances are issued upon a favorable determination of a properly executed investigation.

PROBLEMS

1. You are the FSO for a defense contractor which is authorized to possess classified information at the SECRET level. Some of the material involves nuclear capabilities and intelligence sources. Which three agencies have oversight of the classified material?

2. As a guest speaker at your professional organization you are speaking on the topic of the NISP. Which executive order will you refer to and when was it signed?

3. As FSO, you are working with your management on a plan to win classified contracts. Explain the purpose of the NISP and your company's requirements to protected classified information.

4. Through whom does the Secretary of Defense report costs associate with the NISP?

5. As a security leader, one of your jobs is to provide annual training to your company. You want to introduce them to the NISP and you conduct a search for NISPOM using your favorite search engine. Report on the various hits with information on who originated the information and the topic of the hit.

6. As the FSO, you are continuing to build a great security education program. As part of the program, you want to help your company understand how classified information is designated. Describe the eight qualifications and four conditions that in-

formation must meet before it can be classified.

7. According to Executive Order 13526 there are some reasons that an OCA cannot use to assign a classification. What are some of those reasons?

8. You are providing guidance to an engineer who is deriving a classified product from three different sources. The first source is classified at the CONFIDENTIAL level with a declassification date of 31 December 2022, the second source is classified SECRET with a declassification date of 2024 and the third is also SECRET with a declassification date of 2029. Based on this information, what is the highest level of classification of the final product and what is the duration?

9. What are the two things must a person possess before you can allow them to have access to the classified information?

RESOURCES

1. DoD 5220.22-M *National Industrial Security Program Operating Manual (NISPOM)*, 1-303. Reports of Loss, Compromise or Suspected Compromise, Under Secretary of Defense for Intelligence, 2006

2. O'Connor, John, *TV View; American Spies In Pursuit Of The American Dream*, New York Times, NY, 1990 http://query.ny-times.com/gst/fullpage.html?res=9C0CE6DA133BF937A35751C 0A966958260, Feb 4, 2008

3. The President, Executive Order 12829—*National Industrial Security Program*, Section 101 (a) (Federal Register, Jan 1993)

4. The President, Executive Order 12829—*National Industrial Security Program*, Section 102 (Federal Register, Jan 1993)

5. The President, Executive Order 12829—*National Industrial Security Program*, Section 201 (a) (Federal Register, Jan 1993)

6. *Too Many Secrets: Overclassification As A Barrier To Critical Information Sharing*, (Hearing Before The Subcommittee On National Security, Emerging Threats And International Relations Of The Committee On Government Reform House Of Representatives One Hundred Eighth Congress Second Session

August 24, 2004) Serial No. 108-263, Available Via The World Wide Web: http://frwebgate.access.gpo.gov/cgi-bin/getdoc. cgi?dbname=108_house_hearings&docid=f:98291.pdf.

7. The President, Executive Order 13526, *Classified National Security Information—National Industrial Security Program*, Section 1.3, (Federal Register, Dec 2009)

8. *Engineer Indicted on Spying*, Washington Times, Nov 23,2006, http://www.washingtontimes.com/news/2006/nov/23/20061123-122450-1979r/

9. *United States of America v. Phillip Robert Hanssen*, Affidavit In Support Of Criminal Complaint, Arrest Warrant And Search Warrants, http://www.fas.org/irp/ops/ci/hanssen_affidavit. html, Downloaded Feb 2008

10. The President, Executive Order 13526, *Classified National Security Information—National Industrial Security Program*, Section 1.5, (Federal Register, Dec 2009)

11. The President, Executive Order 13526, *Classified National Security Information—National Industrial Security Program*, Section 1.7, (Federal Register, Dec 2009)

12. The President, Executive Order 13526, *Classified National Security Information—National Industrial Security Program*, Section 1.8b, (Federal Register, Dec 2009)

CHAPTER 2 THE FACILITY SECURITY OFFICER

Introduction

The NISPOM instructs that senior officials of cleared contractor facilities appoint a Facility Security Officer (FSO) [1] The only requirement is that the FSO be a US citizen and has a security clearance at least the same level as the facility clearance. This chapter provides suggested FSO duties and responsibilities that will compliment these minimum requirements.

The Facility Security Officer and Security Clearances

The FSO has a tremendous scope of responsibility in the direction and implementation of a security program designed to protect classified information. They are the link between the government contractor, DSS and the GCA. A defense contractor may not necessarily need to hire a new employee to serve as an FSO. Depending on the workload, it may only be necessary to appoint a competent cleared employee. Sometimes, the owner, an assistant, engineer, program manager, human resources specialist or other cleared employees can assume the additional responsibility. On the other hand, some cleared contractors may have the funding and work to hire additional personnel dedicated entirely to industrial security functions (Figure 2-1).

A Facility Clearance (FCL) is awarded to defense contractor facilities that have a need to perform on classified contracts. The personnel security clearance (PCL) is also awarded based on the contractual need. Both the cleared facility and the FSO must be US entities and have a history of integrity and conduct that prevents or limits exploitation or coercion to release classified material in an unauthorized manner.

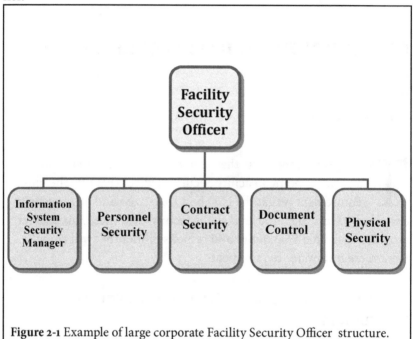

Figure 2-1 Example of large corporate Facility Security Officer structure. These companies can have large numbers of personnel reporting to the FSO or subordinate leaders. In smaller companies, the duties can be delegated to other employees while the FSO maintains program accountability.

The appointed FSO supervises and directs security measures to protect classified information as required by NISPOM. Guidance includes but is not limited to requesting security clearances, coordinating for the approval of closed areas, classified processing, and the proper storage of classified information. Implied tasks include anticipating the level of security effort, infrastructure, supplies and personnel necessary to meet the security requirements. The FSO works for the cleared defense contractor, but the government has oversight of the security program. Any unauthorized disclosure can cause problems such as but not limited to: loss of reputation, loss of contracts, jail time, fines or disciplinary actions against the employee, and loss of security clearance for the employee and the business.

The FSO's security program success depends on developing relationships with employees, managers and executives. This allows the execution of NISPOM requirements found in company policies, security awareness training, volunteer employee reporting of security infractions or change of status, and the proper coordination for the protection of classified information. Any of the above mentioned success milestones are difficult to obtain in a changing employee and contract environment. However, it can be simplified through employee and executive buy-in.

CREATING A SECURITY CONSCIOUS ENTERPRISE

A key trait an FSO should demonstrate is the ability to work within organizational structures to gain executive, manager and work force cooperation. This is critical for integrating the security plan into all business units and company operations. For example, one cause of security violations is the improper introduction or removal of classified material into or from a cleared facility. An FSO can train and write policy but without the enterprise's full cooperation, will find it difficult to enforce (Figure 2-2).

A well integrated security plan ensures that all business units within an enterprise notify the FSO of any change in disposition of cleared employees or classified contracts. This integrated system will trigger the contracts, program manager, business development and other units to coordinate with and keep the FSO informed of expired, current, and future contract opportunities and responsibilities. The coordination allows the FSO to be proactive and able to better support the classified contracts. Having a security program integrated into all aspects of the company produces desired situations and dramatically reduces security violations.

An important task that an FSO faces is the successful implementation of the security program while supporting the company's primary mission; to make money while successfully performing on classified contracts. Security efforts should be risk based and focused while meeting NISPOM requirements. The FSO can direct an award winning program while remaining fiscally responsible.

Figure 2-2 The FSO should incorporate every employee and business unit into the security program.

Companies are investing more in personnel and are able to effectively communicate and realize a return on investment. An FSO with business competency and know how is highly desired. For small contractors, this could mean selecting the most competent employee for the appointed duty. For large organizations, a thorough job description and performance requirements should capture the best candidates. The appointed FSO should be able to safeguard classified material while implementing cost reducing procedures and conducting operations as well as any other professional. The primary purpose of every business is to make money. As such, each employee has the responsibility of identifying new methods, processes and tools to increase efficiency, reduce waste and maintain compliance with cost reduction in mind and without increasing the risk to national security.

The constantly evolving world situation creates an ever changing security environment. Some changes may result in new government policies and guidance. These guidance and policy implementations may provide a changing environment through which the FSO and security staff must be able to negotiate. For the FSO, DSS communicates changes to the NISPOM through Industrial Security Letters (ISL). When changes are identified, the FSO should take advantage of an integrated security plan to notify affected programs and employees to reach a feasible solution.

Reporting Structure

In a best case scenario, the FSO reports to a senior executive. The FSO should foster a credible reputation with management and stakeholders to enable a reporting process and improve the state of security. The senior officers of the company drive the business and could possibly affect classified contracts. The FSO should possess good communication skills and the know how to present information with clarity, reliability and authority.

Large defense contractors may need a structure composed of an FSO with supporting security staff; each employee having a unique discipline. Supporting security staff would focus on one of or a combination of various security descriptions such as: classified contracts, security clearances, physical security, exports compliance, classified computer processing, shipping and receiving and document accountability. In smaller organizations, the FSO could handle all tasks in conjunction with other duties (Figure 2-1).

PERSONNEL SECURITY CLEARANCE REQUEST

Employee:

Title: Business Unit:

Clearance Level Requested

CONFIDENTIAL   SECRET   TOP SECRET

Contract Number:

Justification: (The following questions are not speculative but are based on actual performance requirements.)

DEFINITIONS:

Classified Contract: Requires access to classified information by a contractor or employees in performance of contract.

Classified Information: Official Government information determined to require protection. Common markings include: CONFIDENTIAL, SECRET, TOP SECRET

1.   Is individual required to transport classified equipment/information?
2.   Is individual required to document, transpose or write classified procedures?
3.   Is individual required to sign out, work with, and return classified material?
4.   Is individual required to use classified blueprints to make classified material?
5.   Is individual required to attend classified meetings?
6.   If the answer to any of the above questions is yes, then process the person for a clearance. If no, to all the above, then a clearance is not necessary.

Other Access Required:

NATO	_____	Intelligence Information	_____
Courier Authorization	_____	COMSEC	_____
CNWDI	_____	NATO	_____
STU-II	_____		

Supervisor Request   Date

Dept. Mgr/VP Validation   Date

Date received by FSO/initials

Figure 2-3 Security Clearance Request and Justification

DD Form 254

Work on classified contracts should be executed as specified in the Contract Security Classification Specification (DD Form 254). The FSO works with contracts, engineers, program managers or other departments to ensure that the company understands the customer's security requirements. The DD Form 254 specifies what type of work, how and where the classified work is to be performed. The FSO should review requirements and provide feedback into the completeness, accuracy and clarity of DD Form 254 and how it is applied.

Also important is determining whether or not the FSO implements a plan at a possessing or non-possessing facility. In a possessing facility, classified work is conducted and safeguarded on site. In a non-possessing facility, employees are cleared, but classified work and safeguarding of classified information are conducted at another cleared location. The DD Form 254 will indicate where classified work is to be performed.

Managing Classified Information

Contractors should maintain the minimum number of cleared employees necessary to accomplish the mission [2]. The organizations should also provide personnel clearance justification based on the classified contract. There are many ways to document justification, but an example can be found in figure 2-3. In this case, the manager recommends that an employee receive a security clearance based on a classified contract need. The request is signed by the first executive in their rating chain. Once signed, the request is sent to the FSO. The FSO starts the clearance request process with the justification on file.

Cleared contractors working with classified information in a possessing facility might be required to receive, store, copy, disseminate, destroy, and process classified material according to the specifications of the contract. Control of status and documentation of classified information is usually done by the FSO or supporting security staff members. In a large organization, the FSO and supporting staff can focus on full time industrial security requirements. Small contractors may be just as complex, but again, may only be performed by one appointed employee.

The FSO develops physical security measures either identified in the classified contract or as deemed necessary by the customer or based on an organization's risk assessment. Alarms, access control, storage and closed area or Sensitive Compartmented Information Facility (SCIF) are required for protecting SECRET and TOP SECRET information in certain environments. Otherwise when these security measures are not required the may still be considered based on a risk assessment.

For example, the NISPOM requires that classified information at the SECRET level to be stored in a GSA approved security container. However, open bin storage of the same level of classification requires alarms and monitoring. These efforts are expensive and where the NISPOM does not require additional security measures, the FSO should use the additional security measures based on a risk assessment and if a significant threat exists. Assessment tools can help FSOs make such decisions as unnecessary systems are expensive and cost could be prohibitive for a small company.

In cases where a cleared contractor involves a one-person operation, that person serves as the FSO for that entity. The single employee FSO is as critical as any other FSO. The main difference is that the single employee FSO is the only one who has access to safe or vault combinations and access control and alarm codes. If the employee dies or is incapacitated a backup plan is necessary to better protect the classified material. In cases of sole employees, the FSO will give the combinations to DSS or the home office if part of a larger organization [3.]

How to Conduct the Risk Assessment

The FSO should apply the NISPOM in conjunction with a risk assessment. This helps determine how to safeguard classified information outside of its protected environment. Tools for the risk assessment include police reports, crime statistics and knowledge of threat. This assessment could be conducted in addition to issues affecting life and safety of all employees or simply to provide an extra layer of protection. Either way, the risk assessment is to determine whether or not to provide protection of classified information above and beyond that required by NISPOM.

This protection may also be driven by needs to protect employees and unclassified information and products. The risk assessment should help determine what is needed to protect classified information in all possible situations. In the first step, the FSO should determine what needs to be protected, the second step is identify threat to classified information, the third step is assessing the probability of occurrence, fourth, assess the impact if threat occurs and fifth requires making a decision.

In addition to the five steps, the reader should also keep in mind environmental variables that may produce different results. For example, an FSO in a facility located in a high crime area will have different risks than facility in a no crime area. An FSO in a non-possessing facility will have different concerns as there may be no threat to classified information. Also, more established cleared defense contractors will have different considerations than would a brand new cleared contractor with limited experience protecting classified information. Each risk assessment should be tailored to the environment.

Identifying what needs to be protected

Consider a possessing facility with a contract to perform on and protect classified information at the SECRET level. For the example, the classified information is required to be kept in a GSA container approved for the storage of classified material. The contractor keeps the GSA approved container in room where classified work is conducted. Classified information is often removed and brought to cleared employee offices. The defense contractor is on a tight budget and the facility does not have alarms or enhanced security measures other than a key and lock system. The appointed FSO determines that the classified information is at risk when removed from the security container.

Identifying the Risk to Classified Information

Next, the FSO lists risks to classified information. She might consider threats such as break in, severe weather, fire, employee workplace violence, forgetfulness and espionage. Each threat will have an individual assessment into how real the threat can be.

Assessing Probability of Occurrence

Once the threats are listed, the FSO can check the probability of occurrence by using a rating of 1 through 5. Level 1 could represent a slight risk and level 5 can be significant risk. The identified threats from the above paragraph are provided in the example:

Break in-The FSO pulls police reports based on the facility zip code, she might discover there have been no break-ins or theft in the current and surrounding ZIP codes. Such research can be conducted by contacting local law enforcement or using a search engine. Additionally, the protective measures offered by the GSA container are adequate for preventing theft and list the probability as 1.

Severe Weather-The facility is in an area where severe weather is a reoccurring event. Employees often have to seek shelter against high winds and tornados. In this case, the probability is a 4.

Fire- The safety officer practices fire drills and does a great job at keeping the risk of fire low. However, in the event of a fire or fire drill, an employee may have classified information in their possession. The FSO assigns probability at level 2. Though the risk of fire is low, employees with classified information during and event will have to be addressed.

Employee Workplace Violence-Though a life safety application, such a risk can impact the protection of classified information. When unexpected violence breaks out, the first priority is protection of life. As people react, classified information might be left unprotected and possibly compromised. Violence is not likely, it will be assigned a level 2 for probability.

Employee forgetfulness-The FSO has identified security incidents where classified information has been left unattended during bathroom breaks and over lunch periods. Though further investigation has determined no compromise of classified information, the incidents are severe enough and probable enough to warrant a level of 4. The impact will have to be addressed later.

Espionage-Classified information is protected against espionage. The probability of someone targeting the classified information and breaking in to steal it is a level 1. However, an employee providing unauthorized access is a greater possibility. The FSO gives an overall probability rating of 3.

Assessing Impact of Threat to Classified Information

Once the threats are assessed, the FSO can check the impact by using a rating of 1 through 5. Level 1 represents a low impact and level 5 a significant impact. Let's continue to use the identified threats from the above scenario as an example:

Break in-The probability of occurrence was rated at level 1. Stolen classified information could pose a threat to national security as well as problems for the contractor. The FSO assigns a level of 5 for impact. Multiply the probability by impact for an overall rating of 5.

Severe Weather-In our example, the cleared facility is in an area where severe weather is a reoccurring event. Employees often have to seek shelter against high winds and tornados. As such, the risk level is 4. If severe weather occurs when classified information is outside of the security container, the impact could be significant as it could be disclosed after being transported in all direction by wind, floods and other environmental factors. The FSO might assign the impact level at 5. Multiply the occurrence by the impact for an overall rating of 20.

Fire-The FSO assigns probability at level 2. If a fire or fire drill occurs when classified information is outside of the security container, it could be compromised by emergency responders or uncleared employees. This would not be as severe as a complete loss of classified information so the FSO might assign the impact level at 4. Multiply the occurrence by the impact for an overall rating of 8.

Employee Workplace Violence-The FSO assigns a level 2 for probability. If violence occurs when classified information is outside of the security container, it could be compromised by emergency responders or uncleared employees. The FSO assigns the impact level at 4. Multiply the occurrence by the impact for an overall rating of 8.

Employee forgetfulness-the FSO has assigned a probability level of 4. If employees forget that they have classified information in their possession, it could be compromised by uncleared persons. The FSO assigns the impact level at 4. Multiply the occurrence by the impact for an overall rating of 16.

Espionage-The overall probability rating is 3. If espionage occurs classified information would be compromised by a foreign government. This would be severe so the FSO might assign the impact level at 5. Multiply the occurrence by the impact for an overall rating of 15.

Make a Determination

The risk assessment determines the level of risk from lowest to highest. It is the high ratings that should get the FSOs attention. In our example the risks are from highest to lowest: severe weather, employee forgetfulness, espionage, fire, workplace violence and theft (Figure 2-4). The FSO will then build a security program with security measures supporting NISPOM, but tailored to the facility. They will begin by developing countermeasures to meet the significant threat.

For example, since break in is the least impacting threat, alarms and closed circuit television may not be warranted in the protection of classified information. The protection of classified information alone would not be a justification for such expenses as there is no NISPOM based requirement. If there are other issues such as life safety considerations, they would need to be assessed separately.

From our example, it appears our FSO would spend more time and resources in developing training to address procedures for protecting classified information during severe weather, fire and other emergencies. The countermeasures could also involve rehearsals and other inexpensive solutions.

Employee forgetfulness and espionage countermeasures are almost similar as the cleared employees provide an insider threat. These risky insiders have clearance and access, but because of carelessness or intent to commit espionage they are not trustworthy. Combating such threats include employee security awareness training specific to the problem, posting reminders to cleared employees, conducting random checks of offices and employees as they enter and exit buildings, using a keyword search to check email and computer generated documents to ensure classified information is not leaving through unauthorized channels, conducting robust classified document accountability and etc.

Asset	Risk	Probability (1-5) Lowest to Highest	Impact (1-5) Lowest to Highest	Total Score (Higher Scores Are Greater Risks)	Priority of Focus
Classified Information	Break-in	2	4	8	4th
	Severe Weather	4	5	20	1st
	Fire	2	4	8	4th
	Violence	2	4	8	4th
	Forgetfulness	4	4	16	2nd
	Espionage	3	5	15	3d

Figure 2-4 Sample Risk Analysis Matrix

FOCUSED EFFORT BASED ON NISPOM STRUCTURE

The FSO can focus security efforts and better streamline the security program by determining which parts of the NISPOM apply. The FSO should also understand that the NISPOM is the regulation, but there are waivers available for NISPOM requirements. The NISPOM is a large manual that encompasses many areas and many cleared contractors will apply only some parts of the NISPOM while few may have to comply with all 11 chapters. DSS can help FSOs determine how best to apply the NISPOM within the specific cleared facility.

The risk assessment helps FSOs focus countermeasures to protect classified information from actual identifiable threats by probability. The matrix in figure 2-4 helps the FSO determine how to protect the classified information above and beyond the NISPOM guidance. The same approach should be used in determining which parts of the NI-

SPOM apply to an FSO's facility. For example, a non possessing facility that performs classified work at another facility should not focus security efforts on protecting classified processing. However, they should focus their efforts on NISPOM chapters 1, 2, 3 and 6 parts of chapter 5 and Appendices A and C; the parts of NISPOM that apply to ALL cleared contractors.

The NISPOM's first chapter is dedicated to general industrial security concerns. The chapter is divided into three sections which provide the introduction, general and reporting requirements. Coverage in this chapter includes information concerning the NISPOM's purpose, how the NISPOM is put together, annual reviews, waivers, reporting and other topics.

Chapter two is divided into three sections that cover facility clearances, personnel clearances and foreign ownership control and influence (FOCI) information. In this chapter FSOs can find instructions on how facility clearances are awarded and learn reasons to process personnel clearances and when to do so. Finally, it discusses the factors and procedures to apply when a company is partially or fully under foreign control.

Chapter three instructs how to conduct security training and briefings. It gives detail to what type of training is required and the necessary topics to train.

Chapter five gives proper methods of safeguarding classified information. It provides general safeguarding practices such as oral communication, perimeter controls and emergency procedures.

Chapter six distinguishes between classified visits and meetings and provides information how each is conducted.

Appendix A. Cognizant Security Office Information-lists contact information for the CSOs for the four CSAs under the NISP.

Appendix C. Definitions Provides an alphabetical list of key industrial security definitions. Some terms and phrases have a unique meaning in the context of the NISP.

FSOs can use a simple question and answer session to determine which additional chapters apply to their cleared facilities. These questions are based on the cleared contractor's DD Forms 254. If the answer to any of the following is yes, the FSO can refer to the corresponding

NISPOM chapter or section.

Does the cleared facility provide classification markings? See NI-SPOM chapter 4

Does the cleared facility store, disseminate, or destroy classified information? See NISPOM chapter 5

Is the cleared facility a prime contractor with classified subcontracts? See NISPOM chapter 7

Does the cleared contractor process classified information using an information system? See NISPOM chapter 8

Does the cleared facility have contracts that involve special handling such as Restricted Data (RD), Formerly Restricted Data (FRD), Critical Nuclear Weapon Design Information (CNWDI), Intelligence information or Communications Security (COMSEC) information. See NISPOM chapter 9

Do cleared employees perform international operations, store foreign government information or transfer classified information to foreign entities? See NISPOM chapter 10

Does the cleared facility have contracts that include TEMPEST, Defense Technical Information Center (DTIC) or involved in independent research and development (IR&D) efforts that involve classified information? See NISPOM chapter 11

FSOs should become familiar with the NISPOM. However trying to implement parts of NISPOM that do not apply to the types of classified contracts involved may waste effort and resources. Leading purposeful and efficient security begins with an assessment of both risk and identifying applicable parts of the NISPOM.

Summary

In this chapter covered the role of the Facility Security Officer as related to the NISP. A Department of Defense cleared contractor must appoint an FSO. The role of the FSO is to direct and implement security procedures to protect classified material as identified in the NISPOM.

PROBLEMS

1. Your company president has just informed you that the company has won a classified contract and she wants to appoint you as the new FSO. What are the minimum qualifications that you need to fill the position?
2. According to NISPOM, what are the qualifications an employee must have before being appointed as an FSO?

RESOURCES

1. Department of Defense, DoD 5220.22-M, *National Industrial Security Operating Manual*, section 1-201, February 2006
2. Executive Order 12968—*Access to Classified Information*, section 2-1 (b), Federal Register, August 1995
3. Department of Defense, DoD 5220.22-M, *National Industrial Security Operating Manual*, section 1-203, February 2006
4. Department of Defense, DoD 5220.22-M, *National Industrial Security Operating Manual*, section 2-104, February 2006

CHAPTER 3 SECURITY CLEARANCES

Introduction

Defense contractors are required to have a Facility Clearance (FCL) prior to working on classified contracts. However, they cannot process their own clearances and must be sponsored by a Prime Contractor or Government entity. A Personnel Clearance or PCL is awarded to employees after an investigation and adjudication process. It is the administrative determination that an employee is eligible from a national security basis for access to classified information.

Facility Security Clearances

The FCL is strictly contract based and demonstrates an enterprise's trustworthiness; no organization is guaranteed one. In this section the reader will learn the process of determining facility clearances and how defense contractors qualify for an FCL. The reader will also learn how to maintain the qualification to manage the required FCL and associated documents for future audits.

The FCL is a result of a thorough investigation and the subsequent determination that a company is eligible to have access to classified information. Additionally, if the company is to possess or store classified material, the contract will determine the need and DSS will approve the storage level for that company.

How Uncleared Facilities can Win Classified Contracts

A company can bid on a classified contract without possessing an

FCL as long as they are eligible to receive one. It may be difficult to generate experience necessary to contract with a government customer. However, a defense contractor can team with another cleared defense contractor for sponsorship. For example, suppose a major defense contractor is performing on a classified contract for engineering support. Their core competencies provide much needed results. However, they are in need of a cleared widget maker to make a key piece of hardware. The major defense contractor is familiar with the excellent work performed by a small uncleared defense contractor. The company does not have a clearance but the cleared contractor can award a subcontract and sponsor the company for a security clearance. The uncleared company cannot simply request its own FCL, but must be sponsored by the Government Contracting Activity (GCA) or the prime contractor.

Requirements for obtaining an FCL

The facility clearance is required to be in place prior to the contractor performing on classified work. After the GCA or prime contractor submits the sponsorship letter, the company can begin the process of applying for the clearance. A contractor has to meet five requirements before it can be processed for an FCL[1].

- Be Sponsored
- Sign Department of Defense Security Agreement
- Complete a Certificate Pertaining to Foreign Interests
- Provide Organization Credentials
- Identify Key Management Personnel clearances

Sponsorship-This reflects a need to access classified information. A company cannot apply for a security clearance for business development purposes or to be more competitive. The security clearance process begins with a need which is supported by a legitimate U.S. Government or foreign government requirement and the classified contract will be offered to meet that need. This is in the form of sponsorship.

Department of Defense Security Agreement (DD Form 441)-A security agreement is signed between the US Government and defense contractor. This agreement is legally binding and designates responsibilities of each party to follow procedures established by NISPOM.

Certificate Pertaining to Foreign Interests (SF 328)-Cleared contractors are evaluated to determine whether or not they fall under Foreign Ownership Control or Influence (FOCI) and to what degree. They should not fall under the influence, control or ownership of a foreign entity to the extent that it causes classified information to be in jeopardy of unauthorized disclosure. Cleared contractors that fall under FOCI can still compete for classified work; however, there are measures to be taken to ensure that only U.S. persons control the scope of classified work. DSS and the GCA will be involved in the process.

Organization-the enterprise must be in good business standings and have a history of demonstrating a good reputation and ethical business practices. The company should prove that they are structured and a legal entity under the laws of the United States, the District of Columbia or Puerto Rico and have a physical location in the United States or territories.

Key Management Personnel (KMP)-These are management or senior leaders who influence decisions regarding classified contracts. KMPs can be members of the board of directors, vice-presidents, directors or other upper level managers. Also, neither the company nor key managers can be barred from participating in U.S. Government contracts. A simple review of Federal Acquisition Regulations (FAR) demonstrates the ethics and legal requirements of companies who wish to participate in these contracts.

The Investigation Process

Once a company is sponsored for classified work and meets the requirements as identified above, DSS can begin the process of investigating the business for the FCL. If the company has not already done so, they should to register with the Central Contractor Registration at www.ccr.gov to obtain a Commercial and Government Entity (CAGE) Code. The CAGE code is a form of identification the government assigns to defense contractors. Government agencies use CAGE codes to track and identify defense contractors. Cleared contractors use the CAGE code to search for classified mailing addresses and conduct business with other cleared contractor companies.

In the event of a parent-subsidiary relationship within a corporation, both entities are processed for an FCL separately. Usually, the parent company is granted an FCL at the same or higher level as that of the subsidiary. DSS should determine whether or not the parent will be cleared or excluded based on mission requirements and the contract. If both need clearances, they will be processed separately and as a result, have different CAGE codes.

Oversight

The company being sponsored will fall under the NISP and NISPOM is the guide for DoD cleared contractors. The sooner the company obtains their copy of the NISPOM, the quicker they will begin to understand their expected role in protecting the nation's secrets.

A critical piece of the sponsorship program revolves around DSS having a good understanding of the subject company and their mission. To do this, DSS will review organizational structure and governance documentation to determine which leadership positions can commit the company and make decisions. This information includes: articles of incorporation, stock records, corporate by-laws and minutes.

The senior company officer, FSO and other KMPs, as deemed necessary by DSS, will be processed for a security clearance. This requirement can include board members and committee personnel. Proof of citizenship and other documentation is needed to determine eligibility for a clearance. The other officers and board members may be excluded from the security clearance process if they will not have influence over cleared contractor decisions [2.]

Required Government Forms

Aside from corporate entity documentation; DSS will collect and process additional forms during the FCL process. These forms include, but are not limited to the Department of Defense Security Agreement (DD Form 441) and the Certificate Pertaining to Foreign Interests (Standard Form 328). DSS will advise the contractor on how to fill out the forms and answer any questions the contractor may have.

Department of Defense Security Agreement, DD Form 441

The DD Form 441 is a security agreement between the contractor and the government. It lists the responsibilities of both the cleared contractor and the government. For example, the contractor agrees to implement and enforce the security controls necessary to prevent unauthorized disclosure of classified material in accordance with the NISPOM. The contractor also agrees to verify that the subcontractor, customer, individual and any other person has the proper need to know and possesses the proper security clearance prior to accessing classified information.

The U.S. Government agrees to notify the contractor of the security classification level assigned to classified information. The agreement states that the government will not over classify material and that they will notify the cleared contractor of any changes in the classification level.

The Government will also instruct the contractor on the proper handling, storage and disposition of classified material. The Government also agrees to provide security clearances to eligible contractor employees. Classified contract information is found in the contract related SCG and DD Form 254. The Government will also assess the contractor's ability to protect classified material. For DoD, this is done through a review performed by a designated DSS special agents.

DSS will make an initial determination of a contractor's ability to protect classified information. They will also assess and review at reasonable intervals the security process; procedures and methods the cleared facilities use and determine whether or not they are in compliance with the NISPOM. Typically, DSS inspects based on a checklist and the FSO's security plan. These events are scheduled every 12 months for possessing facilities and 18 months for non-possessing facilities. If the cleared contractor is found not in compliance with NISPOM, DSS will notify the GCA or prime contractor in a written report. On the other hand, if the cleared contractor earns two superior ratings in a row, they are eligible for DSS's Cogswell Award.

Appendage to Department of Defense Security Agreement, DD Form 441-1

The DD Form 441-1 is an additional document used with multiple facility and parent subsidiary companies. The DD Form 441-1 is an additional form providing the government information about the cleared branches or divisions of an organization. These divisions and branches are also included on the DD Form 441 and the SF 328.

Certificate Pertaining to Foreign Interests, Standard Form (SF) 328

The SF 328 is used by the contractor and the CSA to determine whether or not and to what extent the cleared contractor falls under FOCI. The primary concern is always protecting classified information from unauthorized disclosure. As with determining the amount of control a company officer or board member has over classified contracts, the same holds true of foreign entities with which a company may become involved.

In today's changing world it is not unusual for a cleared company to be involved with international business or be owned by a foreign entity. If classified contracts are under the control of a foreign entity, the classified information could be in jeopardy of unauthorized disclosure. If a contractor falls under FOCI, DSS will work with the GCA to evaluate the contractor's ability to mitigate the extent of foreign influence concerning classified information and approve, deny or revoke the FCL.

Granting FCLs

A facility clearance follows the lifecycle of the classified contract. Close coordination and consultation with DSS can help with the speedy processing of the FCL. If DSS determines the company is eligible for access to classified information, they will award the appropriate security level. At that point the company can begin the process of personnel security clearance requests and putting procedures in place required to perform on classified work.

The FCL is a determination that a legal entity is trustworthy and able to safeguard classified information. This FCL relates to an organization and not a physical location or building. For example, a cleared contractor organization can move locations, keep the FCL and the clearance remains in place until either party terminates it. If for some reason the contractor no longer requires access, can no longer protect classified information, is no longer eligible for access to classified material or either party terminates the FCL, the contractor must return or destroy any classified material and provide proof to the GCA [3.]

Personnel Security Clearances (PCL)

The Defense Industrial Security Clearance Office (DISCO) processes security clearances for organizations falling under the NISP. As of this writing there are over 1,000,000 persons with security clearances in this category [4.] According to Executive Order 12968—Access to Classified Information, employees should not be granted access to classified information unless they possess a security clearance, have a need to know the classified information involved, received an initial security briefing and have signed a nondisclosure agreement.

The contractor and DSS have joint responsibilities with the PCL process as they do with the FCL process. Applicants complete a Questionnaire for National Security Positions, also known as Standard Form 86 or SF 86. They submit the application to the FSO who then reviews and forwards to DISCO. An investigation is conducted and the Central Adjudication Facility (CAF) makes a security clearance determination. The determination is then entered into the Joint Personnel Adjudication System (JPAS), the Department of Defense's system where security clearance information is stored. Once entered into JPAS, the FSO can grant access based on need to know and the clearance level [5.]

DSS and FSOs use JPAS to update personnel information. This system allows instantaneous updates of records as well as notification of access, denial or revocation of clearances. At the time of this writing, there are more than 89,000 users of JPAS and 23,000 are from defense contractors [4.]

Not everyone investigated is guaranteed a security clearance. In some instances a clearance can be denied, revoked or suspended. The employee's background is investigated thoroughly for the initial clearance and again every five to fifteen years while maintaining a clearance and depending on the required security clearance level. In the event that a security clearance is denied, suspended or revoked, DSS will also notify the FSO. The FSO will then deny access to classified material to that employee and update JPAS.

Investigation

Prior to granting a security clearance, DSS will ensure the proper security clearance background investigation is conducted. Two primary types of investigation included the Single Scope Background Investigation (SSBI) and the National Agency Check with Local Agency Check and Credit Check (NACLC) [6.]

The SSBI is the most detailed investigation and is used to process TOP SECRET (TS), and Sensitive Compartmented Information (SCI) clearances. The FSO initiates the security clearance request with DSS through JPAS. They then notify the employee to begin the application by completing Electronic Questionnaires for Investigations Processing (e-QIP) Standard Form 86 (SF 86). The federal investigator verifies the information by interviewing references, employers or others who have known the subject socially or professionally. To facilitate an efficient investigation, applicants should complete the SF 86 accurately and completely [7.]

The SSBI will also cover periods of employment and education institutions attended. The applicant should be truthful about the attendance and degrees, certificates or diplomas credited and provide contacts or references as completely as possible. Other areas subject to investigation include places of residence, criminal records and involvement with law enforcement and financial records. The investigators may contact those with social and professional knowledge of the applicant, and divorced spouses.

The NACLC investigation is required for SECRET and CONFIDENTIAL levels of security clearances. Investigations are conducted to determine security and suitability for a clearance, fingerprint classification and a background check using a search of the Federal Bureau of Investigation's (FBI) database. Investigators also conduct a credit check based on residence, employment and education locations. The investigation will also cover law enforcement issues at all locations listed on the SF 86.

Once assigned a case, investigators will use the submitted request to research factors about the employee's life to help determine suitability. The security clearance is not a right, but a privilege based on an employee's ability to protect classified material and not be subject to compromise. The suitability is assessed by a trained adjudicator based on an approved background investigation.

The FSO also forwards supporting documentation for clearance requests. Signature forms authorizing the investigation and fingerprint cards are necessary to begin the investigation process. The FSO collects this information from the applicant and submits it to DSS through the JPAS, facsimile and mail channels. The signature pages are sent through facsimile or JPAS and the fingerprint cards are sent electronically or mailed depending on the technology available to the contractor. Once the investigation is complete and the access is granted or denied the SF 86 has served its purpose. The FSO should then destroy or return it to the applicant. The process of filling out the SF 86 is saved in a protected online national database. The cleared employee can access the SF 86 during the scheduled periodic review (PR).

The granted security clearance investigation is reciprocal and honored across agencies and no additional investigations should be conducted to access classified information at the same level or lower of the PCL. If an employee has a security clearance granted by any agency with an investigation meeting the same or higher requirements, access to classified information can usually be granted without further investigation.

Periodic Reinvestigations

The granted security clearance is part of a continuing evaluation process. Once a security clearance is granted the cleared employee will be periodically reevaluated and reinvestigated if the clearance is to remain in effect. When cleared personnel require access to classified material beyond the scope of the initial investigation, the security office will submit a request for a PR. The adjudicator makes decisions concerning whether or not the subject's allegiance is still to the United States, they can still be trusted to protect classified information and they will still be able to carry out their duties at all times.

The PR for the TOP SECRET clearance is the same level of investigation as was initially conducted. The SSBI-PR is conducted every 5 years as needed. For SECRET, the NACLC is conducted every 10 years and for CONFIDENTIAL the NACLC is conducted every 15 years [8.] Part of the security education process covered in later chapters describes the importance of continuous evaluation of the cleared employee. Part of this evaluation is a requirement for cleared employees to report any information on themselves and other cleared employees that may demonstrate an inability to protect classified information.

Once a cleared contractor determines the employee's need to access classified material, they should verify that the subject is a U.S. Citizen. There are several methods of proving citizenship. The preferred method is a birth certificate containing a raised seal if the state provides a seal. Uncertified birth certificates are unacceptable as well as birth certificates issued more than a year after the actual birth. Supporting documentations such as hospital birth records or circumcision certificates can be used to substantiate unofficial birth certificates. Supplemental information can also be submitted showing baptism records, entry in a bible, and other traditional methods subject to approval. A passport or a record of military service (DD Form 1966) is also acceptable as proof of citizenship. If a person becomes a citizen by naturalization, then the subject can present a certificate of naturalization [9.]

The FSO should submit the clearance request using JPAS and the Electronic Questionnaire for Investigation Processing e-QIP, the applicant completes the online SF 86 and submits it to the FSO for review. The FSO and supporting staff is required to protect the applicant's privacy and personal information from public access. The NISPOM requires that the FSO notify the employee in writing that they will review the SF 86 only for adequacy and completeness. The FSO does not make security clearance granting decisions or pass judgment. That's up to the adjudicator. FSOs simply initiate the clearance investigation through DSS. The notification also includes a statement that the information will not be used for any other reason nor shared with anyone in the company [5].

Cleared contractors usually benefit from hiring employees who already have clearances. This is accomplished by transferring jurisdiction of the new employee's security clearance information in JPAS to the cleared facility. Newly cleared contractors may request clearances investigations for existing employees or well qualified potential employees. In both cases, defense contractors should invest efforts hiring ethical employees up front. Human resources should be involved with the hiring process by initiating employee background checks prior to hiring an employee. Using fair and standard practices to hire ethical and qualified people is a good way to increase the possibility of hiring employees eligible for a clearance. The cleared contractor may have the luxury of hiring a worthy employee and assigning them to other tasks until the needed clearance is granted. However, if the employee is not granted a clearance, the wait can prove to be costly. This is a hard lesson if the employee was not granted a clearance for something the contractor could have discovered using reasonable methods.

Employee background checks should be conducted before any hiring action. They are vital to good company morale, future employee relations, and life safety issues. They can help employers hire qualified employees, but they are not used to determine security clearance eligibility.

Security clearance investigations are more in-depth than typical employee background checks. Investigators report the results of their investigations and the government determines suitability. The results of the investigation are used to determine whether or not the subject is stable, trustworthy, reliable, of excellent character, judgment, and discretion; and of unquestioned loyalty to the United States. The determination is based on 13 investigation criteria [8]:

Allegiance to the United States-The applicant should demonstrate an unquestionable loyalty to the United States. If the investigation reveals that the subject belongs to or has belonged to organizations or individually supporting the overthrow of the U.S. government there is a good chance that a clearance will be denied.

Foreign influence-Ties with foreign nationals are usually not a problem unless the relationship creates a security risk. The employee's relationship with family, friends, and other situations could cause them to compromise classified information. Questionable business partners, banking, investments and other business or financial involvement could cause the employee to be under obligation or duress that could present a national security risk. For example, an employee may be under foreign influence while married to a foreign national spouse with close family ties in an oppressive country. In that situation, the employee could be coerced into providing secrets to spare foreign family members.

Foreign preference-An employee might lean toward being sympathetic to or have idealistic attitudes toward another country greater than that of the U.S. This could present a security risk. Recently a defense contractor cleared employee gave classified information to Israel. Ben-Ami Kadish was recruited by a foreign agent who exploited his sympathy toward Israel. He received no payment, but contributed based on his sentiments [10].

Sexual behavior-Sexual practices or desires of a criminal intent could indicate emotional or personality disorders. Such a person could be under duress, easily influenced, asked to return favors or be under obligation to protect their practices or keep them from being discovered. Examples of risky behavior include: trading sex for drugs or money, becoming obliged to someone to keep practices quiet or a history of arrests for a sex related crime.

Personal conduct-The subject should demonstrate good judgment, trustworthiness, honesty, candor and a willingness to comply with rules. Any behavior otherwise may indicate irresponsibility and unsuitability to safeguard classified material. An example of this is stalking, excess speeding tickets, arrests or terminated from a job for unethical or illegal behavior.

Financial considerations-Investigators will look at financial records, levels of debt or other indicators of ability to meet financial obligations. Unexplained affluence or conducting criminal activities may be indicators of someone who could be tempted to divulge national secrets.

Alcohol consumption-Symptoms of alcoholism, driving under the influence, being drunk on the job or drinking in excess may indicate irresponsibility which could lead to questionable judgment.

Drug involvement-Aside from making poor choices, abuse of prescription drugs is illegal. Inappropriate drug use leads to legal problems, personal problems and judgment issues that may make it difficult for the person to safeguard classified material.

Psychological conditions-Persons suffering under mental, personality and emotional challenges could be unable to perform in normal social or work environments. This could also affect their judgment and suitability for a clearance. Emotional, mental and personality disorders can cause a person to make bad decisions concerning classified information or make them incapable of protecting classified information.

Criminal conduct-Committing crimes or having a criminal record indicates instability, poor judgment and lack of ability to follow rules and regulations. Persons displaying criminal behavior indicate a security risk and may not be suitable to protect classified material.

Handling protected information-Person's who cannot protect privacy, physical inventory or other privileged information may have problems protecting classified material. Employees who have demonstrated willingness to violate security policy could prove a risk to national security.

Outside activities-Sometimes work or activities conflict with the ability to maintain a security clearance. This involvement with outside activities also includes volunteer or non-profit work.

Use of Information Technology Systems-Breaking company policy concerning the use of technology and computer systems can indicate lack of obedience to rules and regulations. Inappropriate use of the internet, computers, fax machines, alarms and networks could indicate that an employee cannot adequately protect classified systems.

Subjects who fall under any of the above criteria will not automatically be denied a security clearance [11.] There are situations where people have committed crimes or used drugs, but have had clearances awarded because of corrective behavior or other mitigating circumstances. They may have sought professional counseling or other types of treatment. Employees who had abused alcohol may have attended rehabilitation. Some may have demonstrated disqualifying behavior because at the time they suffered emotional problems from incidents us as a death or divorce, or the indicated incidences had transpired way back in their personal histories. When considering a person for a clearance, the adjudicator will assess each case based on the whole person concept.

It is important for the applicant to fill out the security clearance request information accurately and completely. The adjudicator will only be able to rely on the information provided in the investigation and the applicant's SF 86. Willful or voluntary disclosure of adverse information can prove helpful during the adjudicative process.

The Continuous Evaluation Process

Cleared personnel should also continue their demonstration of suitability after the security clearance is determined. Cleared employees are responsible for notifying their security offices anytime they or another cleared employee violate any of the criteria. This is referred to as reporting adverse information. Failure to report adverse information could result in risk to national security. On a more personal matter, failure to report adverse information could manifest during the PR. For example, adverse information discovered on a subject during the PR that should have been self-reported, may raise questions of trustworthiness. Self reporting of adverse information demonstrates trustworthiness and helps mitigate the event's impact. Cleared employees with such concerns should seek qualified legal counsel.

The Adjudicative Process

Whether considering an initial investigation or a PR, the adjudicative process requires an authority to consider all evidence and make a decision of whether or not a person is suitable to have a security clearance. The adjudicator weighs decisions based on information the subject provided in the SF 86 as well as the results of the investigation. The adjudicator will use the information to determine whether or not the person is stable, reliable or subject to coercion based on the whole person concept. The whole person concept allows an assessment of many factors that may help mitigate negative findings. In evaluating the relevance of an individual's conduct, the adjudicator will consider the following factors [12]:

The nature, extent, and seriousness of the conduct-There are varying degrees of impact and circumstances of individual conduct. Looking at each incident case by case will provide better details useful in determining whether or not a person is given security clearance.

The circumstances surrounding the conduct-There are situations that may cause someone to take adverse action. People under stress, duress react in different ways. For example, a person is arrested for murder but released after proving self-defense.

The frequency and of the conduct and when it occurred-Conduct may be habitual or a onetime incident. Adjudicators can use the information discovered to make a better determination. For example, a subject has a record of drug counseling from twenty years earlier. The incident occurred in the past and was a onetime occurrence.

The individual's age and maturity at the time of the conduct-Minors are not held accountable for their actions the same way as adults. For example, a subject had several moving violations during the first year after obtaining a driver's license. Incidents may have resulted from immaturity and not a reflection of who the person is now.

The willingness to participate-People can be coerced into doing things they do not want to do. Some people volunteer freely to commit crimes or engage in risky behavior. Both situations are taken into account during the adjudication process. For example, a subject joins a group hostile to the US Government after an invitation is extended; they volunteered freely. Coercion involves a person forced to engage in adverse behavior to avoid certain consequences.

The presence or absence of rehabilitation and other pertinent behavioral changes-Adjudicators may consider whether or not the subject sought counseling or other psychological help with addiction, grief, anger and other behavior issues that can affect the ability to obtain a security clearance. For example, a subject receives counseling to manage their anger.

The motivation for the conduct-The adjudicator may consider the reasons a person behaved adversely. Justice, revenge, anger, self-defense or duress are examples of different types of motivation that can change behavior. For example, a subject attacks and injures a bystander only after friend plies them with alcohol.

The potential for pressure, coercion, exploitation, or duress-There are some situations that can make people vulnerable; peer pressure, alcohol or drug tolerance, coercion and exploitation are a few. These are also taken into consideration to determine whether or not a security clearance and an applicants' situation would create vulnerability. In an earlier example, a subject married to a foreign national from an oppressive country may be coerced to help an adversary obtain privileged information.

The likelihood of continuation or recurrence-Information on a subject is used to determine whether or not the behavior will happen again. For example, a person had been in counseling for an alcohol related event. Both the counseling and the alcohol related event occurred 15 years prior. Since then there have been no further indicators of alcohol abuse. The adjudicator may determine that the likelihood of recurrence is low. Each case will be judged on its own merits, and any doubt concerning personnel being considered for access to classified information will be resolved in favor of national security.

SUMMARY

A defense contractor is required to have an FCL to perform work on a classified contract. The FCL is not a requirement of eligibility to bid on classified contracts, but the process of the FCL is initiated upon award of the contract. A company cannot process their own clearance for the sake of looking competitively attractive, but is a result of sponsorship by the Government or a prime contractor. The FCL is strictly contract based and demonstrates an enterprise' trustworthiness to work on classified contracts.

A PCL is the administrative determination that an employee is eligible from a national security basis for a security clearance. The PCL is based on a contract and the FCL. The FSO provides justification for an employee clearance and submits a clearance request to DSS who then assigns an investigation based on the clearance level. The investigations are thorough and based on 13 criteria to determine eligibility. Once the investigation is complete, the clearance request will go through an adjudication process.

PROBLEMS

1. Aside from corporate documentation, what three government forms will an FSO compile for DSS to begin the process of granting a facility clearance?
2. What characteristics must a company display to qualify for a facility clearance?
3. What determines the security clearance level to which an FSO be cleared?
4. Name three criteria that are considered during the adjudication process.

RESOURCES

1. Defense Security Services, *Checklist for New Facility Security Clearances*, http://www.dss.mil/isp/fac_clear/fac_clear_check. html
2. Department of Defense, DoD 5220.22-M, *National Industrial Security Operating Manual*, section 2-106, February 2006
3. Department of Defense, DoD 5220.22-M, *National Industrial Security Operating Manual*, section 2-110, February 2006
4. Defense Industrial Security Clearance Office, *DISCO Fact Sheet*, https://www.dss.mil/GW/ShowBinary/DSS/about_dss/ fact_sheets/disco_faqsheet.html, Downloaded Jan 2011
5. Department of Defense, DoD 5220.22-M, *National Industrial Security Operating Manual*, section 2-202, February 2006
6. Department of Defense, DoD 5220.22-M, *National Industrial Security Operating Manual*, section 2-201, February 2006

7. Bennett, J W(2011), *Insider's Guide to Security Clearances*, Huntsville, AL: Red Bike Publishing

8. Federal Investigation Notice, Letter No . 97-02, U.S. Office of Personnel Management, July 20, 1997, Downloaded Jan 2011 http://www.opm.gov/investigate/archive/1997/fin9702.asp

9. Department of Defense, DoD 5220.22-M, *National Industrial Security Operating Manual*, section 2-208, February 2006

10. *FBI Claims a Confession in Israel Spy Case*, NY Sun, Joseph Goldstein, April 2008 http://www.nysun.com/national/fbi-claims-a-confession-in-israel-spy-case/75129/

11. Defense Security Services, *Industrial Personnel Security Clearances*, Downloaded Jan 2011, https://www.dss.mil/GW/ShowBinary/DSS/psco/indus_psc_Intrim.html

12. Defense Security Services, *Maintaining an Industrial Security Clearance*, Downloaded Jan 2011, https://www.dss.mil/GW/ShowBinary/DSS/psco/indus_psc_process_applicant.html

Helpful Websites:

e-Qip website
http://www.opm.gov/e-qip
Security Clearances
http://www.dss.mil/isp/fac_clear/fac_clear_check.html
Security Forms
http://www.archives.gov/isoo/security-forms/

CHAPTER 4 CONTRACTING PROCEDURES

INTRODUCTION

The Government Contracting Activity (GCA) or prime contractor should provide the guidelines of the work to be performed in a part of the contract called Statement of Work. A DD Form 254 is issued to describe the level and type of classified work to be performed. This chapter will explain security requirements identified in the NISPOM and addressed in the DD Form 254.

IDENTIFYING CUSTOMER REQUIREMENTS

Whenever the GCA or prime contractor awards classified work to a cleared contractor or subcontractor, they specify the proper safeguarding methods. This security guidance is provided during all phases of the contract negotiations including the Invitation for Bid (IFB) Request for Proposal (RFP), Request for Quotation RFQ or other means of business solicitation [1]. The DD Form 254 (Figure 4-1) is issued by the GCA or Prime contractor and is used to identify the type of classified work the cleared contractor is expected to perform, the classification level of the work to be performed and how to protect the classified information under the cleared contractor's control.

The FSO's role is to work with contracts, engineers, program managers or other involved departments to ensure that the company understands how to protect classified information. The NISPOM requires the contractor to provide input to the DD Form 254 and how it is ap-

DEPARTMENT OF DEFENSE CONTRACT SECURITY CLASSIFICATION SPECIFICATION *(The requirements of the DoD Industrial Security Manual apply to all security aspects of this effort.)*	1. CLEARANCE AND SAFEGUARDING
	a. FACILITY CLEARANCE REQUIRED
	b. LEVEL OF SAFEGUARDING REQUIRED

2. THIS SPECIFICATION IS FOR: *(x and complete as applicable)*

☐	a. PRIME CONTRACT NUMBER		
☐	b. SUBCONTRACT NUMBER		
☐	c. SOLICITATION OR OTHER NUMBER		DUE DATE *(YYMMDD)*

3. THIS SPECIFICATION IS: *(x and complete as applicable)*

☐	a. ORIGINAL (Complete date in all cases)		DATE *(YYMMDD)*
☐	b. REVISED (Supersedes all previous specs)	Revision No.	DATE *(YYMMDD)*
☐	c. FINAL (Complete Item 5 in all cases)		DATE *(YYMMDD)*

4. THIS IS A FOLLOW-ON CONTRACT? ☐ YES ☐ NO. If Yes, complete the following:

Classified material received or generated under _____ *(Preceding Contract Number)* is transferred to this follow-on contract.

5. IS THIS A FINAL DD FORM 254? ☐ YES ☐ NO. If Yes, complete the following:

In response to the contractor's request dated_____, retention of the identified classified material is authorized for the period of_____

6. CONTRACTOR *(Include Commercial and Government Entity (CAGE) Code)*

a. NAME, ADDRESS, AND ZIP CODE	b. CAGE CODE	c. COGNIZANT SECURITY OFFICE *(Name, Address, and Zip Code)*

7. SUBCONTRACTOR

a. NAME, ADDRESS, AND ZIP CODE	b. CAGE CODE	c. COGNIZANT SECURITY OFFICE *(Name, Address, and Zip code)*

8. ACTUAL PERFORMANCE

a. LOCATION	b. CAGE CODE	c. COGNIZANT SECURITY OFFICE *(Name, Address, and Zip Code)*

9. GENERAL IDENTIFICATION OF THIS PROCUREMENT

10. THIS CONTRACT WILL REQUIRE ACCESS TO:	YES	NO	11. IN PERFORMING THIS CONTRACT, THE CONTRACTOR WILL:	YES	NO
a. COMMUNICATIONS SECURITY (COMSEC) INFORMATION	☐	☐	a. HAVE ACCESS TO CLASSIFIED INFORMATION ONLY AT ANOTHER CONTRACTOR'S FACILITY OR A GOVERNMENT ACTIVITY	☐	☐
b. RESTRICTED DATA	☐	☐	b. RECEIVE CLASSIFIED DOCUMENTS ONLY	☐	☐
c. CRITICAL NUCLEAR WEAPON DESIGN INFORMATION	☐	☐	c. RECEIVE AND GENERATE CLASSIFIED MATERIAL	☐	☐
d. FORMERLY RESTRICTED DATA	☐	☐	d. FABRICATE, MODIFY, OR STORE CLASSIFIED HARDWARE	☐	☐
e. INTELLIGENCE INFORMATION:			e. PERFORM SERVICES ONLY	☐	☐
(1) Sensitive Compartmented Information (SCI)	☐	☐	f. HAVE ACCESS TO U.S. CLASSIFIED INFORMATION OUTSIDE THE U.S., PUERTO RICO, U.S. POSSESSIONS AND TRUST TERRITORIES	☐	☐
(2) Non-SCI	☐	☐	g. BE AUTHORIZED TO USE THE SERVICES OF DEFENSE TECHNICAL INFORMATION CENTER (DTIC) OR OTHER SECONDARY DISTRIBUTION CENTER	☐	☐
f. SPECIAL ACCESS INFORMATION	☐	☐	h. REQUIRE A COMSEC ACCOUNT	☐	☐
g. NATO INFORMATION	☐	☐	i. HAVE TEMPEST REQUIREMENTS	☐	☐
h. FOREIGN GOVERNMENT INFORMATION	☐	☐	j. HAVE OPERATIONS SECURITY (OPSEC) REQUIREMENTS	☐	☐
i. LIMITED DISSEMINATION INFORMATION	☐	☐	k. BE AUTHORIZED TO USE THE DEFENSE COURIER SERVICE	☐	☐
j. FOR OFFICIAL USE ONLY INFORMATION	☐	☐	l. OTHER *(Specify)*	☐	☐
k. OTHER *(Specify)*	☐	☐			

DD FORM 254 Front

Figure 4-1a DD Form 254, front side

plied in the company [1]. The FSO should at least review the DD Form 254 with cleared employees to ensure it is accurate, clear and that everyone performing on the contract understands the security requirements. Additionally, the FSO should ensure they receive the Security Classification Guide (SCG) from the GCA or prime contractor customer. The performing cleared contractor should abide by requirements in

12. PUBLIC RELEASE. Any information *(classified or unclassified)* pertaining to this contract shall not be released for public dissemination except as provided by the *(NISPOM* or unless it has been approved for public release by appropriate U.S. Government authority. Proposed public releases shall be submitted for approval prior to release

☐ Direct ☐ Through *(Specify):*

to the Directorate for Freedom of Information and Security Review, Office of the Assistant Secretary of Defense (Public Affairs)* for review.
*In the case of non-DoD User Agencies, requests for disclosure shall be submitted to that agency.

13. SECURITY GUIDANCE. The security classification guidance needed for this classified effort is identified below. If any difficulty is encountered in applying this guidance or if any other contributing factor indicates a need for changes in this guidance, the contractor is authorized and encouraged to provide recommended changes; to challenge the guidance or the classification assigned to any information or material furnished or generated under this contract; and to submit any questions for interpretation of this guidance to the official identified below. Pending final decision, the information involved shall be handled and protected at the highest level of classification assigned or recommended. *(Fill in as appropriate for the classified effort. Attach, or forward under separate correspondence, any documents/guides/extracts referenced herein. Add additional pages as needed to provide complete guidance.)*

14. ADDITIONAL SECURITY REQUIREMENTS. Requirements, in addition to NISPOM requirements, are established for this contract. *(If Yes, identify the pertinent contractual clauses in the contract document itself, or provide any appropriate statement which identifies the additional requirements. Provide a copy of the requirements to the cognizant security office. Use Item 13 if additional space is needed.)* ☐ Yes ☐ No

15. INSPECTIONS. Elements of this contract are outside the inspection responsibility of the cognizant security office. *(If Yes, explain and identify specific areas or elements carved out and the activity responsible for inspections. Use Item 13 if additional space is needed.)* ☐ Yes ☐ No

16. CERTIFICATION AND SIGNATURE. Security requirements stated herein are complete and adequate for safeguarding the classified information to be released or generated under this classified effort. All questions shall be referred to the official named below.

a. TYPED NAME OF CERTIFYING OFFICIAL	b. TITLE	c. TELEPHONE *(Include Area Code)*
d. ADDRESS *(Include Zip Code)*		**17. REQUIRED DISTRIBUTION**
		☐ a. CONTRACTOR
		☐ b. SUBCONTRACTOR
		☐ c. COGNIZANT SECURITY OFFICE FOR PRIME AND SUBCONTRACTOR
e. SIGNATURE		☐ d. U.S. ACTIVITY RESPONSIBLE FOR OVERSEAS SECURITY ADMINISTRATION
		☐ e. ADMINSTRATIVE CONTRACTING OFFICER
		☐ f. OTHERS AS NECESSARY

Figure 4-1b DD Form 254, reverse side

the DD Form 254, SCG and NISPOM. It is the cleared contractor's responsibility to ensure the organization understands and applies the security requirements. DSS will inspect the contractor to determine how well they understand and apply the NISPOM and requirements identified in the DD Form 254 [2].

FSO responsibilities include providing a good assessment of any security product and service costs necessary to meet requirements. For example, the defense contractor agrees to abide by the NISPOM. Therefore, the contractor pays for all of the costs required to implement the NISPOM.

Interpreting Requirements in the DD Form 254 and NISPOM

A cleared contractor can help reduce costs by preparing ahead of time. This is where an FSO can anticipate expenses, perform risk assessments while implementing NISPOM and advise on ways to reduce costs while being compliant. The earlier into the process the assessment is conducted the better the company performs. Conducting a cost impact analysis or coordinating with DSS after committing to the contract may place the contractor in the tough position building closed areas, ordering more GSA approved containers (safes) and meeting tough governmental compliance with short notice. Lack of planning could prove costly.

The FSO should form a team of key players consisting of key players such as: program managers, engineers, security, contract and others responsible for developing business with the prime contractor or GCA. This team should be able to make decisions to bring to the company leadership before they commit to perform as the contract specifies. The FSO contributes by providing information and guidance on protecting classified information in the process and such planning could translate into significant cost reduction.

Understanding how to advise and assist in the development of the DD Form 254 provides the ground work for ensuring the customer security requirements are clear, applicable and understood. Since the government provides the protection requirements, getting in on the ground level development can only benefit the contractor.

The DD Form 254 requirements can be a baseline to help the FSO assess the current state of security to determine whether or not the company has enough classified storage space, the right type of storage space, whether or not alarms are needed and other physical security needs to support the contract. Other performance requirements may indicate the need for classified computer processing, upgrading facility and personnel clearances, and increasing storage level and capability.

The DD Form 254 could be used to identify training needs concerning how to perform on the classified work. Training should be contract specific to protect the classified information while meeting the customer's needs. Training topics include familiarization with the SCG, details specific to the DD Form 254, and a refresher of the initial security training topics as they could be impacted with the new work. Depending on the requirements, DSS may have to provide additional briefings to the FSO such as NATO, COMSEC, intelligence and others. In turn, the FSO will be expected to brief designated cleared employees.

Interpreting the DD Form 254

Non-possessing facilities

In most situations, non-possessing facilities are not authorized to store classified information on site. The DD Form 254 will specify the contract requirements for possessing and non-possessing facilities. As an example, a fictional company called XYZ Contractor will illustrate requirements of a sample DD Form 254. Beginning at the top of the page, items 1-8 (Figure 4-2) are administrative and list important information concerning the organization's identity, clearance level and oversight agency. Item 1 indicates the highest level of facility clearance a contractor is expected to have before performing on the contract. The expected clearance level is identified by the appropriately checked box indicating CONFIDENTIAL, SECRET or TOP SECRET [3]. The contractor will require valid facility clearance at the level indicated to perform on the contract. This is arranged by the sponsor if the contractor is not already cleared at the appropriate level.

Part 1b indicates the highest level of classified storage required for performance on the contract. The storage level should be the same or lower than the facility security clearance level indicated in 1a. If classified storage is not required, the prime contractor or GCA will write "Not Applicable". In XYZ Contractor's situation, the contract requires the company to have a TOP SECRET facility clearance, but no classified storage requirement. The FCL is granted at TOP SECRET and cleared employees will be eligible to perform on the contract at another facility. However, no classified information will authorized for storage on site.

DEPARTMENT OF DEFENSE	1. CLEARANCE AND SAFEGUARDING
CONTRACT SECURITY CLASSIFICATION SPECIFICATION	a. FACILITY CLEARANCE REQUIRED TOP SECRET
(The requirements of the DoD Industrial Security Manual apply to all security aspects of this effort.)	b. LEVEL OF SAFEGUARDING REQUIRED Not Applicable

2. THIS SPECIFICATION IS FOR: (x and complete as applicable)

☒	a. PRIME CONTRACT NUMBER ABC1230-00-7-A-0000	
☐	b. SUBCONTRACT NUMBER	
☐	c. SOLICITATION OR OTHER NUMBER	DUE DATE *(YYMMDD)*

3. THIS SPECIFICATION IS: (x and complete as applicable)

☒	a. ORIGINAL (Complete date in all cases)		DATE *(YYMMDD)* 09/10/22
☐	b. REVISED (Supersedes all previous specs)	Revision No.	DATE *(YYMMDD)*
☐	c. FINAL (Complete Item 5 in all cases)		DATE *(YYMMDD)*

4. THIS IS A FOLLOW-ON CONTRACT? ☐ YES ☒ NO. If Yes, complete the following:

Classified material received or generated under —————————————— *(Preceding Contract Number)* is transferred to this follow-on contract.

5. IS THIS A FINAL DD FORM 254? ☐ YES ☒ NO. If Yes, complete the following:

In response to the contractor's request dated_____, retention of the identified classified material is authorized for the period of_____

6. CONTRACTOR *(Include Commercial and Government Entity (CAGE) Code)*

a. NAME, ADDRESS, AND ZIP CODE XYZ Contractor 123 Bramlet Drive Huntsville Alabama 35802	b. CAGE CODE 34567	c. COGNIZANT SECURITY OFFICE *(Name, Address, and Zip Code)* Defense Security Services 100th Lane Great Government Facility, Huntsville, Alabama 35824

7. SUBCONTRACTOR

a. NAME, ADDRESS, AND ZIP CODE	b. CAGE CODE	c. COGNIZANT SECURITY OFFICE *(Name, Address, and Zip code)*

8. ACTUAL PERFORMANCE

a. LOCATION Cleared Building Cleared Address Redstone Arsenal, AL	b. CAGE CODE	c. COGNIZANT SECURITY OFFICE*(Name, Address, and Zip Code)* Same as 6c

9. GENERAL IDENTIFICATION OF THIS PROCUREMENT

Perform assembly of Gravy Fighter Systems and Research and Development on Gravy Radar

Figure 4-2 Sections 1-9 of the DD Form 254

In item 2a, the issuing activity will enter the contract number. This contract number provides authorization for the facility and personnel security clearance request, upgrade, or maintenance and the current level. If a prime contractor is issuing a subcontract, the issuing authority will fill out item 2b. In that case, they provide the original prime contract in item 2a (Figure 4-3). Item 2c is filled out for Requests for Proposal, Requests for Quote, Invitations for Bid or other requests for business (Figure 4-4).

Figure 4-2 demonstrates XYZ Contractor's DD Form 254. XYZ

Contractor has been awarded a Government contract, ABC1230-00-7-A-0000. This contract authorizes the classified work to be performed and indicates the facility clearances and the storage level. Storage of classified information is not authorized at the contractor location. There are no subcontracts and this is not a final contract award, items 2b and 2c will not be completed.

2. THIS SPECIFICATION IS FOR: (x and complete as applicable)		3. THIS SPECIFICATION IS: (x and complete as applicable)		
☐ a. PRIME CONTRACT NUMBER ABC1230-00-7-A-0000		☒ a. ORIGINAL (Complete date in all cases)		DATE (YYMMDD) 09/10/22
☒ b. SUBCONTRACT NUMBER A111111111		☐ b. REVISED (Supersedes all previous specs)	Revision No.	DATE (YYMMDD)
☐ c. SOLICITATION OR OTHER NUMBER	DUE DATE (YYMMDD)	☐ c. FINAL (Complete Item 5 in all cases)		DATE (YYMMDD)

DD FORM 254 Front

Figure 4-3 Example of a DD Form 254 for a subcontract

2. THIS SPECIFICATION IS FOR: (x and complete as applicable)		3. THIS SPECIFICATION IS: (x and complete as applicable)		
☐ a. PRIME CONTRACT NUMBER		☒ a. ORIGINAL (Complete date in all cases)		DATE (YYMMDD) 09/10/22
☐ b. SUBCONTRACT NUMBER		☐ b. REVISED (Supersedes all previous specs)	Revision No.	DATE (YYMMDD)
☒ c. SOLICITATION OR OTHER NUMBER a10-1966-T	DUE DATE (YYMMDD) 150131	☐ c. FINAL (Complete Item 5 in all cases)		DATE (YYMMDD)

DD FORM 254 Front

Figure 4-4 DD Form 254 identifying request for quote, bid or other business

DEPARTMENT OF DEFENSE CONTRACT SECURITY CLASSIFICATION SPECIFICATION (The requirements of the DoD Industrial Security Manual apply to all security aspects of this effort.)	1. CLEARANCE AND SAFEGUARDING
	a. FACILITY CLEARANCE REQUIRED TOP SECRET
	b. LEVEL OF SAFEGUARDING REQUIRED Not Applicable

2. THIS SPECIFICATION IS FOR: (x and complete as applicable)		3. THIS SPECIFICATION IS: (x and complete as applicable)		
☒ a. PRIME CONTRACT NUMBER ABC1230-00-7-A-0000		☐ a. ORIGINAL (Complete date in all cases)		DATE (YYMMDD) 09/10/22
☐ b. SUBCONTRACT NUMBER		☒ b. REVISED (Supersedes all previous specs)	Revision No. 1	DATE (YYMMDD) 11/23/22
☐ c. SOLICITATION OR OTHER NUMBER	DUE DATE (YYMMDD)	☐ c. FINAL (Complete Item 5 in all cases)		DATE (YYMMDD)

DD FORM 254 Front

Figure 4-5 *Section identifying a revised DD Form 254*

Item 3 offers several choices of status; original, revised, or final. It allows for only one check mark for options a, b, or c. Original is checked to indicate the type of contract. The original document is retained on file and all additional future changes or revisions will refer to this original document.

The "Revised" choice is selected when there is a change to the DD

Form 254 (4-5). In the case of a revision, the revision number and the date of the revised DD Form 254 are entered. Since the original DD Form 254 is always the source, the date of the original DD Form 254 is entered in Item 3a. Both DD Forms 254 are filed and accounted for in a manner facilitating quick reference and access.

DEPARTMENT OF DEFENSE CONTRACT SECURITY CLASSIFICATION SPECIFICATION *(The requirements of the DoD Industrial Security Manual apply to all security aspects of this effort.)*	**1. CLEARANCE AND SAFEGUARDING**		
	a. FACILITY CLEARANCE REQUIRED TOP SECRET		
	b. LEVEL OF SAFEGUARDING REQUIRED Not Applicable		
2. THIS SPECIFICATION IS FOR: (x and complete as applicable)	**3. THIS SPECIFICATION IS:** (x and complete as applicable)		
☒ a. PRIME CONTRACT NUMBER ABC1230-00-7-A-0000	☐ a. ORIGINAL (Complete date in all cases)		DATE (YYMMDD) 09/10/22
☐ b. SUBCONTRACT NUMBER	☐ b. REVISED (Supersedes all previous specs)	Revision No.	DATE (YYMMDD)
☐ c. SOLICITATION OR OTHER NUMBER DUE DATE (YYMMDD)	☒ c. FINAL (Complete Item 5 in all cases)		DATE (YYMMDD) 12/01/11
DD FORM 254 Front			

Figure 4-6 The date of the original DD Form 254 will be completed in Item 3a

In some cases classified material is authorized for retention for a period of longer than the two years if authorized after the associated contract closes. When retention is necessary, the contractor should request an extension from the GCA or prime contractor. Upon approval, the issuing authority submits a final DD Form 254 to reflect the change. In that case, Final (Item 3c) will be selected and the new DD Form 254 date is annotated. The date of the original DD Form 254 will be completed in Item 3a (Figure 4-6).

Item 6 is required when the Government issues a contract to a prime contractor. The contracting activity enters the contract company name, Commercial and Government Entity Code (CAGE), and the DSS address in items 6a through 6c. Item 7 requires the same information when it is a subcontract. In our example, XYZ Company is located in Huntsville, Alabama and their CAGE Code is 34567. DSS is also located in Huntsville, Alabama.

Item 8 notifies the contractor the location where actual classified work will be performed. If work is performed in the contractor company or the subcontractor company, "Same as Item 6a or 7a" is annotated. In our example, work is performed at the US Government Address. If work is performed in multiple locations, that information is added in Item 13 to include company name, CAGE code and the serving CSO organization is completed. A copy of the DD Form 254 is submitted to the FSOs of the other companies. When work is performed on a government facility, the information is listed in Item 13.

The GCA or prime civilian contracting officer provides a clear, unclassified description of the work to be performed in items 9 and 10 (Figure 4-7). Descriptions and titles should be unclassified when at all possible to provide a means of cataloging, filing and retrieving and for ease of access. If a classified description is entered, then the DD Form 254 itself would be classified. A possible security violation could arise if the actual DD Form 254 were not stored in an approved location. Per Item 9, XYZ Contractor will "Perform assembly of Gravy Fighter Systems and Research and Development on Gravy Radar".

9. GENERAL IDENTIFICATION OF THIS PROCUREMENT						
Perform assembly of Gravy Fighter Systems and Research and Development on Gravy Radar						

10. THIS CONTRACT WILL REQUIRE ACCESS TO:	YES	NO	11. IN PERFORMING THIS CONTRACT, THE CONTRACTOR WILL:	YES	NO
a. COMMUNICATIONS SECURITY (COMSEC) INFORMATION	☐	☒	a. HAVE ACCESS TO CLASSIFIED INFORMATION ONLY AT ANOTHER CONTRACTOR'S FACILITY OR A GOVERNMENT ACTIVITY	☒	☐
b. RESTRICTED DATA	☐	☒	b. RECEIVE CLASSIFIED DOCUMENTS ONLY	☐	☒
c. CRITICAL NUCLEAR WEAPON DESIGN INFORMATION	☐	☒	c. RECEIVE AND GENERATE CLASSIFIED MATERIAL	☐	☒
d. FORMERLY RESTRICTED DATA	☐	☒	d. FABRICATE, MODIFY, OR STORE CLASSIFIED HARDWARE	☐	☒
e. INTELLIGENCE INFORMATION:	☐	☒	e. PERFORM SERVICES ONLY	☐	☒
(1) Sensitive Compartmented Information (SCI)	☐	☐	f. HAVE ACCESS TO U.S. CLASSIFIED INFORMATION OUTSIDE THE U.S., PUERTO RICO, U.S. POSSESSIONS AND TRUST TERRITORIES	☐	☒
(2) Non-SCI	☐	☐	g. BE AUTHORIZED TO USE THE SERVICES OF DEFENSE TECHNICAL INFORMATION CENTER (DTIC) OR OTHER SECONDARY DISTRIBUTION CENTER	☒	☐
f. SPECIAL ACCESS INFORMATION	☐	☒	h. REQUIRE A COMSEC ACCOUNT	☐	☒
g. NATO INFORMATION	☐	☒	i. HAVE TEMPEST REQUIREMENTS	☐	☒
h. FOREIGN GOVERNMENT INFORMATION	☐	☒	j. HAVE OPERATIONS SECURITY (OPSEC) REQUIREMENTS	☐	☒
i. LIMITED DISSEMINATION INFORMATION	☐	☒	k. BE AUTHORIZED TO USE THE DEFENSE COURIER SERVICE	☐	☒
j. FOR OFFICIAL USE ONLY INFORMATION	☐	☒	l. OTHER (Specify)	☐	☒
k. OTHER (Specify)	☐	☒			

DD FORM 254 Front

Figure 4-7 An unclassified work description is provided Item 9.

Item 10 provides all the information that the contractor needs to know and the access they are required to maintain on the contract. The access blocks are marked with an "X" indicating "Yes" or "No" for access requirement. The FSO or appointed representative may need to provide security briefings for the different types of required access levels. Coordination should be made between program managers and security offices to ensure understanding and compliance.

Item 10 addresses sensitive information determined to require additional protection. The NISPOM primarily addresses CONFIDENTIAL, SECRET and TOP SECRET. However, item 10 covers areas that may require additional security countermeasures. This book will not address security requirements for Item 10, but an affected contractor can get more in depth guidance from the government customer or prime contractor and DSS. In this example of a cleared contractor of a non-possessing facility, all checks in item 10 will indicate "No" or no special types of access required.

Moving on to Item 11 we discover how to perform on the contract. Item 11 identifies where and how classified information should be accessed. For example, all the access listed earlier is not necessarily required to occur on company campus. In some cases, a DD Form 254 will identify that a company will have a facility clearance and no storage requirement. In the example our non-possessing facility has no special access and will perform all work at a US Government location.

Item 11a indicates whether or not access to classified information ONLY occurs at another facility. The word "ONLY" indicates that the work will be performed elsewhere and not be conducted on the company campus. In the example, the answer is yes and Items 11b through 11f are marked "No". Since 11a is yes, then Item 13 may indicate the location of classified access.

When the contractor is afforded the use of the Defense Technical Information Center (DTIC), then "Yes" will be indicated in Item 13g. When the opportunity comes for a contractor to gain access to DTIC services, the government agency's GCA or the prime contractor will sponsor the company for access. The DTIC access is tied to a contract. The GCA will submit the Registration for Scientific and Technical Information Services, DDForm1540, to the DTIC [9]. The prime contractor submits the request form through the GCA for verification of need to know. Once registered with DTIC, the contractor can apply for access to unclassified, military critical data from Department of Defense. The request is sent using Military Critical Technical Data Agreement, DD-Form2345, to the Defense Logistics Service Center.

Item 11g through 11k are marked indicating that accounts and access to COMSEC, TEMPEST, OPSEC and Defense Courier Services are not necessary.

The cleared contractor should seek approval from the GCA prior to releasing information to the public. The NISPOM also requires contractors to seek approval before releasing certain unclassified information relating to a classified contract [3]. Because of the nature of classified contracts, even the release of some unclassified information related to the contract could compromise a program. All release of any information concerning a classified contract should be discussed with and approved by the GCA or prime contractor.

The GCA or prime contractor provides specific classified performance guidance and how to implement security measures in Item 13 (Figure 4-8). The contractor or subcontractor has an equal responsibility to understand the security requirements identified on the DD Form 254. The contractor should review each item and ensure they have an understanding of how to safeguard the classified items and what exactly is classified. The contents of Item 13 should be clear to the user such as where classified work will be performed and at what level. The information in Item 13 should include clarification on the existing SCG, identification of source and what makes the information or product classified, and any other information to let the contractor know just what to protect and how to protect it while performing classified work off-site.

Item 14 is identified as early as possible. Additional security requirements could increase costs. The earlier costs are identified the better. The contractor or subcontractor is responsible for ensuring that they are able to provide the specified additional requirements. These additional requirements are reflective of precautions necessary for intelligence and special access. Good coordination between the GCA, contractor and DSS conducted early will ensure the contractor is prepared to implement the required level of security without providing undue burden.

The final pieces consist of certification, signature and distribution. The signature and certification represent that the DD Form 254 has been staffed and is complete and accurate. If done correctly, this last part is more of a formality after a great coordination effort and understanding of all parties involved. The contractor should not be reviewing the completed DD Form 254 for the first time at this point, but should have been involved with the coordination throughout the creation. Additionally, they should not be left to filling out their own requirements for the GCA or prime contractor to approve.

12. PUBLIC RELEASE. Any information *(classified or unclassified)* pertaining to this contract shall not be released for public dissemination except as provided by the NISPOM or unless it has been approved for public release by appropriate U.S. Government authority. Proposed public releases shall be submitted for approval prior to release

☐ Direct ☒ Through *(Specify):*

GCA, 44th Aviation Brigade to the Directorate for Freedom of Information and Security Review, Office of the Assistant Secretary of Defense (Public Affairs)* for review.
  *In the case of non-DoD User Agencies, requests for disclosure shall be submitted to that agency.

13. SECURITY GUIDANCE. The security classification guidance needed for this classified effort is identified below. If any difficulty is encountered in applying this guidance or if any other contributing factor indicates a need for changes in this guidance, the contractor is authorized and encouraged to provide recommended changes; to challenge the guidance or the classification assigned to any information or material furnished or generated under this contract; and to submit any questions for interpretation of this guidance to the official identified below. Pending final decision, the information involved shall be handled and protected at the highest level of classification assigned or recommended. *(Fill in as appropriate for the classified effort. Attach, or forward under separate correspondence, any documents/guides/extracts referenced herein. Add additional pages as needed to provide complete guidance.)*

Products developed during the Research and Development process will be classified up to TOP SECRET. Compilation of classified material derivative information to the classified level up to
TOP SECRET.
The contractor will need to perform in a Government provided sensitive compartmented intelligence facility to properly protect the classified the proper level on Red Stone Arsenal.
Contractors will need to proper clearance to access the information off-site.
All working on the program will refer to the "Gravy Security Classification Guide", DTD 29 Aug 2007.

14. ADDITIONAL SECURITY REQUIREMENTS. Requirements, in addition to NISPOM requirements, are established for this contract. *(If Yes, identify the pertinent contractual clauses in the contract document itself, or provide any appropriate statement which identifies the additional requirements. Provide a copy of the requirements to the cognizant security office. Use Item 13 if additional space is needed.)* ☒ Yes ☐ No

Contractor will have to access and protect classified material on Red Stone Arsenal.

15. INSPECTIONS. Elements of this contract are outside the inspection responsibility of the cognizant security office. *(If Yes, explain and identify specific areas or elements carved out and the activity responsible for inspections. Use Item 13 if additional space is needed.)* ☒ Yes ☐ No

All products, services and work on project Gravy are carved out of DSS inspection.

16. CERTIFICATION AND SIGNATURE. Security requirements stated herein are complete and adequate for safeguarding the classified information to be released or generated under this classified effort. All questions shall be referred to the official named below.

a. TYPED NAME OF CERTIFYING OFFICIAL	b. TITLE	c. TELEPHONE *(Include Area Code)*
Jim Contractor	Government Contracting Officer	(555) 555-5555

d. ADDRESS *(Include Zip Code)*	17. REQUIRED DISTRIBUTION
43d Aviation Brigade Redstone Arsenal Alabama 35824	☒ a. CONTRACTOR ☐ b. SUBCONTRACTOR ☒ c. COGNIZANT SECURITY OFFICE FOR PRIME AND SUBCONTRACTOR
e. SIGNATURE	☐ d. U.S. ACTIVITY RESPONSIBLE FOR OVERSEAS SECURITY ADMINISTRATION ☐ e. ADMINISTRATIVE CONTRACTING OFFICER ☒ f. OTHERS AS NECESSARY

DD FORM 254 Reverse

Figure 4-8 DD Form 254 identifying requirements in Item 13

Possessing Facilities

Possessing facilities are authorized to maintain and work on classified information at the defense contractor location. Let's use XYZ Contractor again, but this time as a possessing facility performing classified work on-site. In this case they are required to store and perform on TOP SECRET work on site and everything remains the same except for Items 1b, 8 and 10-13. This storage level and facility clearance is required for the contract and Item 1b is marked as TOP SECRET to indicate XYZ Contractor is authorize to store the classified information on-site (Figure 4-9).

Item 10 (Figure 4-10) provides all the information that the contractor needs to know and the access they are required to maintain on the contract. The access blocks are marked with an "X" indicating "Yes" or "No" for access requirement. The FSO or appointed representative may need to provide security briefings for the different types of required access levels. Coordination is made between program managers and security offices to ensure understanding and compliance with the requirements of the government or primary contract holder.

DEPARTMENT OF DEFENSE CONTRACT SECURITY CLASSIFICATION SPECIFICATION *(The requirements of the DoD Industrial Security Manual apply to all security aspects of this effort.)*			**1. CLEARANCE AND SAFEGUARDING** a. FACILITY CLEARANCE REQUIRED TOP SECRET b. LEVEL OF SAFEGUARDING REQUIRED TOP SECRET			
2. THIS SPECIFICATION IS FOR: *(x and complete as applicable)*			**3. THIS SPECIFICATION IS:** *(x and complete as applicable)*			
☒	a. PRIME CONTRACT NUMBER ABC1230-00-7-A-0000		☒	a. ORIGINAL (Complete date in all cases)		DATE (YYMMDD) 09/10/22
☐	b. SUBCONTRACT NUMBER		☐	b. REVISED (Supersedes all previous specs)	Revision No.	DATE (YYMMDD)
☐	c. SOLICITATION OR OTHER NUMBER	DUE DATE (YYMMDD)	☐	c. FINAL (Complete Item 5 in all cases)		DATE (YYMMDD)
4. THIS IS A FOLLOW-ON CONTRACT? ☐ YES ☒ NO. If Yes, complete the following: Classified material received or generated under _____ *(Preceding Contract Number)* is transferred to this follow-on contract.						
5. IS THIS A FINAL DD FORM 254? ☐ YES ☒ NO. If Yes, complete the following: In response to the contractor's request dated_____, retention of the identified classified material is authorized for the period of_____						
6. CONTRACTOR *(Include Commercial and Government Entity (CAGE) Code)*						
a. NAME, ADDRESS, AND ZIP CODE XYZ Contractor 123 Bramlet Drive Huntsville Alabama 35802		b. CAGE CODE 34567	c. COGNIZANT SECURITY OFFICE *(Name, Address, and Zip Code)* Defense Security Services 100th Lane Great Government Facility, Huntsville, Alabama 35824			
7. SUBCONTRACTOR						
a. NAME, ADDRESS, AND ZIP CODE		b. CAGE CODE	c. COGNIZANT SECURITY OFFICE *(Name, Address, and Zip code)*			
8. ACTUAL PERFORMANCE						
a. LOCATION Same as 6a.		b. CAGE CODE	c. COGNIZANT SECURITY OFFICE *(Name, Address, and Zip Code)* Same as 6c			
9. GENERAL IDENTIFICATION OF THIS PROCUREMENT Perform assembly of Gravy Fighter Systems and Research and Development on Gravy Radar						

Figure 4-9 DD Form 254 identifying TOP SECRET Level of Storage

If COMSEC requirements are annotated in 10a, accounts are created for COMSEC items that with National Security Agency's Central Office of Records (NSA COR) oversight [4]. The GCA will have to approve a subcontractor's access prior to a prime contractor awarding the affected contract. The NSACOR requires notification prior to bargaining for the contract requiring access to COMSEC. This coordination is necessary for sponsorship to enable the approved companies to apply for and receive the COMSEC accounts. Keep in mind that some COMSEC material may not require the contractor to have a COMSEC account.

10. THIS CONTRACT WILL REQUIRE ACCESS TO:	YES	NO	11. IN PERFORMING THIS CONTRACT, THE CONTRACTOR WILL:	YES	NO
a. COMMUNICATIONS SECURITY (COMSEC) INFORMATION	☒	☐	a. HAVE ACCESS TO CLASSIFIED INFORMATION ONLY AT ANOTHER CONTRACTOR'S FACILITY OR A GOVERNMENT ACTIVITY	☐	☒
b. RESTRICTED DATA	☒	☐	b. RECEIVE CLASSIFIED DOCUMENTS ONLY	☐	☒
c. CRITICAL NUCLEAR WEAPON DESIGN INFORMATION	☒	☐	c. RECEIVE AND GENERATE CLASSIFIED MATERIAL	☒	☐
d. FORMERLY RESTRICTED DATA	☒	☐	d. FABRICATE, MODIFY, OR STORE CLASSIFIED HARDWARE	☒	☐
e. INTELLIGENCE INFORMATION:	☒	☐	e. PERFORM SERVICES ONLY	☐	☒
(1) Sensitive Compartmented Information (SCI)	☒	☐	f. HAVE ACCESS TO U.S. CLASSIFIED INFORMATION OUTSIDE THE U.S., PUERTO RICO, U.S. POSSESSIONS AND TRUST TERRITORIES	☐	☒
(2) Non-SCI	☒	☐	g. BE AUTHORIZED TO USE THE SERVICES OF DEFENSE TECHNICAL INFORMATION CENTER (DTIC) OR OTHER SECONDARY DISTRIBUTION CENTER	☒	☐
f. SPECIAL ACCESS INFORMATION	☐	☒	h. REQUIRE A COMSEC ACCOUNT	☒	☐
g. NATO INFORMATION	☒	☐	i. HAVE TEMPEST REQUIREMENTS	☐	☒
h. FOREIGN GOVERNMENT INFORMATION	☒	☐	j. HAVE OPERATIONS SECURITY (OPSEC) REQUIREMENTS	☒	☐
i. LIMITED DISSEMINATION INFORMATION	☐	☒	k. BE AUTHORIZED TO USE THE DEFENSE COURIER SERVICE	☐	☒
j. FOR OFFICIAL USE ONLY INFORMATION	☒	☐	l. OTHER (Specify)	☐	☒
k. OTHER (Specify)	☐	☒			

DD FORM 254 Front

Figure 4-10

When COMSEC accounts are required by the DD Form 254, the FSO appoints a cleared employee as a COMSEC custodian. The COMSEC Custodian does not have to be the FSO or other senior leader. Any appropriately cleared employee capable of performing the job is eligible. The appointed employee attends training and develops a compliant accountability program depending on the type of COMSEC and the classification level assigned. The custodian is responsible for conducting periodic inventory, conducting employee COMSEC briefings and other administrative actions. DSS conducts briefings for the FSO, COMSEC and Alternate COMSEC custodians. The FSO or COMSEC custodian in turn briefs the company employees [5].

Items 10b, c and d are designated for access to additional security measures, information and items affected by the Department of Energy and Nuclear Regulatory Commission. RESTRICTED DATA (RD) and FORMERLY RESTRICTED DATA (FRD) require structured briefings prior to accessing the information.

The DD Form 254 indicates that XYZ Contractor needs access to RD, FRD and Critical Nuclear Weapon Design Information (CNWDI). Recall that, CONFIDENTIAL and SECRET clearances require NACLC clearances and TOP SECRET requires an SSBI. However RD has different background investigation requirements. SECRET RD requires a favorable SSBI where plain SECRET requires only a NACLC [6]. The FSO should ensure the proper security clearance is requested through JPAS based on the identified DD Form 254 need.

The FSO should use the DD Form 254 requirements to prepare for the receipt and storage of new material. This is where they provide return on investment to their employers. Knowing the requirements of the DD Form 254 will help them prepare for budgetary requirements that come from company overhead, not customer provided. Heightened preparation includes anticipating supplies on hand in anticipation of properly marking classified information. In addition to the classification markings, the FSO should prepare for other marking capability to indicate special handling instructions. As an example, consider a document that contains RESTRICTED DATA, a statement will indicate; "RESTRICTED DATA, This document contains RESTRICTED DATA as defined in the Atomic Energy Act of 1954. Unauthorized disclosure subject to administrative and criminal sanctions." If the document contains FORMERLY RESTRICTED DATA, the statement will show: "FORMERLY RESTRICTED DATA, Unauthorized disclosure subject to administrative and criminal sanctions. Handle as RESTRICTED DATA in foreign dissemination. Section 144b, AEA 1954" [7].

Item 10e falls under the jurisdiction of the Director of National Intelligence (DNI). However, the GCA ensures security requirements identified by DNI are implemented in the contractor security procedures. As with earlier items, releasing agency approval is necessary prior to a contractor providing a subcontractor access to the intelligence information [8].

If access to SCI is required, then special security requirements are necessary to protect intelligence information. The contractor or sub contractor will need to know what physical security, access control, alarms, briefings and other measures are necessary to protect the classified product. DSS typically has the responsibility of inspecting the contractor's ability to protect classified information. However, DSS will not have oversight of this particular area without an agreement in place with DNI. When an agreement has not been made, the DNI has oversight and DSS is "carved out".

Access to intelligence information is identified as requiring either SCI or Non-SCI. XYZ Contractor will need access to a Sensitive Compartmented Information Facility (SCIF) to protect intelligence sources and methods. The FSO should be prepared to protect classified information by investing time, money and personnel to prepare and properly mark (when necessary) such intelligence markings. The FSO should use the DD Form 254 to identify security requirements and resources such as stamps and ink pads and other equipment necessary to properly mark generated classified material.

Item 10f notifies the contractor whether or not access to Special Access Programs (SAP) is necessary. The GCA's Program Security Office approves all contractors for access to program material. Any additional security requirements should be identified in item 13. Whether or not the CSA is "carved out" or deemed not responsible for inspecting the program will be noted in Item 15 (Figure 4-8).

In our example 254, SAP access is required. The contractor and sub contractor gets guidance in Item 13 as well as special security requirements as identified in Item 14. Were SAP inspections are not conducted by the DSS, Item 15 will be marked to indicate "Yes" for Inspection to indicate that DSS will not be providing the inspections.

Though not addressed in NISPOM, the DD Form 254 preparation guide instructs that NATO and Foreign Government Information both require GCA approval prior to a contractor granting access to a subcontractor 3. The FSO will also give briefings prior to granting access to contractor employees. Item 10i no longer applies and will therefore always have "No" selected. FOR OFFICIAL USE ONLY requires GCA to provide security guidance as it is not classified and is not covered in the NISPOM. The GCA provides the guidance in Item 13. Item 10k is filled out if there are other access requirements not identified in the DD Form 254. If there are any, the "Yes" box is selected and the specifics are provided in Item 13.

As Figure 4-9 indicates, XYZ Contractor will have access to COMSEC, RESTRICTED and FORMERLY RESTRICTED DATA, CNWDI, SCI and non-SCI Intelligence information, NATO, Foreign Government Information and For Official Use Only material. Each access will require separate briefings. Recall that DNI has oversight over intelligence information and DoE and NRC has oversight over RD and CNWDI. Each access will also have different agency oversight and inspection requirements unless an agreement between agencies is in place.

Moving on to Item 11 we discover how to perform on the contract. Item 11 identifies where and how classified information is to be accessed. For example, all the access listed earlier is not necessarily required to occur on company campus. In some cases, a DD Form 254 will identify that a company will have a facility clearance and no storage requirement. If that is the situation, then work will be identified to take place at other locations and Item 10 describes the access levels. There will not be security instructions for work performed outside of the facility. Additionally, companies that perform work on site have in depth security instructions to best safeguard classified information.

Item 11a indicates whether or not access to classified information ONLY occurs at another facility. The word "ONLY" indicates that the work will be performed elsewhere and not be conducted on the company campus. If the answer is yes, then Item 11b should be marked "NA" or "none". If 11a is yes, then Item 13 may indicate the location of classified access.

For Item 11b, the contract issuer will indicate whether or not the company will ONLY receive classified information. This is opposite of Item 11a, meaning that the access identified in Item 10 is to occur on the company campus and that the company will ONLY receive the information and not generate classified material. In some cases the scope of work may require the company to generate classified material. Since it is difficult to predict the possibility, the contract issuer can add flexibility by annotating Item 13. "Situations may require the generation of classified material. Always mark classified material to the level of the source material."3

If a contractor will be authorized to receive and generate classified material, the GCA or prime contractor selects "Yes". If the contractor is to receive and generate classified material as outlined in Item 10, additional security classification guidance is necessary. The guidance is added to Item 13 and provided in the associated SCG.

The contractor may be required to fabricate, modify or store classified hardware. If so, "Yes" is selected in Item 11d. Detailed information is vital to the proper security of the hardware. Item 13 is used to include information such as how much hardware, use of Closed or Restricted areas and any other information to indicate what type of storage is necessary.

Item 11e identifies whether or not the access to classified information is for services only. If "Yes" is checked, then the type of services should be identified in Item 13. For example, the type of service examples may indicate some of the following situations:

Editing only- Services to perform include editing classified documents for accuracy of content, technical information, and grammar. Classification markings are already provided.

Janitorial – Services to perform involve cleaning rest rooms, hallways and closed areas. Cleaning employees are cleared at the SECRET level.

Quality - Consult on how to improve first time yield of manufactured parts. These parts are classified at the CONFIDENTIAL level.

When situations arise where the cleared contractor will have access to classified information outside the U.S., Puerto Rico, U.S. Possessions and Trust Territories, the "Yes" block will be checked. Item 13 could have the location of the work to be performed to include the city, state and country of the performance. The contractor company will provide a DD Form 254 to DSS.

When the contractor is afforded the use of DTIC, then "Yes" will be indicated in Item 13g.

Item 11g is marked indicating whether or not a COMSEC account is necessary. A COMSEC account is required when a company is engaged in using accountable Communication Security equipment or devices. The GCA informs the contractor of the need to have a COMSEC account and the contractor will inform DSS of the names of primary and alternate COMSEC custodian and the FSO to the NSA Central Office of Record and the GCA.

The GCA may require the contractor to provide Operations Security (OPSEC). The OPSEC plan is designed to help a contractor identify areas of weakness that could be exploited by an adversary. The OPSEC plan is designed to deny an adversary unclassified information. The OPSEC information is usually unclassified, but would cause some damage to a company or individual. For example, a contractor may forbid customers or vendors from taking notes or bringing cell phones into meetings in efforts to protect proprietary information. The government may specify that a company must have a plan in place to shred all unclassified material associated with a certain contract.

If a contractor is required to use the Defense Courier Service, the GCA will approve it. The prime contractor will seek this approval prior to requiring it from the sub contractor [10]. Item 11k is for additional information not covered in earlier items. Specifics are usually included in Item 13.

The contractor should seek approval from the GCA prior to releasing information to the public. The NISPOM also requires contractors to seek approval before releasing certain unclassified information relating to a classified contract [3]. Because of the nature of classified contracts, even the release of some unclassified information related to the contract could compromise a program. All release of any information concerning a classified contract should be discussed with and approved by the GCA and DSS.

The GCA or prime contractor provides significant guidance on how the contractor or subcontractor is to protect the classified information and work provided by the contract. The DD Form 254 is the venue for providing such guidance and how to annotate security measures in Item 13. The DD Form 254 provides the technical guidance for protecting our nation's secrets, but should also relay the spirit of intent.

The contractor or subcontractor has an equal responsibility to understand the security requirements identified on the DD Form 254. The contractor should review each item and ensure they have an understanding of how to safeguard the classified items and what exactly is classified. The contents of Item 13 should be quite clear to the user. The information in Item 13 should include clarification on the existing SCG, identification of source documents whether or not classified hardware will be produced or provided, what makes the information or product classified, and any other information to let the contractor know just what to protect and how to protect it.

Item 14 is identified as early as possible. Additional security requirements could increase costs. The earlier costs are identified the better. The contractor or subcontractor is responsible for ensuring that they are able to provide the specified additional requirement reflective of precautions necessary for intelligence and special access. The final pieces consist of certification, signature and distribution.

SUMMARY

The fundamental tool for company to develop and implement and security program to protect classified information is the DD Form 254. This is designed to identify the GCA or prime contractor or subcontractor and the access necessary to perform on the classified work. The GCA or the prime contractor will also inform how and where the contractor will work on the classified work and protect the classified information. The completed DD Form 254 is the result of cooperation between the two parties for the successful implementation and execution of a security program to protect classified information.

PROBLEMS

1. Your company has just won a major contract supporting the Department of Defense. A program manager is sure that your company will not need to access classified material on campus, but needs verification. Where will you find that information?
2. What type of information should be included in Item 13 of the DD Form 254?
3. Explain why the DD Form 254 is important to a company's ability to protect classified material.
4. Who provides the security briefings to the FSO and COMSEC Custodian?
5. An FSO should be prepared to point out to senior executives any additional security requirements and the impact. What are some things an FSO should consider when preparing for storage of SCI information. In other words, what are some expenses to consider that go above and beyond non-SCI security?

RESOURCES

1. Department of Defense, DoD 5220.22-M, *National Industrial Security Operating Manual*, section 4-103, February 2006
2. Department of Defense, DoD 5220.22-M, *National Industrial Security Operating Manual*, section 1-206, February 2006
3. Defense Security Service Academy, *A Guide for the Preparation of a DD Form 254*, Defense Security Services Academy, MD, http://dssa.dss.mil/seta/documents/aguide254dssaaug2006.pdf, downloaded Sep 2008
4. Department of Defense, DoD 5220.22-M, *National Industrial Security Operating Manual*, section 9-403, February 2006
5. Department of Defense, DoD 5220.22-M, *National Industrial Security Operating Manual*, section 9-404, February 2006
6. Department of Defense, DoD 5220.22-M, *National Industrial Security Operating Manual*, section 9-104, February 2006
7. Department of Defense, DoD 5220.22-M, *National Industrial Security Operating Manual*, section 9-108, February 2006
8. Department of Defense, DoD 5220.22-M, *National Industrial Security Operating Manual*, section 9-303, February 2006
9. Department of Defense, DoD 5220.22-M, *National Industrial Security Operating Manual*, section 11-202a, February 2006
10. Department of Defense, DoD 5220.22-M, National Industrial Security Operating Manual, section 5-402a, February 2006

HELPFUL WEBSITES

DD Form 254 Guide
http://dssa.dss.mil/seta/documents/aguide254dssaaug2006.pdf
DSS Website
http://www.dss.mil

CHAPTER 5 RECEIVING CLASSIFIED MATERIAL

INTRODUCTION

Protecting classified information begins with the proper introduction of classified information into a cleared facility and ends with the successful removal through return to customer, destruction or dissemination of classified information. This chapter demonstrates how to properly receive classified material. Also included is a recommended organizational structure to ensure only cleared personnel have access to classified material.

THE INFORMATION MANAGEMENT SYSTEM (IMS)

The cleared contractor is required to protect all classified material and be able to retrieve it within a reasonable amount of time [1]. Though the NISPOM only requires the cleared contractor to keep accountability of TOP SECRET information, cleared contractors should keep a document trail for all classified information. The NISPOM requires receipting action whenever SECRET and TOP SECRET information is transferred to or from a cleared contractor. However, it is a good practice to track deliveries and send receipts for outgoing CONFIDENTIAL information as well. Confirmation of receipt and visibility of the internal transfer of classified information will also help an FSO be able to retrieve classified information or identify its location. A defense contractor can possess anywhere from a few to thousands of classified documents. An IMS should help track and find classified material at any time no matter how much classified information .

Classified information can arrive at a cleared contractor in many different ways. Delivery through cleared contractor employees, government employees, contractually related customers, Defense Courier Service, secure fax, secure email, US Postal Service, overnight delivery services and other approved means of transmission, delivery or other methods of disseminating classified information. Regardless of how classified material arrives, the FSO should provide for the proper reception of classified material by authorized cleared employees. The receiver of classified material plays a role in both safeguarding classified material after it arrives as well as identifying discrepancies and security violations that may have occurred in transit.

CENTRALIZED CLASSIFIED INFORMATION PROCESSING

FSOs should control the introduction and dissemination of classified information with a centralized document control system. The process directs the arrival of visitors, couriers, mail carriers, overnight delivery companies, and others who could potentially convey classified information. Through a process of document control, FSOs receive classified information, inspect it, sign receipts, document its arrival, safeguard it or make it available for authorized employees.

Without such controls, classified information could be vulnerable to unauthorized disclosure, loss, or compromise. Possible scenarios include classified information on site but: not contract related, improperly marked, improperly stored, provided to unauthorized employees, or even removed from the premises without authorization. To prevent the unauthorized delivery of classified information, classified deliveries should be made to ONLY the classified mailing address. This address should be synonymous with the centralized classified information processing location.

A facility registers for and obtains a CAGE code through the Central Contractor Registration System (CCR). They also provide a classified mailing address as part of the clearance processing. These addresses are listed in DSS's Industrial Security Facility Database (ISFD). Multiple receiving locations in a facility can cause confusion during deliveries. However, providing guidance to cleared employees on where to deliver classified information will help resolve any confusion.

Reporting Security Violations

The uncontrolled introduction of classified information can cause serious accountability problems, potential security violations and compromise of classified material. The FSO conducts investigations into security violations to determine whether classified information is lost, compromised or suspected to be compromised. Many security incidents are investigated internally and resolved at the lowest level. However, if the investigation reveals that classified material is lost, compromised or suspected to be compromised, the information should be reported to DSS.

Train Cleared Employees How to Introduce Classified Information

The FSO should create company policy demonstrating how classified material is introduced and removed properly from the company and train cleared employees on the procedures. The intent is to establish an enterprise where everyone has a clear understanding of policy and minimize any customer generated security violations. For example, the FSO can ensure that the government customer understands that classified deliveries are to be made through the cleared contractor's security department and not directly to the cleared engineer. Assuming that cleared employees will know what to do without verifying that knowledge can lead to the security program's failure.

One trigger point to plan the reception of classified information is upon notification of a classified visit request. When cleared employees visit another cleared facility, their organization submits the visit request through JPAS. At that point, the receiving FSO can coordinate directly with the sending security manager for proper delivery of classified material. Furthermore, if a classified visit or meeting is taking place the FSO or representative can provide a security briefing covering accountability of all classified notes or other items necessary for the meeting.

Restrict Flow of Visitor Traffic

A follow on method of controlling the introduction of classified information is to restrict or direct the flow of visitor traffic into the cleared facility. Cleared facilities may have multiple entry points and visitors should have access to only designated entry points. To help with maintaining control of the classified environment, FSO's can employ information technology or human controls to direct pedestrian traffic into their facility. Access controls with biometric, pin card or data card access provide an excellent opportunity to flow all traffic through an authorized area. When budget does not permit the purchase or subscription to expensive information technology, high security hardware such as door locks and crash bars are adequate to prevent entry into unauthorized doors.

When controls are in place, pedestrian traffic is filed through a reception area where visitors are received warmly and reminded to check in with the security or reception desk for all classified deliveries. Additionally the NISPOM requires the prominent display of signs notifying employees and visitors to a cleared facility that their personal effects are subject to inspection [2]. Human resources and legal corporate entities should be consulted and actions coordinated to ensure that privacy is respected and laws are followed. The technology and physical security measures are designed for the FSO to control who enters the facility, the reason for entry, and the further control of introduced classified material.

Inspecting Classified Information Deliveries

The FSO should ensure all arriving classified information is inspected and received into accountability. This due diligence is conducted to ensure that classified information has not been compromised, is related to a contract, and is properly marked. Regardless of transmission methods of physical items (mail, courier, overnight, hand carry and etc.) classified material should be double wrapped. Each layer serves to protect the classified material from inadvertent and unauthorized disclosure and should be properly addressed.

The classified information should be wrapped and sealed in opaque material or envelopes. The NISPOM does not cover seams of wrapped items, but a good practice is to cover seams with rip-proof opaque tape or other material that prevents and detects tampering. All seams of the outer layer should be sealed with opaque tape in an effort to create a solid layer of covering. The item should be wrapped and sealed with the first layer containing the proper classification level and to and from address lines. Two copies of receipts should either be attached to the first layer or inside the first layer. The outer layer should not contain classification markings and be addressed to a cleared contractor and not a person's name [3].

A good security practice allows for the sender to contact the receiver that classified material is being sent to their facility. This alerts the receiver to expect the delivery. Many times program managers, engineers or other technical employees are anticipating the delivery, but may not have all the details of delivery times and dates. However an FSO to FSO coordination can provide all the information of the transaction in advance.

Detailed Inspection Requirements

Regardless of transmission methods, the recipient should examine the outer wrapping for evidence of tampering or to otherwise to inspect that there has been no compromise of classified material. Classified material should be double wrapped or in other words have two independent layers of protection. Each layer consists of opaque material such as: an envelope, paper, box or other strong wrapping material. The first part of the inspection should be conducted to look for evidence of tearing, ripping, re-wrapping or some other means of unauthorized access to the material.

Next, the shipping label should be reviewed for full approved classified mailing address, return address. There should be no classification markings on the outer layer of the item; the outer layer should not draw attention to the classified material inside. Classification markings on the outside of a package are a security violation.

The inner layer should be inspected the same way as the outer layer for evidence of tampering or unauthorized disclosure (Figure 5-1). However, the inside wrapping should contain the full address of the recipient as well as classification markings on the top, bottom, front and back (Figure 5-2). TOP SECRET and SECRET material should have a packing list or receipt of contents either on the outside or inside of the container. Receipts are not necessary with the shipment of CONFIDENTIAL material. If a receipt is included, the receiver should sign it and return it to the sender.

Figure 5-1 This package is ripped. The receiver would notify the sender that the shipment packaging was damaged. It may be necessary to investigate and determine whether or not classified information was compromised.

The receiver should then check the receipt against the contents to ensure the item has been identified correctly and all items are accounted for. The properly filled out receipt should list the sender, the addressee and correctly identify the contents by an unclassified title and appropriate quantity. Since the receipt may be filed for administrative and compliance purposes, the inspector should ensure it contains no classified information. If the receipt contains a classified title, the sender may be able to coordinate for an unclassified title for internal use. Listing classified titles in an unclassified IMS data base is a security violation. Also, since the receipt contains a classified title, it must be protected as classified. The receiver should prepare to store the receipt long term in a GSA approved container because of the classification level.

Figure 5-2 This inner layer is addressed and stamped correctly. It is typical of the inner wrapper of a package a cleared facility might receive via mail, delivery or courier. Notice the anti-rip tape on all major seams.

If a signed receipt is to be returned to the sender, the FSO should ensure it is prepared properly for delivery. The receiver should compare the classification identified in the receipt with that annotated on the inner wrapper. These markings ensure the package is handled correctly once the outer wrapping has been opened or removed. The receiver should compare the classification marking on the contents with the wrapper and the receipt to once again verify the classification level and prevent unauthorized disclosure. Once all the checks and verifications are complete, the receiver can then sign a copy of the receipt and return to the sender, thus closing the loop on the sender's accounting responsibilities (Figure 5-3).

Items to inspect when receiving classified deliveries:

1. Outside layer:
   - Evidence of tamper
   - Seams sealed with anti-rip tape
   - Label is addressed to organization (not individual)

2. Inside layer:
   - Evidence of tamper
   - Seams sealed with anti-rip tape
   - Inside label addressed to recipient
   - Inside wrapper is marked with appropriate classification
   - Receipts / packing list included for SECRET and above
   - Compare receipt/packing list against contents
   - Ensure items are classified properly
   - Sign receipts and return to sender

Figure 5-3 The FSO should ensure that all classified deliveries are inspected prior to bringing them into accountability. Such checks are necessary to ensure items were sent properly, were not tampered with in transit, contain correct items and are authorized for storage in the classified holdings

---

Top Secret Control Official

Cleared contractors that are granted a TOP SECRET Facility Clearance (FCL) and are authorized to maintain a TOP SECRET inventory are required to appoint a TOP SECRET control official (TSCO). All transactions involving TOP SECRET information require documentation through access and accountability records. This requirement is for the lifecycle of the information and includes reception, transmission, destruction and storage. Additionally, the contractor is required to perform an annual accountability inventory unless a waiver for the requirement is on file.

For example, all TOP SECRET information and material is documented by numbering them in a series. This allows the contractor and owner of the classified information to know exactly how many there are and what to look for during inventory. Any incoming material, copies generated or faxes transmitted are documented with the number and accounted for by the TSCO using the numbering and a continuous receipt system.

Reporting Requirements

It is the sender's responsibility to ensure classified information arrives at the intended destination. They should track the classified deliveries until they receive a receipt or verify arrival. The receiver should report discrepancies to the sender, notifying them of a possible problem with their shipping policy. The sender can then take the opportunity to investigate the root problem. Once the root of the security infraction is discovered they can conduct training, review policy and otherwise put measures into place to improve their security program. If the notification responsibility or the report itself is ignored, then more severe problems could develop.

Security violations resulting in loss, compromise or suspected compromise of classified material, should be reported to DSS. There is value added with sharing discrepancy information with the right agencies and parties. The primary reason for reporting is to prevent loss, compromise, suspected compromise or unauthorized disclosure of classified information and determine its impact. Also, a reporting process is used to provide feedback from which all parties concerned can benefit to better implement and direct security policies to protect classified information.

Safeguarding the Classified Information

The FSO should design a policy to maintain strict control over classified material. The NISPOM requires accountability and control of classified information at the TOP SECRET level [4]. However, all material entering the facility, produced, reproduced or entering the facility in any fashion should be brought into possession for control, audit and inventory purposes. Contractors should maintain an IMS to protect and control classified information [4]. This provides visibility over the classified material and allows for preventative measures against unauthorized disclosure or identification of security violations.

The FSO should employ a security training and discipline program to compel cleared employees to act as force multipliers increasing security effectiveness. In that role, cleared employees will know to deliver all newly introduced classified material to the FSO for accountability purposes and into the IMS. When security personnel practice good customer service and enforce procedures, good relationships develop making procedures easy to follow as well as rewarding for all employees.

Once the material is received and the delivery inspected against the receipt, the FSO or security specialist can input the information into a retrievable database or IMS. This database can be something as simple as logging the information into a notebook or through technology such as software sold on the market. As a reminder, caution should be taken to ensure only unclassified information is entered in to an unclassified database.

An example of a classified information accountability record can be seen in Figure 5-4. An accountability record is an excellent tool for controlling classified information introduced into the defense contractor facility. With the accountability record, documents are managed with additional receipting action. Some accountability records track document status from introduction to dissemination on the same record. Contractors are not limited to a certain method of document control other than the ability to track the status of classified information the cleared facility possesses.

Date of Receipt	How Received	Contract No.	Document No.	Title	Classification	Copy No.	Location
2/11/2011	Express Mail	ABC1230-00-7-A-0000	08-012	Gravy SCG (U)	SECRET	1	Safe 12875

Figure 5-4 Sample Information Management System record.

Because of the positive identification and control involved, inventories should be conducted for all classified information. This enhances protection of classified information. If during the course of inventory, a document cannot be easily located, a more thorough search takes place. Input into the IMS record as documents are used or moved throughout the organization provides information for a growing data warehouse that may prove beneficial in finding the misplaced product.

Commercially available IMS use information technology to create a detailed database that helps FSOs track classified material through many dispositions from receipt, inventory requirements and final disposition. Some produce receipts, tie to a barcode scanner, report statistical data that can help determine use and much more. For example, if an inventory reveals missing classified information, the database can provide valuable information to help reconstruct the classified information's history.

Databases can be tied to scanner software. Barcodes can be printed and applied to classified items for scanning. If an item is destroyed, shipped, filed, loaned or returned, it can be scanned and the status updated. These databases provide reports identifying when and where the barcode on the classified document was scanned and the last disposition. The FSO can use the technology to research dates, methods of receipt, contract number, assigned document number, assigned barcode, title, classification, copy number, location, and name of the receiver as follows:

Date of Receipt or Generation-This information is recorded to indicate the day the document arrived. It can be used as the countdown date for an inventory requirement or as a time line or search method in case an employee needs to retrieve it. If a document cannot be easily traced, those conducting the inventory can use the date in reference to narrowing down search locations or options

How Received-Did the classified item arrive through USPS mail, overnight delivery, courier, hand carry, electronic means, derived from other research, printed or duplicated? This information is important to the FSO for use during DSS's annual review of the contractor's ability to protect classified material. This column can be linked to the receipting action bringing the classified document to the company from external locations or perhaps from an internal customer request.

Contract Number-Contract numbers are important in situations where a contractor may have hundreds of classified contracts including directions that the material classified at certain levels must be stored separately. This added column can assist with determining need to know, quick retrieval of receipts, records or the classified item itself. Additionally, the FSO can pull documents by contract number to return to customer during contract closeout.

Document Number-Cleared contractors operating an IMS can generate an internal document number for classified information entering the company. This system generates a unique number that allows for quick filing and retrieval by that designation. Each contractor may assign a unique internal document number.

Barcode-The barcode is an excellent tool for document filing, retrieval, inventory and internal tracking for cleared contractors with large inventories of classified information. Classified information is received, assigned a barcode number and a physical code is placed in an easy to scan location. The barcode reader is used to scan the item during inventory and any other transactions. An FSO can assign any value to the document record necessary to know the status of any classified material at any time. Major retail stores use the same technology in their inventory and logistics process.

Unclassified Title-Because the title information could be stored in an unclassified computer, file cabinet, desk top or drawer, unclassified titles should be used. If a receipt arrives with a classified title, the receipt will have to be protected as classified. However, the receiver can make arrangements to assign a new unclassified title with little confusion. If an unclassified title is not possible or desired, arrangements will have to be made to protect all records and receipts with the classified information annotated. The classified title cannot be put on an unclassified database.

Classification Level-Data with the classification identified at the TOP SECRET, SECRET, or CONFIDENTIAL level helps during the retrieval process. Classified information with the additional designations or caveats of: FGI, NOFORN, INTEL, NATO and others should be filed separately according to regulations and contract requirements.

Copy Number-Copy numbers are used for multiple copies of existing classified material. For example, five copies of the same type of classified document could arrive or be duplicated on site. Each duplication should be safeguarded at the same level as the original document. For example, XYZ Contractor number's their documents sequentially. Document number 35601-02 is the 35,601st document entered into the system. Additionally, the -02 identifies it as the second copy of that document.

Location or Disposition-The exact location of classified material helps with the easy retrieval. To log a document into accountability with no location is fine for companies possessing a limited amount of documents. Those contractors or agencies with multiple documents and possible locations will want to identify the assignment for quick retrieval. An additional data field can be used to input shelf, GSA container, room or building number. The more details the better. Additional comments and supporting documentation is necessary when the classified material leaves the accountability system by dissemination, destruction, declassification or downgrade.

FSOs may also want to track the use of classified information checked out of a central location. This is similar to what a library does. Tracking the check out dates can help reconstruct where and when a document is used to find lost documents, help enforce need to know and provide better document control.

SUMMARY

A good security program designed to protect classified material begins with the proper reception of classified information. Classified information should be delivered to an approved mailing address. Prior to delivery, the sender should contact the receiver and notify them of the intended delivery. The receiver should then prepare for the delivery and ensure that only the proper employee cleared to the appropriate level receives the classified delivery. The receiver should inspect the delivery for proper wrapping, address, and delivery method. After inspection, they should sign a receipt and return it to the sender. The inspector should then enter the classified items into an IMS. Once filed, they can make the information available for use to those with clearance and need to know.

PROBLEMS

1. After receiving classified material, the receiver inventories the contents and inspects the package. Name three items for possible inspection?
2. You have just received a classified package. Upon comparing the contents of the package with the receipt, you notice a misspelled title. What should you do?
3. Who should the FSO or senior security specialist notify in the event of a potential or suspected compromise of classified material?

RESOURCES

1. Department of Defense, DoD 5220.22-M, National Industrial Security Operating Manual, section 1-303, February 2006
2. Department of Defense, DoD 5220.22-M, National Industrial Security Operating Manual, section 5-103, February 2006
3. Department of Defense, DoD 5220.22-M, National Industrial Security Operating Manual, section 5-406, February 2006
4. Department of Defense, DoD 5220.22-M, National Industrial Security Operating Manual, section 5-201, February 2006

CHAPTER 6 MARKING CLASSIFIED MATERIAL

Introduction

Marking classified material is a method of warning and informing of classification level, the exact information to be protected, of downgrading and declassification instructions, reasons for classification and sources of classification, and special access, control or safeguarding requirements (Figure 6-1). In classified documents, the classification level is applied to the front and back covers, top and bottom of pages, paragraphs, figures, tables and charts. They are placed in conspicuous locations on objects, computers and other types of media. This chapter demonstrates how to inspect classified items for proper markings and how to properly mark classified items originally created or derived.

Guidance for Marking Classified Material

Executive Order 13526 delivers guidelines for assigning classification levels to objects and information. The Government classifies information to provide proper safeguarding and prevent unauthorized disclosure, loss or compromise of classified information [1]. The amount of classified information should be kept to the minimum needed to direct the appropriate amount of protection.

When receiving classified information, the FSO should check it against a receipt, inspect it for proper identification and markings and bring it into an IMS. If there are marking discrepancies, the receiver should rectify the situation by either sending it back or fixing the mistake themselves according to directions in the appropriate security classification guide (SCG).

Reasons for Applying Classification Markings

Classification markings can be found on the top and bottom, front and back of classified items. Markings are also found in internal pages, paragraphs and other locations inside documents, books, manuals and other paper based products.

- Warn and inform a user that an item is indeed classified or sensitive
- Conveys what exactly needs protection
- Identifies levels of classification or sensitivity
- Provides vital information and instruction on when to downgrade or declassify the material
- Gives sources and reason for classifying the item
- Warns of special access, control, dissemination or safeguarding requirements

Figure 6-1 Reasons for Classification

Security violations could occur if classified information is not marked properly. Suppose an engineer of XYZ Contractor goes to the company's centralized document storage area and signs out a document classified as SECRET. According to company information management policy the user is to return the item to document control prior to the end of the work day, or when they leave the office. The engineer takes the document back to his office and works with it. After a while his eyes get tired and he grabs his day planner to check his schedule.

He is reminded of an upcoming meeting with the social committee and begins to reflect on the near term company picnic. He gets up and walks to the window to look at proposed picnic location. While gathering his thoughts, he hears a knock at the door and walks over to open it. As he passes his desk his eyes glance at the document's markings of SECRET on the top and bottom of the opened pages. He then closes the classified book and picks it up. With the book closed and firmly secure in his hands and the outside protected by a cover sheet he opens the door and sees his buddy from across the hall. They both have clearances, but are working on two different contracts. His buddy has no need to know of the contents of the book.

In the example, the markings served to remind the engineer of the classified information in his possession and ensured that he maintained proper control and accountability. The marking also reminded the cleared employee of the responsibility of verifying clearance and "need to know" before disclosing classified information.

Classified markings also convey what exactly needs protection. For example, a cleared employee reviews a classified document and is able to determine from the portion markings which information is TOP SECRET, SECRET or CONFIDENTIAL. This information is important as a cleared employee would need to correctly transfer the classification of any information derived from the document to incorporate into a new document (derivative classification). Additionally, if any UNCLASSIFIED information needs to be removed for a sanitized product, the information will be properly identified in the portion markings.

Downgrade and Declassification

Classification markings also convey information and instruction on when to downgrade or declassify the material. These instructions are identified with "Declassify on:" and "Downgrade on:" followed by an event or a date. The downgrade and declassification instructions assist cleared employees in keeping classified material to the minimum necessary [2].

Executive Order 13526, directs that the OCAs assign a date or event for the declassification based on the sensitivity. Once the date or event transpires, the information should be declassified. This date or event should occur within the following 10 years and be annotated on the "Declassify on:" line. If declassification within the next ten years will still be sensitive enough to cause a measure of damage to national security, the OCA can extend "10-year rule" to a total of 25 years [3]. E.O. 13526, does offer exceptions to this rule which could extend the time past 25 years.

SECRET

For training purposes only

(U) Classified Material Marking Guide

Classified by: Jon Dow RBP/1022 DDMA

Reason: 1.4(e)

Declassify on: 31 July 2021

SECRET

For training purposes only

Figure 6-2a Front Cover

SECRET

For training purposes only

(U) Classified Material Marking Guide

SECRET

For training purposes only

Figure 6-2b Cover Page

SECRET

For training purposes only

(U) Classified Material Marking Guide

(U) First Page Markings

(U) Since this is the first page of the main part of the document, classification markings will be applied to the top and bottom that reflect the highest level of overall classification.

(C) For training purposes, this porting is classified CONFIDENTIAL but the page will be marked with SECRET on the top and bottom. The classification level of the portion markings on the first page have no bearing on the classification marking of the page.

SECRET

For training purposes only

Figure 6-2c First Page

SECRET

For training purposes only

SECRET

For training purposes only

Figure 6-2d Back Cover

Marking a Sample Classified Document

Figure 6-2 shows the overall marking requirements for a classified document. Here, the document is designated with a classification level of SECRET. In classified documents, the overall classification level is applied to the front and back covers, the title page and the first page of the document. The front cover page has an unclassified title as indicated by the portion marking (U) applied just before the title text. The "By:" line is on the cover page. Jon Dow of the fictional RBP Agency office designation 1022 DDMA provided the classification based on guidance from section 1.4 of Presidential E.O. 13526. The OCA listed Reason as 1.4 (e) (Figure 6-3) because the document contained information that would reveal "… scientific, technological, or economic matters relating to the national security, which includes defense against transnational terrorism" [4]. In this example, assume that the current date is 31 July 2011. He also assigned a declassification date for a duration of within the next ten years hence "Declassify on: 31 July 2021".

In another example of a classification "By:" line, information could be classified if unauthorized revelation could compromise military plans, weapon systems, or operations. In such cases a document or item assigned a classification because of this reason could have the statement "Reason: 1-4a". The 1-4a refers to section 1-4 of the E.O. 13526 (Figure 6-3). The reason line could also read, "Reason: Military plans, weapon systems or operations". The "Declassify on:" line could carry a date as indicated in the above paragraph, or an event such as "Declassify on: When the Ambassador Smith returns from her posting."

The top right page of Figure 6-2 is an example of the title page also with the "SECRET" markings on the top and bottom of the page. The page classification level is indicated by the "(U)" for UNCLASSIFIED as shown in the title. However this is one of the mandatory four pages reserved for the markings of the highest level of classification, therefore the overall classification marking is SECRET.

The page on the bottom left is also to be marked with the overall classification even though the OCA has indicated that the highest level of the page is a paragraph marked with the "(C)" for CONFIDENTIAL. The back cover is the final page requiring overall markings. This page will also indicate the highest level even if the highest level markings are the only classification markings on the page.

Sec. 1.4. Classification Categories

Information shall not be considered for classification unless it concerns:

(a) military plans, weapons systems, or operations;

(b) foreign government information;

(c) intelligence activities (including special activities), intelligence sources or methods, or cryptology;

(d) foreign relations or foreign activities of the United States, including confidential sources;

(e) scientific, technological, or economic matters relating to the national security, which includes defense against transnational terrorism;

(f) United States Government programs for safeguarding nuclear materials or facilities;

(g) vulnerabilities or capabilities of systems, installations, infrastructures, projects, plans, or protection services relating to the national security, which includes defense against transnational terrorism; or

(h) weapons of mass destruction..

Figure 6-3 Reasons for original classification authority to assign a classification.

SPECIAL HANDLING

Special access, control, dissemination or safeguarding requirements and warnings are also identified in the classification markings. These alert the holder of special handling instructions in addition to protection provided by the classification level. These handling instructions are more precisely "need to know" oriented. Some other warnings may require additional briefings beyond the induction required for standard TOP SECRET, SECRET and CONFIDENTIAL clearances.

MARKING CLASSIFIED INFORMATION

Cleared contractors are not OCAs. However, they may have a contract to produce classified documents or items based on a contract.

The cleared contractor should apply appropriate markings as classified items are generated, reproduced or compiled. Failure to apply timely markings could lead to inadvertent security violations such as forgetting to lock classified items in a GSA approved container, vault or other approved storage; improper processing to include mailing or delivering in an unauthorized manner and unauthorized disclosure to those without clearance and need to know. The lack of proper notification could lead to compromise, suspected compromise, loss and theft of classified material.

Classification markings are required on all classified material regardless of the type of information or media [5]. Documents such as reports, books, white papers and notebooks are physically easier to apply classification marking to. But because of the multiple pages and portions, they may require a greater volume of markings. Objects such as computers, machinery, weapons and other large end items require fewer markings, usually on the top and bottom of each side. Computer software and media such as floppy discs, flash drives and CDs require small labels. Smaller items are very difficult to apply classification markings and exceptions exist. However, every effort is made to ensure that classification level is clearly identified. DSS can assist and advise in the proper procedures for non conventional marking issues.

Caution

Working on classified projects may seem intimidating at first. Overtime, the work may quickly become routine and perhaps mundane. The cleared employee can quickly go from being impressed with their responsibilities and alert in their actions to having a more relaxed attitude as they become accustomed to the work. Soon the classified items and the markings can become invisible and ineffective. Many modern examples of security violations include cleared employees leaving classified information unattended at their desks, lunch rooms and other areas. Such actions have led to possible compromise as security containers have even been left open and unattended or accidentally removed from a cleared facility with classified information still inside.

REMINDERS

Markings should not be the "stand alone" security measure. FSOs might be tempted to add additional markings to already cluttered media hoping to prevent a user lapse in judgment. Once again the effectiveness begins to wear off and man hours are wasted on efforts that may not increase awareness. To counter the effects, the holder of the classified material must remain vigilant and aware of their surroundings and situation at all times. This is a proactive posture and requires a bit of imagination. Such security is accomplished with solid training and reminders of responsibilities while possessing classified information.

Simple Solutions

Simple acts such as maintaining a clean desk policy has helped reduce security violations. In this situation, an employee removes everything from the tops of their working surfaces or desks except for the classified material. That simple practice could make a busy employee more aware that any articles on the desk requires extra diligence and must never be left unattended. When no longer needed, classified information should be locked up in a security container or closed area. If a desk is empty, the cleared employee can also assume that there are no classified items out. This discipline creates an environment that reduces the chances of the employee leaving a classified item vulnerable to compromise if they forget to secure it prior to taking a break or leaving for the day. Also useful is the posting of a desk tent and door hanger with an important reminder that classified items are left out. As the employee leaves their work area, they will encounter the warnings on their desk or door handle.

TYPES OF CLASSIFICATION MARKINGS

Classification markings are broken down into categories to assist with proper protection and control. These categories of markings help reduce the risk of security violations, loss, compromise or suspected compromise. The categories are as follows:

- Identification Marking
- Overall Marking
- Page Marking
- Component Marking
- Portion Marking
- Subject and Title Marking
- Derivative Marking

Identification Marking

Identification markings provide the contact information of those responsible for preparation of the classified material and the date of classification. This is usually completed by the original classification authority (OCA) or the person assigning derivative classification markings.

Overall Marking

Overall markings display the highest level of classified information contained in the document. The overall markings are conspicuously placed to allow for easy identification and protection of the highest level of classified information. Classification markings should be more prominent than any other letters, characters or otherwise stand out for easy identification. Classified information can be applied with a stamp, hand written, branded, printed on labels or any other method of permanently identifying the classification level.

The overall classification is placed on the top and bottom of the outside front cover, the title page, first page and the outside back cover (Figure 6-2). The overall classification provides the highest level contained in the document. For example, if a document contains CONFIDENTIAL, SECRET and TOP SECRET information, the overall classification of the document is marked TOP SECRET. Computers, discs, drives and other objects, are also marked on the top, bottom, front and back. If this is not possible, markings should be placed in such a manner that there no doubt of the classification.

Page Marking

Page markings are for classified documents with single and multiple pages such as books, notebooks or other multi-page manuals. Except for those pages reserved for overall markings, the remaining document's pages are marked on the top and bottom with the highest classification level contained on that particular page. For example, if a page in the TOP SECRET document contains only CONFIDENTIAL information, the page will be marked "CONFIDENTIAL". If the page contains SECRET and CONFIDENTIAL information, then the page marking will be "SECRET" even though the overall document classification will be TOP SECRET (Figure 6-4) 6 .

Component Marking

Component markings refer to documents with stand alone sections such as annexes, appendixes or other components. These could be parts of plans, programs or projects with attachments. In the case of a major section containing UNCLASSIFIED material, only the top and bottom of the first page should be marked "UNCLASSIFIED". A statement is included with wording such as "All portions of this component (identify the component as an appendix, section, letter, annex, etc.) are UNCLASSIFIED 6.

Portion Marking

Subject and title markings should be unclassified. When the unclassified title or subject is marked in a classified document the (U) will be inserted at the beginning or end depending on the OCA's requirements. This unclassified title allows for documenting, filing and adding to other unclassified databases. If a classified title is used, the database or files would have to be protected as classified.

Figure 6-4a demonstrates how page and portion markings should be applied. The markings on the page on the upper left corner carry the highest classification of the material found in the paragraphs and portions. Here, the second paragraph is classified at the CONFIDEN-

CONFIDENTIAL

For training purposes only

(U) Pages are marked top and bottom according to the highest classification on the page. Mark with material that will stand out from the rest of the document.

(C) The marking on the top and bottom of the interior page reflects the level of the paragraph or portion with the highest classification.

CONFIDENTIAL

For training purposes only

Figure 6-4a Portion Markings

UNCLASSIFIED

(U) Even though the overall classification may be SECRET, this page is marked UNCLASSIFIED.

(U) Each portion is UNCLASSIFIED, therefore the entire page will be marked as such.

UNCLASSIFIED

Figure 6-4b Overall Markings

SECRET

For training purposes only

(U) Portion markings reflect the classification of each part, paragraph or portion of an item.

(C) Depending on agency, portion markings can be put to the front or behind the actual portion.

(S) Abbreviate (TS) for TOP SECRET, (S) for SECRET and (C) for CONFIDENTIAL when marking portions.

SECRET

For training purposes only

Figure 6-4c Portion Markings

SECRET

For training purposes only

(U) The term "portion" also includes charts, graphs, pictures, etc. The following table has a full portion marking inside the table and an abbreviated marking in the caption.

Vehicle	Speed	Ceiling
Helicopter	100 KPH	12,000 Ft
Airplane	150 KPH	15,000 Ft
Jet	450 KPH	30,000 Ft
Rocket	17,000 KPH	22 Mi

(U) Aircraft capabilities   SECRET

SECRET

For training purposes only

Figure 6-4a Graphics

TIAL level, marked with a (C) [7], and the classification is transferred to the top and bottom as the overall page marking. Primarily, pages are marked at the highest level of classified information found on that page.

Figure 6-4b provides an example of a page within a classified document containing unclassified information. All portion markings are marked with "(U)" indicating that the highest level of classification on the page is indeed UNCLASSIFIED. The overall marking of the page is therefore UNCLASSIFIED.

Figure 6-4c is classified at the SECRET level and marked as such on top and bottom. This marking is directly linked to the portion marked with "(S)". Portion markings containing text use abbreviations of the classification and are placed either before or after the portion depending on agency requirements. TOP SECRET is abbreviated with "(TS)", SECRET is abbreviated with "(S)" and CONFIDENTIAL with "(C)" [7].

Finally, Figure 6-4d is classified SECRET because of the table's classification. Portion markings on tables, charts, figures, diagrams, illustrations, etc, should not be abbreviated but spelled out and placed conspicuously as to indicate the classification level [7]. The text identifying the feature uses abbreviations as seen in "(U) Aircraft capabilities".

Though these examples have demonstrated overall markings on certain required pages and page markings throughout the document, some GCAs may require that all pages are marked with the overall classification regardless of the highest classification on that page. For example, if the overall classification of a document is Secret, then the each page will be marked SECRET even when the highest level of classified information on the page is CONFIDENTIAL.

Derivative Marking

According to the NISPOM, "Contractor personnel make derivative classification decisions when they incorporate, paraphrase, restate, or generate in new form, information that is already classified".

Original classification occurs when information meets classification criteria as described in Executive Order 13526, *Classified National*

Security Information. Classification determination is usually considered as events, programs or missions develop. Remember, the product of original classification is a security classification guide, classification markings and the DD Form 254.

SECRET

For training purposes only

The Testing Agency

Washington, DC

June 21, 2011

MEMORANDUM FOR CHIEF

From: Deputy of Development

Subject: Test Results

(U) This is the original classified document. If a cleared employee conducts research based on this and/or other documents, then they will transfer the classified information.

(S) The classification level of the information used will determine the classification level of the new document

Classified by: Jon Dow RBP/1022 DDMA

Reason: 1.4(e)

Declassify on: 31 July 2021

SECRET

For training purposes only

Figure 6-5a Page markings on original document

Derivative classified information occurs when information is used that has already been determined to be classified and is provided in a new product such as report, item, or event. Information is already known to be classified. In this case a security classification guide or previously classified information is used to identify the existing classification level. The product of derivative classification is properly based on guidance in the DD Form 254, Security Classification Guide and/or previously marked source documents.

SECRET

For training purposes only

Local Research Park

Decatur, IL

October 2, 2011

MEMORANDUM FOR DIVISION

From: Jon Smith, Senior Engineer

Subject: Fireworks

(U) This paragraph contains original information from independent research. The information is unclassified.

(S) The classification level of the information used will determine the classification level of the new document. This information was extracted from the document Subject: Test Results.

Classified By: John Jones, Engineer

Derived From: Memorandum dated June 21 2009

Subj: Test Results

The Testing Agency

Declassify on: 31 July 2021

SECRET

For training purposes only

Figure 6-5b Page markings on derivative document

Where the government makes classification determinations, contractors carry over classification markings on existing classified information. Copying or duplicating classified information is not considered derivative classification. It's just copying. A new product or application using existing classification better fits the derivative classification description.

The following is an example of derivative classification. While writing a report to enhance the "Gravy System", XYZ Contractor engineers pull three classified documents from the classified holding area. They conduct background research based on the documents and begin to understand not only how the system works, but how they can improve the system to work better in rain storms. The engineers are working with a document classified SECRET and two documents classified at the CONFIDENTIAL level. By the time they completed the report, they had used portions of all three documents thus the finished product is classified SECRET.

Derivative classification products are marked the same as any other classified product. The top, bottom, front and back of objects and the front and back covers, title and first pages of documents are marked with the highest overall level. The difference between original documents and derived documents exists in the area reserved for information about the classification. Derived documents also have a "Classified by:" line and a "Derived from:" line (Figure 6-5b). The "Derived from:" line provides a connection between the original source document or security classification guide and the new document. In some cases there are multiple security classification guides or source documents, thus the contractor should simply state "multiple sources". When using the "multiple sources" designation, the derivative classifier documents the sources to preserve a continuous record of the derived document and the basis for classifying the product.

Derivative classifiers are trained every two years 1. Since the definition of deriviative classification covers all production, assembly, paraphrasing, word for word transition, and many other tasks, this training is significant; no training, no work performance. Employees performing derivative classification must also be cleared at the appropriate level, have need to know and have access to classification guides or other references to provide sources of proper markings.

Previous Classification Guidance

There are still many documents, machines, objects, computers and other products that have been classified by an OCA using previous Presidential Executive Orders. The markings on such classified material are sufficient if they are legible and provide proper safeguarding and identification notification. There is no guidance to re-mark such material and the task may prove to be a tremendous burden on contractor and government personnel [8]. In such cases where this classified information is still available, it can be stored and worked with no changes. If there is a need to re-mark the documents the responsibility falls on the OCA. These previously classified documents can be used as source documents.

Where the documents have no portion markings or page markings, the derived document will carry over the markings of the overall source document classification. If classification guidance or markings need clarification, the holder should inquire with the Agency responsible for the original classification [9]. Every effort should be made to clarify any confusion about classified information to prevent unauthorized disclosure or compromise. The "Declassify on:" line uses dates and other information contained in the DD Form 254 and the SCG or from the original source documents [10].

WHEN TO APPLY CLASSIFICATION MARKINGS

Part of good IMS is a formal request process for copying, creating, transmitting and destroying classified material. The NISPOM requires hand receipt action for the transfer of material classified at SECRET or above and also require accountability measures for items classified at the TOP SECRET level [11].

An FSO can control the use of classified information using many techniques. One way is to create and implement forms for each classified transaction executed by the cleared employees. For example, when cleared employees compile classified research projects into a new document they can submit a request to the classified document custodians for those originating classified documents. On the request they would specify the name of the new document, the sources of compilation by in-house document number, type of media the document will be create on (disk, CD, data stick, book, etc). The FSO can then properly prepare the derived classified document as they assign a new document number and either add the required classification markings to the new media, or review the new document to ensure proper markings have been applied. The FSO can also create a process and implement request forms for destruction, transmission, duplication and other transactions.

Alternative Marking Methods

There are exceptions to marking guidance as not every product follows a typical form or structure. Items can be too small, large, odd shaped or bulky, thus preventing the application of classified markings in the directed method. In all cases, the NISPOM requires a clear identification of the protection level regardless of the shape or form.

The NISPOM does provide information on how to mark various forms of classified material. Classified files, folders, envelops, binders, and etc are to be marked in an obvious method with the proper classification. Markings must be placed directly on the object and a cover sheet should be provided when removed from a closed area or security container [11]. Classified email should also be properly marked within the message. The first words on the first line should contain the classification level. Also included in the email should be the "Derived from" line. Certain agencies may also require a "classified by:"and "Reason for classification:" lines. More contract specific classification information is available in the program SCG. If the email is printed, then the classification marking should stand out above the other print in the document [12].

Objects that are too small to be read with the human eye should be marked such that the markings can be seen when read with magnification equipment. For example, microfiche items should be marked in such a way to be immediately recognized, and the storage container should be marked to protect it from unauthorized disclosure. Since the print is small on the original document, other markings large enough to be read with the unaided eye should be placed on the container. The original classified document should be marked in such a way as to be recognized when magnified.

Transmittal Papers

Transmittal papers accompany a document while it is transferred from one location to the other. It provides administrative data about the classified product being transmitted. The transmittal document should be marked at the highest classification level of the information in the entire document packet. A statement of the classification level when classified attachments are removed from the compiled document should be included. For example, if there are unclassified attachments included with the classified document, the statement would read: "Unclassified when separated from classified enclosures." In another example, attachments could include those classified with higher classification documents included. This would include the statement, "CONFIDENTIAL or SECRET when separated from enclosures." (Figure 6-6) [13].

CONFIDENTIAL

For training purposes

(U) Understanding Marking Requirements-Unclassified Transmittal Documents

When an unclassified transmittal document is attached to a classified document, mark the transmittal document with the highest classification level transmitted to include all attachments. Some agencies do not require portion markings on the unclassified transmittal document.

(U) Include the statement: "This document is UNCLASSIFIED when removed from the package."

Enclosures

This document is UNCLASSIFIED when removed from the package

CONFIDENTIAL

For training purposes

Figure 6-6 Transmittal Documents

Compilation

In the event unclassified items are grouped with other unclassified items, the SCG may identify the compilation to be classified. When events warrant such classification, the compilation will carry markings of the highest level and a statement of the reason for classification will be affixed to the item in a visible location. Unlike other documents, portion markings on compiled information are not necessary [14].

Unclassified information can be developed while working with classified information. In this case, the material should be protected at the overall classification level. For example, suppose a company is making a classified item. Some of the by-products, or rejected products may not be usable and will be destroyed. Until then, they should be treated as classified material [15].

Training Aids

Training is vital to an organization's improvement. They are great resources as students are able to observe and participate in exercises to help improve their skills and performance on the job. Where employees practice protecting classified material they may need to use training aids labeled with classified markings. Unclassified training material is marked to indicate that it is UNCLASSIFIED but is assigned a classification for training purposes only. For example an unclassified document is marked to portray a secret memorandum. Here, the preparer or trainer may mark the document to indicate it is unclassified, but deemed classified for training purposes with the following or similar markings: "UNCLASSIFIED SAMPLE", "SECRET FOR TRAINING OTHERWISE UNCLASSIFIED", "CONFIDENTIAL for exercise only", etc [16].

Declassifying Information

When the classification duration has expired according to the markings on the classified material, the holder of the information should begin the process of declassifying. Contractors should coordinate with the GCA before beginning the declassification or downgrading process [17]. Regardless of the approval method, when the holder of the classified material is authorized to begin declassifying or downgrading, they should re-mark appropriate areas. For documents, the holder cancels the old classification markings and re-applies the new downgraded markings (Figures 6-7 and 6-8). This action also depends on how the involvement impacts operation. If the impact is too great, the GCA's can provide guidance for alternative markings or notices. A classified document with multiple pages may look as depicted in Figure 6-9.

~~SECRET~~

UNCLASSIFIED

For training purposes

(U) Classified Material Marking Guide

Classified by: Jon Dow

RBP/1022DDMA

Reason: 1.4(e)

Declassify on: 31 July 2008

~~SECRET~~

UNCLASSIFIED

For training purposes

Figure 6-7 Example of a document that has been marked as UNCLASSIFIED after the "Declassify on:" date has passed. Original classification has been crossed out and the new UNCLASSIFIED marking has been added.

~~SECRET~~

CONFIDENTIAL

For training purposes

(U) Classified Material Marking Guide

Classified by: Jon Dow

RBP/1022DDMA

Reason: 1.4(e)

Downgrade to Confidential on: 31

July 2008

Declassify on: 31 December 2020

~~SECRET~~

CONFIDENTIAL

For training purposes

Figure 6-8 Example of a document that has been marked as CONFIDENTIAL after the "Downgrade to:" date has passed. Original classification has been crossed out and the new CONFIDENTIAL marking has been added.

Upgrading Information

Some activity, discovery or action could indicate that the classification assigned does not offer the correct level of protection necessary for safeguarding the classified material. In these cases the GCA may require that the document be upgraded and re-marked from CONFIDENTIAL to SECRET or TOP SECRET or from SECRET to TOP SECRET [18]. The person responsible for the re-marking should cross out the old classification and re-mark with the upgraded classification in all the appropriate locations. They then enter the information of the authority responsible for the upgrade and the reason for the upgrade and notify all users of the information.

CHALLENGING CLASSIFIED MATERIAL

Users of classified information have an obligation to report any confusing classifications or wrongly marked classified material [19]. This is challenging the classification. Measures are in place to prevent employees from suffering any form of punishment or retribution for raising the issues. This reporting assists with proper markings, preventing over classification and ensuring that classification is based on legitimate reasons.

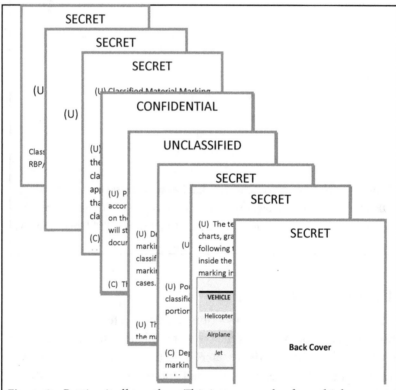

Figure 6-9 Putting it all together. This is an example of a multiple page document (composed of figures from this chapter). The front, back, title and first pages are marked with the overall classification. The internal pages are marked with the highest level on each page. (Each page is classified for training purposes).

Those who discover classification discrepancies should challenge the classification. The SCG provides information on challenging classification with the GCA.

SUMMARY

Cleared employees who perform on classified contracts should be able to recognize what is classified and know how to protect the classified material based on the markings provided. Classified information comes in many forms. Classified objects and products are marked on the top, bottom, sides, front and back. If the item is bulky, odd shaped or otherwise a size and configuration that makes mandatory marking difficult, the markings should be placed as clearly as possible to convey the proper classification level. Multiple page classified documents have many places reserved for classification markings.

Additionally, the source of classification, reason for classification, and duration are applied to classified items. Derived classifications will have a statement indicating from where the classified information came. While working with classified items, cleared employees are responsible for challenging any classified information that has been incorrectly or unnecessarily classified, should be downgraded or upgraded to another classification level or that security classification guidance is incorrect or not sufficient.

PROBLEMS

1. As a document custodian, your responsibilities involve receiving and inspecting documents for proper classification markings. You receive a properly wrapped classified document from a Government agency with the following characteristics:
    *   Contains UNCLASSIFIED, CONFIDENTIAL and SECRET information
    *   Created on June 21, 2007
    *   Reason for Classification is 1.4 (a)
    *   Contains 400 pages
    *   Classified by: Jon Wain, RBP, 1022 DDMA
    *   Classification guidance is found in the Gravy Security Classification Guide

1a. Based on the above description, what are the major areas you would expect to see classification markings?

1b. Write out the "By:" line describing who classified the material, reason for classification and the declassify on date.

1c. Which classification marking would you expect to find on the overall marking?

2. Your security team is conducting an annual inventory of your company's classified holdings. In the course of the inventory, they come across a 30 page document entitled *Weather Capabilities (U)*. The document is slightly worn but otherwise in good condition. Your team notifies you that a page is loose and that the document needs to be repaired. They also ask your opinion on some findings concerning internal illustrations; none of the graphs, pictures or containers contains classification markings. Additional information for the document follows:

   - Created in 1986
   - Contains the following marking on the first page:
   - Classified by: RBP, 1022 DMDA
   - Reason for classification: Military capabilities
   - Declassify on: OADR
   - Contains overall classification of CONFIDENTIAL.

   2a. What would you direct your team to do concerning the portion markings?

3. An engineer is about to print a report based on classified information. This report is a summary of information found in two different documents. As you prepare to help her correctly mark the derivative document you take into consideration the two source documents that she has provided. The source documents are the same as example questions 1 and 2.

   3a. The derived document contains information classified SECRET, how would the "Classified by:" line be filled out?

   3b. What should be put on the "Reason for classification:" line?

   3c. What would be the duration of classification?

4. You are making the rounds of your security team's area and overhear a heated discussion between your team members and

a technical writer. In order to diffuse the situation, you politely interrupt the conversation and ask the technical writer if you can be of any help. He informs you that "your" security specialist has rejected acceptance of the document based on classification marking errors. He states that it is a good product and no one would notice the mistake anyway. What would you say to him?

5. A program manager knocks on your door and asks if you have a moment for something important. He asks you to take a walk with him to a secure area where he shows you a piece of hardware. The object is small enough to fit in your hand. You notice a commercial CONFIDENTIAL label; the kind that a manufacturer might install at the factory. The manager lets you know that he has been informed that the object is not classified at all, but that the manufacturer installed the labels as classified material would be added at a later date. The program manager would like to bring the item to an unclassified meeting seeing that "it's not classified anyway." You notice that the object is well worn and does not look new at all.

5a. Where can you go to discover whether or not the item is classified?

5b. Are there any other sources?

5c. After speaking with the right people and consulting the authoritative documents, you are now more confused than ever. You decide to challenge the classification to seek the clarification you need to properly protect the item. Describe the process you would employ.

RESOURCES

1. Department of Defense, DoD 5220.22-M, National Industrial Security Operating Manual, section 4-200, February 2006
2. Department of Defense, DoD 5220.22-M, National Industrial Security Operating Manual, section 4-205, February 2006
3. The President, Executive Order 13526, Classified National Security Information—National Industrial Security Program, section 1.5, (Federal Register, Dec 2009)

4. The President, Executive Order 13526, Classified National Security Information—National Industrial Security Program, section 1.4e, (Federal Register, Dec 2009)

5. Department of Defense, DoD 5220.22-M, National Industrial Security Operating Manual, section 4-201, February 2006

6. Department of Defense, DoD 5220.22-M, National Industrial Security Operating Manual, section 4-205, February 2006

7. Department of Defense, DoD 5220.22-M, National Industrial Security Operating Manual, section 4-206 February 2006

8. Department of Defense, DoD 5220.22-M, National Industrial Security Operating Manual, section 4-209, February 2006

9. The President, Executive Order 13526, Classified National Security Information—National Industrial Security Program, section 1.8, (Federal Register, Dec 2009)

10. Department of Defense, DoD 5220.22-M, National Industrial Security Operating Manual, section 4-208, February 2006

11. Department of Defense, DoD 5220.22-M, National Industrial Security Operating Manual, section 5-201, February 2006

12. Department of Defense, DoD 5220.22-M, National Industrial Security Operating Manual, section 4-210, February 2006

13. Department of Defense, DoD 5220.22-M, National Industrial Security Operating Manual, section 4-211, February 2006

14. Department of Defense, DoD 5220.22-M, National Industrial Security Operating Manual, section 4-213, February 2006

15. Department of Defense, DoD 5220.22-M, National Industrial Security Operating Manual, section 4-214, February 2006

16. Department of Defense, DoD 5220.22-M, National Industrial Security Operating Manual, section 4-215, February 2006

17. Department of Defense, DoD 5220.22-M, National Industrial Security Operating Manual, section 4-216, February 2006

18. Department of Defense, DoD 5220.22-M, National Industrial Security Operating Manual, section 4-217, February 2006

19. Department of Defense, DoD 5220.22-M, National Industrial Security Operating Manual, section 4-104, February 2006

CHAPTER 7 WORKING WITH CLASSIFIED

INTRODUCTION

A good security program protects classified information from unauthorized disclosure. Otherwise national security could face varying degrees of damage depending on what information is disclosed and how it was used. We have seen how classified information is identified with markings and protected from unauthorized disclosure. An IMS helps the FSO know the disposition of classified information and security containers and closed areas protect classified information when not in use.

PROTECT ORAL TRANSMISSION

Protecting classified information spoken in conversation or presentation is a baseline security requirement that applies to both possessing and non-possessing cleared facilities. A classified conversation may occur during a classified visit or meeting and should be conducted only as necessary and in controlled environments. For example, classified conversations are authorized in areas where access and need to know have been verified. These classified communications should never take place in hallways, around the water cooler, in public places or car pools. Just as the holder of classified documents verifies a receiver's need to know and security clearance before transferring it, the same is true for releasing classified information verbally.

MEETINGS AND VISITS

As an example, suppose a GCA desires to sponsor a classified meeting at XYZ Contractor as part of contractual requirements. The government holds and controls the release of classified information while XYZ Contractor provides the facilities and controls the access. The government organizes the meeting and provides the need to know. They also verify that access controls are in place. Their responsibilities include setting up the meeting and authorizing the release of classified information. The attendees then use the approved method of filing a visit authorization through JPAS.

On the day of the meeting, an XYZ Contractor cleared employee verifies the identification and clearance levels of all authorized attendees based on the information provided by the points of contact. Once verified, the visitor is given a pass and escorted to the conference room which has been previously approved for conducting classified discussions.

Prior to the start of the meeting the FSO ensures that someone provides a security briefing notifying attendees of the classification level of information to be discussed, whether or not taking notes is permitted and if so, how classified notes will be controlled. When classified notes are permitted, they will have to be properly marked and prepared for dissemination (hand carry with the attendee, faxed or mailed at a later date).

In situations where classified conversations are required over telephone, radio, or other means, each party must be in a location authorized for classified conversation. Additionally, the discourse must occur while using devices authorized for classified discussions such as the National Security Agency (NSA) approved Secure Telephone Unit (STU) or Secure Telephone Equipment (STE).

END OF DAY SECURITY CHECKS

Non-possessing Facilities

End of day checks apply to facilities where classified work is conducted and or classified meetings have taken place. The primary purpose is to protect classified information by double checking that it has been returned to classified storage. Non-possessing facilities should implement this practice in situations where classified conversations and note taking have occurred or any instance where classified information has been carried into the facility. It is also a good idea to implement such checks to protect other sensitive or critical information or for life safety issues.

Possessing Facilities

The following is an example of a typical workday involving classified documents signed out from the company's central classified document repository. At the end of the day, the FSO reviews an IMS database to identify any classified material not returned. Satisfied of the accountability, she closed her safe and left for the evening. A few hours later, the contracted guard service informs the on call security specialist of a possible security violation. The FSO has left a classified document unattended on top of a security container.

To prevent the above violation, end of day checks serve as a precaution against leaving classified material unattended. The designated responsible employee should complete a check list prior to leaving an area where classified material is used, stored, transmitted or is otherwise accessed. The checklist should address secure containers, tabletops, walking surfaces, printers, copiers, and computers to ensure that no residual classified material is left unattended. The end of day checks are not required when an area is manned 24 hours per day, seven days per week [1].

Though not required by NISPOM, government forms are available as methods of strengthening of security programs. Companies are free to use these forms or create their own. One such form available is the Activity Security Check List, Standard Form 701. The FSO can adapt it by removing inapplicable information or even adding to the checklist. For example, the government form includes a block for checking whether or not coffee pots are turned off. This may or may not be important to the FSO. Regardless of the system used, the security checks are effective measures and have proven successful. Unsecured classified information would have otherwise been susceptible to compromise.

MAGNETS AND REMINDERS

When conducting end of day checks, the designated, last to leave or other responsible person determines whether or not the security containers are locked. This involves spinning the dial and attempting to open the security container. They should inspect the security container check sheet, Standard Form 702 to ensure it has been properly annotated with initials, date and time of persons locking the container and sign the SF 702 as the checker.

The inspection continues with searching tables, desks, printers, trash cans and other areas where classified material may be left unattended. Removable hard drives, classified papers left in printers and copiers, and other materials that may be classified, and other classified material should be properly stored before departing. Then they should check doors and windows for proper operation and to ensure they will lock properly. Finally, they should set locks and alarms, ensure magnets display the CLOSED side, and annotate the end of day check sheet. These SF Forms 702 are not required, but do have useful fields for annotating the date and time opened, initials for person opening the lock, date and time closed with initials of person securing the lock and the date and time verified that the lock is indeed closed with the verifier's initials. The final fields are for guards to annotate their checks if necessary.

Other Inspection

The following does not pertain to non-possessing facilities. Perimeter controls are required for certain areas containing classified information in possessing facilities. Such controls set the tone for the successful security program. Perimeter controls provide an additional physical security layer between unauthorized persons and classified material. Controls begin with an assessment of the risk facing the classified information in the holder's possession. Depending on the assessment results and contractual or NISPOM guidance controls may manifest in the installation of cameras, alarms, reaction force and physical reinforcements to deter and detect forced entry.

The NISPOM requires physically inspecting employees in possessing facilities [2]. Inspections enhance classified document accountability and the myriad compromise opportunities while working with classified information. Establishing a system to deter, detect and deny the unauthorized introduction or removal of classified material is critical. Such a system notifies employees, visitors, contractors and vendors entering and exiting a cleared facility that they are subject to inspection. Posting signs and performing random inspection gives the organization an active measure to set the stage for compliance. Laptops, electronic items and other materials where classified information is stored should be searched. Searching electronic data such as laptops, disks, or other storage devices with a keyword list can also help detect and prevent the unauthorized removal of classified information. Sample keywords might include "secret, program, proprietary, export," or other words that could tip off security that unauthorized information resides in the information system or storage device.

Such measures encourage and remind others not to remove or introduce classified material without going through proper channels. These measures make economic and intelligence espionage more difficult. However, FSOs consult with legal council before conducting inspections of persons or their belongings.

DEVELOP EMERGENCY PROCEDURES TO PROTECT CLASSIFIED INFORMATION

On September 11, 2001 a jet, slammed into the Pentagon. Fuel, fire and concussion waves smashed into the most secured of areas. Sensitive and Classified military information and material, communications equipment and secure containers became vulnerable to loss or compromise. In 2005 Hurricane Katrina flooded much of the Alabama, Mississippi and Louisiana low areas. Residents and businesses evacuated the area leaving classified information locked in security containers. Flood waters caused tremendous damages that could have left unprepared businesses with unsecured classified material.

Regardless of the type of disaster, man-made or natural, those in possession of classified material should have a procedure for protecting it based on the risk analysis. Life safety is the top priority. However, when possible, classified information must be protected. Creating emergency procedures and rehearsing them regularly can save lives and protect classified information. Such procedures should support the overall security program and be in harmony with the risk assessment and practical enough to execute. The contingency plan includes written policy and rehearsals to ensure everyone understands their role in protecting classified material.

For example, an FSO may use the risk analysis to discover that fire and severe weather are the biggest and most disastrous of threats. Any emergency causing the evacuation of the facilities makes classified information vulnerable. Risk analysis helps the FSO develop a plan to account for any classified material that could be in use and otherwise vulnerable when disaster strikes. Such an effort requires the implementation of a team of all affected business units to map out a written policy and scheduled rehearsals.

What happens when a disaster occurs while classified information is in use and not properly stored in a secure container? The resulting emergency requires that when possible, cleared personnel will evacuate their work areas with classified material. Time permitting, identified cleared employees should lock security containers and grab emergency kit bags (Figure 7-1) and classified document sign out sheets. All employees should report to their designated assembly areas where security representatives relieve them of their classified material and provide adequate protection from unauthorized disclosure.

Classified Information Accountability Process

The NISPOM requires cleared contractors to maintain access and control of TOP SECRET information. Since the unauthorized disclosure or compromise of TOP SECRET information has the potential to cause exceptionally grave damage to national security, the cleared contractor must designate a Top Secret Control Official (TSCO) [3].

Emergency Kit Bags

- Marking supplies (Pen, stamp, preprinted labels, etc)
- Opaque bag or wrapping paper
- Opaque security tape
- Cleared personnel roster
- TOP SECRET, SECRET and CONFIDENTIAL cover sheets

Figure 7-1 Suggested contents of emergency kit bags. These bags should be kept up to date and readily available during emergency evacuations.

This official maintains records and accountability of TOP SECRET information entering and leaving the facilities. They also conduct an annual inventory and maintain a chain of custody on actions pertaining to the TOP SECRET holdings. Receipts, records and accountability of all items are continuous from reception to destruction. Additionally, destruction and reproduction receipts should be maintained for two years [4].

The TSCO tracks the movement of the TOP SECRET information. They know at all times where an item is stored or located at any given time. Each TOP SECRET item is cataloged and numbered in a series. This includes items photocopied, derived, courier, electronically, or otherwise properly received. As the item is stored, moved, disseminated and or destroyed, the paper trail and catalog numbers are annotated accordingly. This tracking system allows for constant status surveillance.

TOP SECRET Control Officials are authorized to:

- Receive
- Transmit
- Maintain access and accountability
- Conduct annual inventory

Information Management Systems (IMS)

Though NISPOM directs the duties and appointment of a TSCO, it is a good practice to control all classified information. Receipting actions, reproduction, destruction, and other activities concerning classified information should be documented. This can aid in the control, protection and investigations concerning locating discovering disposition of classified information. Also, NISPOM identifies the IMS, but does not provide implementation details [5].

Basically, the IMS should allow for documenting receipting actions, transmission, receptions, storage location and other transitions involving all classified information. IMS can be a spreadsheet or for complicated inventories, software is available from vendors and may be worthwhile for contractors with large classified holdings inventory.

Working Papers

The accounting process for TOP SECRET includes any unfinished products such as notes, files and workbooks used for more than 30 days or transmitted outside of a facility. The creator should mark working papers with the date created, the classification level and annotate "Working Papers". These TOP SECRET working papers become finalized after 30 days and a control number and documentation by the TSCO should begin. Working papers at the SECRET and CONFIDENTIAL classification levels are finalized at 180 days and again when sent outside of the facility [6]. The working papers should become a final product at the end of the time period. If not needed they should be destroyed.

Classified information not a finished product? No problem
- Mark date created
- Mark classification level
- Annotate "Working Papers"
- Working papers are to be marked as finished document when:
  - Over 30 days old for TOP SECRET
  - Over 180 days for SECRET and CONFIDENTIAL
  - Sent outside of facility

Classified Material Storage

TOP SECRET material is normally required to be stored in a GSA approved security container. If items are too large or bulky, they can be stored in approved vaults or closed areas with supplemental controls. SECRET material can also be stored in the same manner as TOP SE-CRET except that it can be stored in a safe (figure 7-2), a steel file cabinet or safe type container with automatic locks [7]. Supplemental controls are intrusion detection systems or an approved guard force and are required for SECRET stored in closed areas and all TOP SECRET information. However NISPOM does not require supplemental controls standard SECRET as long as it is in GSA approved container.

Figure 7-2 Classified information should be stored in GSA approved security container unless open bin storage is approved.

Classified Reproduction

Classified information should only be reproduced in response to a contractual requirement such as in the performance of a deliverable. Reproduction should not be made as a matter of convenience as it puts classified information at unnecessary risk and it requires dedicated resources. The FSO can enforce resource discipline with procedures to ensure classified information is reproduced only as necessary and using only approved equipment. They can also ensure only trained and authorized personnel are able to reproduce classified information. This control should include procedures to govern the use and type of designated reproduction equipment.

Copy machines, scanners and other reproduction equipment should be identified and designated for classified information reproduction. All other enterprise equipment should be off limits to classified reproduction. This can be accomplished through signs identifying authorized equipment as "Approved for Classified Production at the _____ level". Other equipment would be identified as "Not authorized for the reproduction of classified information".

TOP SECRET information is authorized for reproduction to meet contractual requirements such as when directed provide them to the customer. Any other use should be approved by the GCA. SECRET and CONFIDENTIAL information should also be reproduced only as part of a subcontract in furtherance of a contract or as part of a business proposal or in the preparation of a patent.

The FSO should consider the type of equipment the company purchases, leases or rents. When service contracts expire, repairs are needed, equipment is to be replaced or other transactions replacing or removing the equipment occur, the hard drive or memory should be destroyed or wiped in an approved manner to remove all stored classified information. DSS can help determine this approved method and guidance is available in Chapter 8 of the NISPOM.

Cleared employees should understand that only trained and authorized persons are authorized to make classified copies. The FSO can make the determination of how many and who to authorize. This can be based on contractual needs, workload or other valid reason. However, procedures should be established that identify authorized persons and train them how and when to copy classified information and how to protect it. Procedures should include detecting and deterring unauthorized reproduction of classified information, documenting copies according to the IMS procedures, marking, storing and disseminating the classified information.

In large enterprises the FSO might limit access to classified information as they create an environment where classified information is stored in a central area and issued to engineers by document custodians. On a smaller scale, classified information might be stored in a security container where a few cleared employees possess the combination. Additionally, classified reproduction can be limited to a designated copier where access is controlled and a code is provided before copies can be made. In this situation, the FSO can control who can make copies as well as audit authorized access.

But the real threat may exist when an employee copies classified information in uncontrolled environments. Limiting reproduction to authorized equipment and personnel only protects classified information reproduced honest employees. It does not protect against acts of espionage where employees access classified information and copy it at uncontrolled copiers, load them to unauthorized disks, fax them using unauthorized machines all in an effort to remove it from the company undetected. This can also be controlled by requiring a login code on reproduction equipment, putting all reproduction equipment in access controlled areas, or controlling all copying functions. However, the ultimate protection resides with controlling who accesses classified information, when they access it and what they do with it.

Reproduced classified information should only be done as a last resort. When copies are made, it generates the need to protect additional classified material that employs resources and functions of an IMS. Copies have to be afforded the same protection as the original and may require re-marking, additional storage space or dedication of security focused man hours. Also, FSOs should assign document numbers to track the amount of copies made. For example, if a copy of a document assigned an internal document number 401 is copied, the new number might be 401 copy 1 or 401-01.

Restricted Areas

Restricted areas provide temporary solutions for performing classified work and may apply in both possessing and non-possessing facilities. These are designated areas, but not dedicated areas. In other words, they are temporary and can be created from existing locations. These locations can then be returned to their original function almost immediately. A cleared employee may find it necessary to use a restricted area in the performance of a contract. This may arise from many reasons to include emergencies, because the product or process is large, bulky or of other unique size and such that work cannot be performed in the normal work area. When the need for working in a temporarily classified location arises, the cleared employees and FSO can create and occupy a restricted area.

Restricted areas should be clearly identified and access controlled to prevent unauthorized entry or compromise of classified material [8]. Physical barriers such as walls, doors, or barricades are not necessary, but access control should be present to prevent unauthorized personnel from entering and to keep control of classified material prior to introduction and removal. The restricted area can be as simple as stringing yellow caution tape around an accident site, or as complicated as using a hardened area such as a room or cafeteria. Cleared employees should challenge all who enter and verify clearance and need to know. Since restricted areas are temporary, all classified material should be returned to secure storage when no longer needed.

The creation of temporary restricted areas can solve problems of growing companies. In situations where closed areas are non-existent, work can be performed in a designated restricted area. Additionally, restricted areas can be created in non-possessing companies when the need arises to have a classified meeting or conversation. Restricted areas can be created for the introduction of classified information when needed and returning it to proper storage when no longer required or at some point before the work day ends.

Reminders should be posted in the restricted area to remind cleared employees to control access and to ensure classified material is returned to secure storage. Depending on the company's mission, warning signs could be posted outside of the restricted area to notify employees that only those with the appropriate clearance and need to know will be granted access.

Restricted areas are used when controlling access to classified material in a large area

- Temporary areas
- Only used during working hours
- Used for unique size, mission or other issues
- Classified material must be returned to proper storage prior to end of shift
- Employees challenge all who enter to ensure clearance and need to know

Closed Areas

Closed areas are a more permanent solution for possessing facilities and when classified items are difficult to store in a GSA approved container. When unique sizes and shapes do not fit into conventional GSA container storage capability, the FSO should seek approval from DSS for open shelf or bin storage.

Closed areas are necessary for storing bulk information. However, TOP SECRET material should be stored in a GSA approved container with supplemental protection such as a guard force and or intrusion detection systems are required for TOP SECRET in all cases 9. SECRET material also requires supplemental protection in a closed area when not stored in a GSA approved security container. As with restricted areas, closed areas require access control either with an ever present, cleared employee checking a roster or through a supplanting access control system such as biometrics, access card, pin number, and retina scan readers. Supplemental protection is not necessary at the time when the work area is occupied.

Physical security measures employed in a closed area prevents unauthorized access at any time. Reinforced doors, windows and other access points should be installed to prevent anyone from easily breaking in or going around current security precautions. DSS approves new construction, modifications, and repairs of closed areas. When building closed areas, the FSO should ensure pictures of progress are taken as evidence of compliance with construction requirements.

The construction standards require that all hardware is of heavy-gauge material and the hinges and jams are pinned, brazed or spot welded to prevent removal. Walls, windows, doors and ceilings are made of materials that can detect and resist unauthorized entry. Barriers should be constructed to prevent removal and access to classified material 10.

Closed areas are used to store classified material that won't fit into a GSA approved container

- Access is controlled
- Supplemental protection for SECRET and TOP SECRET
- Qualify structural integrity at required intervals
- CSA approves open shelf/bin storage of SECRET and CONFIDENTIAL
- No open shelf or bin storage of TOP SECRET

Vaults

When constructing vaults, the FSO should also ensure pictures of progress are taken as evidence that the contractor is in compliance with construction requirements. Vaults have additional construction requirements outlined in the NISPOM to offer a protection level necessary for the classified material stored. The doors and frames are GSA approved furnishings.

Openings to the vault are constructed the same as with openings of closed areas and designed to prevent and reveal evidence of tamper. Wire mesh, screens and other efforts installed to provide barriers that prevent people or objects from entering. These barriers must not be easily removed and should detect and prevent forced entry. Pipes and conduits should be installed during construction to maintain better integrity. Construction gaps remaining between the pipes and conduit should be filled with waterproof and tamper resistant caulking or material [11].

Security Containers, Locks and Combinations

The GSA approved security containers provide the appropriate amount of protection as identified on the level of classification markings. The containers are rated to withstand break-ins and detect attempts of break-ins. Security containers come in many forms and sizes ranging from single drawer to five drawers. Containers can have one locking drawer to secure the entire container or each drawer can have a separate lock.

Security containers are available in many makes and models, but unauthorized modification can degrade the security level of the container. For example, painting the container to match the office décor or removing the large GSA label will cause the container to lose its certification.

Security containers should be used only for storing classified material. Though not addressed in the NISPOM, alcohol, tobacco, firearms, personal items and valuables should never be kept in a GSA approved security container. Also, the classification level of the contents must never be displayed on the outside of the security container [12]. The tops and the surface of security containers should be free of debris, books, plants and anything else other than the SF 702 and the OPEN/CLOSED or combination reminder magnets. The proper use of classified information and the protection using GSA approved storage containers help to prevent security infractions.

The containers are certified and so must the maintenance and upkeep of the security container. All maintenance should be performed by approved repair persons using approved parts or approved cannibalized parts and approved methods. Repairs are either performed using authorized cleared employees or by escorting authorized technicians [13]. Once the repairs are made, the authorized repair technician issues a certificate of repair and the certificate is kept in local files. Unless the repair person is a cleared employee with a need to know, they should never be allowed to change or set the combination. Combinations are classified at the same level as the contents of the security container. Providing combinations to unauthorized personnel is a security violation.

Key and Combination Control

The amount of authorized employees having knowledge of combinations or access to keys to locks security classified information should be kept at the minimum amount necessary. FSOs should maintain a roster of those who have access to the combination and remind those who sign for the combinations to protect the combinations based on the highest classified level of the contents.

The FSO should either perform as or assign someone as a combination control person to maintain administrative records and combination control to protect classified information [12]. The FSO should also maintain a log of those with knowledge of combinations. A good practice is using the Security Container Information Form, Standard Form 700. The SF 700 can be filled out every time the combination is changed. When used, a copy is stored inside the locking drawer of the security container. The SF 700 tear sheet is stored in a separate security container approved for storage at the same level of the container contents. The SF 700 is a great tool for controlling security container access and keeping records up to date.

When in possession of multiple security containers, vaults and closed areas, FSOs could make a combination access binder. This binder can be used to keep up with who has access to the combinations, serial numbers of the containers and when the locks were last changed. Where facilities have multiple security containers, this binder can serve as a reminder of combinations. Instead of remembering every combination, the list of combinations can be stored in a security container with equal or greater security classification storage capacity.

Combinations are meant to be memorized and not written down or stored in computers, phones or Personal Data Assistant devices. The combination should be protected at that same level of the contents in the security container. For example, if the contents of the security container are CONFIDENTIAL, then so is the combination. To ease in memorization combinations can be created with six letter words or the first six letters of longer words. Instead of memorizing a long six digit number, they create a word and use a phone for the corresponding numbers.

Magnetic combinations reminders similar to telephone touch pads are also available. For example the number 2 corresponds with ABC, three with DEF, etc. When cleared employees have access to multiple safes, word reminders help prevent security violations that occur when cleared employees write the combinations down for personal use. Using combination word clues and providing an administrative security container helps reduce the risk of such violations.

According to NISPOM, combinations should be changed upon initial use, change in status of authorized users, compromise or suspected compromise of container or combination, when safe is left open or when required by FSO or DSS [14].

When a security container is brand new or has been pulled out of service for repair or resale, it should be set to an industry standard combination of 50-25-50. This universal combination allows the resale, reuse or temporary disposition until needed later. Upon initial use and after ensuring the certification of the container, the new owners of the security container should reprogram a new combination. The new combination is issued to authorized personnel and those having knowledge of the previous combination will no longer provide a security vulnerability.

Employees having knowledge of combinations and who can no longer protect the classified material or otherwise no longer have clearances and need to know provide a significant security risk. When an employee having access to a combination has had their clearance revoked or suspended, is transferred away or loses employment or otherwise has a change in status affecting their eligibility to provide the proper security of the classified information, the FSO should change the combination.

Security violations occur when combinations are revealed to unauthorized or non-cleared persons. Combinations spoken out loud, written down, or otherwise broadcast in an unauthorized manner put classified material at risk of compromise. Likewise security containers that no longer work properly or have suffered damage significant enough to affect the required security capability may make compromise a possibility. When the combination or security container has been compromised or is suspected of being compromised, then the combination must be changed and an investigation conducted.

Keyed Locks

The procedures, recommendations and security effectiveness of padlocks and keys are similar to managing and accounting for classified combinations. FSOs using padlocks and keys must maintain a registry of those who have possession of keys and locks. A monthly change of custody key and lock inventory ensures that keys remain on the premises and are stored to offer the correct level of protection [15].

The key and lock roster is the administrative accountability and assignment document. The FSO should ensure that only the amount of cleared personnel necessary is assigned access to keys and locks. Their role is to provide classified storage and accountability of classified material inside the security container. The key and lock custodian keeps account of persons and the specific keys and locks for absolute access control. The register is helpful during inventories, investigations, or when someone loses the assigned locks or keys.

Keys and locks protecting classified information should be inventoried regularly. FSOs should conduct this inventory monthly to ensure keys are secured properly and are where they should be [14]. If any keys are missing or are not stored to offer the proper level of protection an investigation should be initiated to determine whether or not classified information has been compromised. Keys and locks should also be inventoried when reassigned to new or additional cleared employees.

Keys should remain in the secure facilities. Putting keys on personal key rings or bringing them home is equivalent to writing down a security container combination and keeping it in a wallet or other unauthorized location. Such actions are violations and increase the potential for loss or compromise of classified material escalates. To provide better control the locks are changed or rotated annually and replaced when keys become lost or compromised. Master keys must not be duplicated as key control could be lost and thus degrade security and lead to the possible compromise of classified material.

Control keys and locks to classified containers
- Appoint a custodian
- Maintain register of lock and keys
- Audit keys and locks monthly
- Inventory keys upon change of custody

- Keep keys on premises
- Protect at the level of contents
- Rotate or change locks annually and replace when keys become lost or compromised
- Keep tight control of inventory and never make master keys

ACCESS TO CLASSIFIED INFORMATION

The possessor of classified information is required to protect it from unauthorized access [15]. According to the NISPOM, the term access is the ability and opportunity to gain knowledge of classified information [16]. This results from a determination that a person is trustworthy as proven in a thorough background investigation. Recall that there are varying degrees of background investigation depending on the level of classification the person is required to access. For example, a person with access to information at the SECRET level has had a NACLC conducted. Once a person is determined to be trustworthy, the clearance will be granted and the individual signs a non disclosure agreement, Standard Form 312.

A successful background check conducted and a clearance granted is just part of the process. A cleared person also has to have need to know. Need to know can be determined by using an access roster, information on the DD Form 254, statement of work, the SCG and other documents listing the classified work requirements. Typically, an FSO will have a way to verify the security clearance. Need to know is trickier, but usually resolved with familiarity of who works on a classified program or verification from another cleared employee.

SECURITY AWARENESS TRAINING

The NISPOM, Executive Orders covering the NISP and access to classified anformation and training resources found on the DSS website can help the FSO create a good training program. This program should remind cleared employees how items are classified, properly marked, how to use security related resources such as the Contract DD Form 254 and the Security Classification Guides. The FSO can personalize this education by demonstrating the company's compliance with the security classification system.

All cleared employees should attend security awareness training [17]. The training reminds cleared employees to properly safeguard classified information and the possible criminal, civil and administrative sanctions reserved for those who violate their safeguarding responsibilities.

The NISPOM lists training topics that FSOs should train cleared employees on prior granting access to classified material. These requirements include a threat awareness briefing, the defensive security briefing, and overview of the security classification system, employee reporting obligations and requirements and the security procedures and duties applicable to the employee's job [17].

Threat Awareness Briefing

The threat awareness briefing addresses dangers to national security, classified information and anything specifically detrimental to a company's employees and business. Training resources for threat briefings can be found in reports from the DSS, FBI, counter-intelligence analysis and local police reports as it pertains to a defense contractor's geographical area.

Defensive Security Briefing

A defensive security briefing includes information on what cleared employees may encounter while traveling to a foreign country. Cleared employees cannot control the environment they are in while traveling, but they can control their actions. Consequently, cleared employees should understand foreign officer recruiting techniques, crime statistics of the foreign country to be visited, embassy information, and health care and customs concerns relating to their visit. The FSO would also do well to remind employees of export compliance requirements which is found in the International Traffic and Arms Regulation (ITAR). Information for defensive security briefings can be found at the State Department's website: www.state.gov. Country specific briefings can also be found at the Central Intelligence Agency's website at www.cia.gov.

Reporting Requirements

Cleared employee reporting obligations should be emphasized in a cleared defense contractor organization. Each cleared employee is responsible for reporting information about themselves and fellow cleared employees that may demonstrate an inability to protect classified information. An example of such information includes illicit drug use, arrests, relations with foreign nationals, debt, foreclosure and other issues [18]. Such reporting is difficult and many may wonder why they should report adverse information on themselves or others. This requirement is found in NISPOM and based on an agreement that cleared employees make when they sign the Nondisclosure Agreement of Standard Form (SF) 312. Additionally, during the periodic review, the investigator may discover the adverse information and inquire into why it hadn't been reported earlier.

Task Oriented Training

Cleared employee training should focus on security procedures as they apply to their job. The cleared employee supervisor should follow initial training with effective security management while on the job. FSOs should provide a reminder of the SF 312 that they have signed and review the procedures for introducing and removing classified material to and from the facilities. The Industrial Security Oversight Office has created an SF 312 briefing agenda for download at http://www.archives.gov/isoo/industry/index.html.

A demonstration of the procedures for working with classified material, equipment and emergency procedures specific to the company helps every cleared employee understand their role. The FSO should give new employees a good overview of the security program and the foundation they need to prepare for the on the job training with their supervisors. Additionally, the cleared employees should attend annual security awareness refresher training. The refresher training covers the topics mentioned above as well as any new changes to the NISP.

SUMMARY

The FSO creates a security program and trains the employees on the proper procedures to protect all disciplines of classified work. Whether the work is conducted in a closed area, restricted area, vault, or other location of the facility, care is taken to ensure no unauthorized persons have access to the classified information. All cleared employees are responsible for protecting classified information. Restricted areas are used for temporary work and not authorized for permanent classified information storage. Defense contractors should use closed areas and vaults to work with and store classified information designed as a permanent working solution. Finally, the FSO should provide training for cleared employees.

PROBLEMS

1. You are an FSO of a growing defense contractor. One of the executives approaches you about the need for more space to conduct classified work. He is agreeable to implementing your recommendation to use a restricted area and would like you to prepare a security briefing for his team. Prior to your briefing, you conduct the necessary research. Describe the reason for a restricted area and when cleared employees would use a restricted area. Keep in mind access control and storage requirements.

2. You have just sat down to eat lunch and receive a phone call from a cleared employee. She tells you that the security container's drawers are closed, but the dial on the combination lock has not been engaged. She explains further that according to the SF 702, the container had been locked and checked 20 minutes earlier. She is sure that was "about the time everyone left for lunch." What would you direct her to do?

3. Your colleagues leave for the day. On their way out, they inform you that you are the last to leave. The facility is autho-

rized to store classified materials. What will you check for prior to leaving?

4. As part of the building project, you are responsible for providing input into the projected classified contracts and the required work space and storage requirements. As you put together a presentation you research the requirements of a much needed closed area. Describe how a closed area should be constructed. Who approves the construction requirements?

REFERENCES

1. Department of Defense, DoD 5220.22-M, National Industrial Security Operating Manual, section 5-102, February 2006

2. Department of Defense, DoD 5220.22-M, National Industrial Security Operating Manual, section 5-103, February 2006

3. Department of Defense, DoD 5220.22-M, National Industrial Security Operating Manual, section 5-201, February 2006

4. Department of Defense, DoD 5220.22-M, National Industrial Security Operating Manual, section 5-603, February 2006

5. Department of Defense, DoD 5220.22-M, National Industrial Security Operating Manual, section 5-200, February 2006

6. Department of Defense, DoD 5220.22-M, National Industrial Security Operating Manual, section 5-203, February 2006

7. Department of Defense, DoD 5220.22-M, National Industrial Security Operating Manual, section 5-303, February 2006

8. Department of Defense, DoD 5220.22-M, National Industrial Security Operating Manual, section 5-305, February 2006

9. Department of Defense, DoD 5220.22-M, National Industrial Security Operating Manual, section 5-306, February 2006

10. Department of Defense, DoD 5220.22-M, National Industrial Security Operating Manual, section 5-801 a-h, February 2006

11. Department of Defense, DoD 5220.22-M, National Industrial Security Operating Manual, section 5-802 a-e, February 2006

12. Department of Defense, DoD 5220.22-M, National Industrial Security Operating Manual, section 5-308, February 2006

13. Department of Defense, DoD 5220.22-M, National Industrial

Security Operating Manual, section 5-311, February 2006

14. Department of Defense, DoD 5220.22-M, National Industrial Security Operating Manual, section 5-309, February 2006
15. Executive Order 12968—Access to Classified Information, section 6.2, Federal Register, August 1995
16. Department of Defense, DoD 5220.22-M, National Industrial Security Operating Manual, Appendix C, February 2006
17. Department of Defense, DoD 5220.22-M, National Industrial Security Operating Manual, section 3-106, February 2006
18. Department of Defense, DoD 5220.22-M, National Industrial Security Operating Manual, section 1-302, February 2006

Helpful Websites:

Access to DSS Training
https://www.dss.mil/GW/ShowBinary/DSS/diss/enrol-intro.html
Area Studies/World Fact Book
http://www.cia.gov
Federal Bureau of Investigation
http://www.fbi.gov
ITAR
http://www.ddtc.gov
http://www.redbikepublishing.com
NISPOM
http://www.redbikepublishing.com
Training Pamphlets
http://www.archives.gov/isoo/training/
Travel Advisory and Travel Briefing Information
http://www.state.gove
Security Container Magnets
http://www.redbikepublishing.com
Various Security Forms
http://www.archives.gov/isoo/security-forms/

CHAPTER 8 CLASSIFIED COMPUTER SECURITY

Introduction

For orientation purposes, the reader should remember the requirements for safeguarding classified material. The practice is the same with protection of documents at different security classification levels but the execution is different. Safeguarding classified information on computer systems or information systems (IS) is similar in concept as protecting classified physical items (Figure 8-1).

The classified information is not to be disclosed to unauthorized persons or in an unauthorized manner. Just as combinations and keys to classified security containers are protected, so should the passwords and authenticators be that allow access to classified IS.

Information system protection also includes the requirement to appoint an Information System Security Manager (ISSM). The ISSM can be the FSO or any other cleared employee capable of performing information security duties. The ISSM is involved in assessing risk to classified information, filing reports, applying for certifications and authorizations, installing access controls, protecting data according to classification level, assigning password and authentication requirements.

Government Certifications and Approvals

DSS approves and certifies IS prior to a cleared defense contractor conducting classified processing. ISSMs will not introduce classified information to the IS until the classification and sensitivity of the IS has been identified. ISSMs submit this for approval in a request that demonstrates the protective measures are already in place. The designated approval authority established by the DSS reviews the request and determines whether or not to approve the defense contractor to operate IS with classified information.

Figure 8-1 Just like other classified information, classified Information systems and media must be protected in a security container or closed area.

Required Audits

The ISSM performs audits of the systems. Whether the system is stand alone or serving as part of a network, the audits are conducted to verify function and the effectiveness of security measures.

Information systems allow businesses to increase work productivity at blinding speeds [1]. Documents, images, and media can be duplicated, printed, emailed and faxed much faster than technology allowed just a few years ago. The lightening speed capabilities enable enterprises to perform on contracts more efficiently and in less time. However, because of fast distribution and processing speeds, measures must be in place to prevent unauthorized disclosure, spillage and compromise of classified information. Classified information must only be processed on approved information systems. The approved IS should have classification markings applied as with documents and other classified objects. For example, if the IS is setup to store or process CONFIDENTIAL, SECRET or TOP SECRET data, it should be marked as such.

The ISSM and FSO look at the effectiveness of protection measures as they relate to the computer or system and as it affects the entire organization mission and national security. The FSOs should keep management involved and informed of the risk management process and results. Additional help and resources in risk management are available with DSS, counter-intelligence units, FBI, Homeland Security, local law enforcement and professional organizations.

ACCREDITATION

ISSMs should demonstrate that IS is protected through accreditation and certification. This work is performed by the designated ISSM, who could be the FSO or other designated cleared employee with the approved level of training [2]. Accreditation is a determination that the information systems can operate at a required level of security in a particular environment [3]. The accreditation is conducted to ensure that the risks are mitigated to the fullest extent possible. The risk should be reduced to the minimum degree possible without affecting the capability of the systems to support mission requirements.

The designated accrediting/approving authority is authorized to grant IS accreditation. DSS manages the approval process through the Office of Designated Approval Authority (ODAA) [3]. The approval authorities take into consideration the purpose, costs, and the acceptable level of risk while still conducting business effectively. They also assess the damage and impact if classified spillage or compromise occurs. Accredited systems demonstrate that the approval authority has considered what would happen should a loss of any three critical system capabilities occur. These critical capabilities are confidentiality, integrity and availability [4].

Confidentiality-This control measure ensures the protection of privileged and classified information processed by the computer system. It prevents unauthorized disclosure of information through the use of passwords and personal identification numbers. If confidentiality fails, unauthorized persons can access the system and gain knowledge of classified information.

Integrity-A control used to protect all components of hardware and software used during classified programming and prevent any modification of the information system. With integrity in place, only authorized persons can add or delete information, documents or software, increase capabilities or perform other modifications to the systems. If integrity is not enforced, classified information can be printed, copied, added, and modified through bypassing security policy. Violations could make IS vulnerable to unauthorized access and the introduction of mal-ware.

Availability-Allowance of timely access to information and protecting the computer from mal-ware and natural disasters. The information system should allow authorized access when and where needed. If systems are not available, unscheduled interruptions could affect access controls, the protection measures concerning classified information and degrade performance and capabilities.

CERTIFICATION

Certification is an assessment of security control effectiveness as implemented in the IS certification [5]. Those authorized to approve the certification assess the management, operational, and technical security controls identified in the accreditation. They review the accreditation and the security controls to determine the adequacy and whether or not the risk is mitigated. They then determine whether or not to authorize classified processing with the IS.

The first assessment focuses on the security management. The assessment answers the question of whether or not policies and procedures are in place to effectively mitigate risk without compromising performance. This assessment also involves discovering whether or not the system or item is adequately protected during and after work hours.

If the ODAA cannot determine that the IS is managed properly based on the risk assessment process and the accreditation, then they will not issue IS certification.

The security plan provides controls to limit possibilities of spillage or compromise of classified data during classified processing. Such security provides for access control mechanisms, separation of privileged and user program code, and audit capabilities. Information security measures allow constant surveillance and accountability of those who perform classified work on the information systems.

The technical security controls include encryption systems, firewalls, and other devices to prevent adding or deleting files, installation of mal-ware and other efforts to compromise classified information. The certification and accreditation is conducted to validate the ISSM's plan after the information system is established and the protective measures are in place. The process reviews the plan to determine its effectiveness and that the security measures are functioning as indicated. The certification authority will use the results of the certification to provide input to the accreditation decision.

DSS authorizes and approves the risk management and the certification and accreditation process. This authority also pertains to the training, oversight and program review of the information system. DSS then conducts risk analysis based on the security plan, facilities and classification and sensitivity level of the processed information [6].

The ISSM

The cleared contractor assigns ISSMs to publish and put into affect the security and IS policy [7]. ISSMs should complete DSS training as they are responsible for assessing whether or not the facilities are in compliance based on the physical security and storage requirement of the classified information. They also establish procedures to train and hold the user accountable for protecting the classified information. The ISSM provides the security policy and certifies that everything is working properly. They also notify DSS when the IS is no longer being used to process classified information as well as when significant changes have occurred that impact the established security accreditation. The

ISSM also provides the risk analysis to identify and document threats and IS vulnerabilities [8].

Other ISSM responsibilities include providing security education, awareness and training for all appropriate managers, IS personnel, and authorized users. This training includes information about proper classification marking and processing, removing, transporting, sanitizing, reusing, and destroying media and equipment activities. The controls include using authentication and passwords and the detection of malicious code, viruses and other forms of mal-ware.

All IS security incidents should be reported to the ISSM and FSO for an assessment of whether or not compromise or suspected compromise of classified information occurred. If classified information compromise or suspected compromise occurred the FSO notifies DSS. In some cleared facilities, an ISSM may be able to ensure the security of IS either alone or with the assistance of Information System Security Officer (ISSO). Where work is more abundant, the ISSM may determine the need for an ISSO to share the responsibilities and help run the IS security program in a leadership role not just as an assistant [8].

Designated IS Users

Two types of users are identified for classified information systems and are determined by the type of access required. A privileged user has almost complete control of the system and the ability to create and administer accounts. They can also control how information is sent over IS equipment. These users perform important IS functions such as administering and changing other users' access. The general user has much more limited capabilities and cannot control and administer accounts or authenticators or change parameters on key IS equipment [9].

Security and Protection Requirements

Information system protection integrates both physical and information security. Physical security involves access control and other measures designed to prevent unauthorized persons from physically accessing the IS or data stored in a closed area or security container. This protects employees; prevents unauthorized entry to facilities, IS and media; protects against espionage, sabotage, vandalism and theft; and prevents or reduces probabilities of service interruptions. These protection measures should include barriers to entry, declassification of IS prior to removal from a secure area, adding access controls designed to protect the classified data at the designated level and constructing facilities storing classified IS to the standards outlined for closed areas and vaults.

Sound security countermeasures ensure that removable hard drives, software and other media are stored in an approved security container and workstations are locked when not in use. Depending on classification level and type of system, the workstations should require authentication [10]. The ISSMs incorporate imbedded security to prevent unauthorized persons from gaining access as well as recognize and record login attempts, successful logins and track user activity as they use the system.

Information systems used to store or process classified information are considered classified until that information is removed or the information and classified media are properly destroyed. The classified product such as printouts, hard drives, tapes, and flash drives should be marked with the proper classification and stored accordingly.

Cleaning and Sanitization

DSS provides instructions for the clearing, sanitation and release of IS and media [11]. This ensures everyone working with classified IS understands how classified information is to be introduced and removed from the cleared facility. Sometimes a cleared contractor may have useful hard drives but no longer have a need for the classified data it contains. Instead of destroying the entire hard drive, they can remove the classified information and reuse the hard drive. Destroying hard drives can be expensive and time consuming especially if the possessor does not have in house capability, requiring preparation for transmitting the classified hard drive off site.

Cleaning

Cleaning can save time and resources and involves wiping information from a disk or drive before reusing it again in a secure environment. The information is removed or cleared to deny access to it at a later date. For example, XYZ Contractor has successfully completed a project requiring analysis of data on a classified IS. In this case, the program manager and engineers used a removable hard drive classified at the SECRET level. When working on classified information, the engineer removed the hard drive from a security container and installed it in the classified computer. He then logged in to conduct the classified processing. Once finished, he logged out, shut down the IS and returned the hard drive to the security container.

Now, the project is complete and the information on the hard drive no longer needed. The program manager notifies the ISSO or ISSM that the information is to be removed, but the hard drive itself is to be re-used at the SECRET level. The ISSO should then clean the hard drive. Once complete, the data is no longer accessible but the hard drive is still available for other classified processing.

Sanitization

Sanitization is the complete removal of information from a disk or drive before re-using the media for unclassified work or an area with a lower level of security protection [11]. The data is properly removed to declassify or downgrade the classification level of the disk or drive. Suppose XYZ Contractor no longer needed the hard drive as discussed in the cleaning example. The program is complete and the hard drive can be used on a different effort classified at the confidential level. Just as a CONFIDENTIAL document cannot contain pages marked at the SECRET level, the hard drive must be downgraded to store information classified at the CONFIDENTIAL level. This means all data containing SECRET information should be removed. The ISSO or ISSM will sanitize and either re-label the media with the new classification level or notify the security department to conduct the reclassification administrative functions.

Inspections

Other protection measures involve inspecting hardware and software. Prior to putting hardware or software on an IS, an examination is made to ensure the items operate as they should. This examination is also conducted to determine that there is nothing attached or loaded that could cause harm to the IS or the information stored or processed. Software should be checked to ensure that there is no threat to the security of the IS. Hardware should also be checked to determine whether or not a threat exists to the security operation of the IS.

Identification and Authentication

Verifying authorized users requires authentication and identification management to control how the classified information is made available and to whom it is made available. Just as a badge reader is employed or guard is posted at the entry to a closed area, access to IS is controlled by identification and permission. Each user is issued a unique identity that informs the IS of who is requesting entry.

Not only must those accessing closed areas produce identification, but should provide a fingerprint, retinal scan or personal identification number (PIN). The same applies as users log on to the secure IS. Once the user provides identification associating them as someone requiring access, they also enter a PIN or other method of proving who they are. For example, a pickpocket steals a traveler's wallet and identification card. They now have the name, address and other personal information of the hapless victim. However, just because they possess the identifying documents does not mean they are authorized to sleep in the person's bed or walk into their house and have dinner with the family.

Without the family's recognition and approval, the newcomer is nothing more than an unwelcome imposter and will not be able to get access to the house by showing the credentials. With access control, just having a card or other form of identification does not give an unauthorized user logon capability. The user verifies their identity and authorization as authentic with a password, smart card, PIN, fingerprint or other biometric requirement [10].

Audits

Information system audits provide an accountability of user access to the IS. The accountability should provide enough information or computer forensics to reconstruct a documented history of IS use. According to NISPOM, audit trails are not required for single user stand alone systems [12]. They are required when multiple cleared employees require access to an IS. Audit protection is used for discovering which activities occurred on an IS and who performed them [13]. The audit trail should provide the identity of the user and date and time of access and user activity including attempts to bypass, modify or disregard IS security.

How to Use Identification and Authentication

Key control custodians maintain accountability of combinations, locks and keys used in the storage of classified material. Likewise an ISSM controls the authentication and identification and ensures measures are in place for the proper access of the classified information stored or processed on the IS [2]. The authentication, user identification and logon information acts as "keys" controlling when the classified information is used on the system. Without the control, there is no way to prevent unauthorized persons from getting to the data stored in computers or components.

Classified information is restricted to only those with the proper clearance and need to know. Each user has the ability to access only the data authorized. The segregation of access and need to know for each user can be implemented on individual systems or components dedicated to only one access requirement. The ISSM or ISSO can protect the authentication data by making it unreadable or segregating it.

Just as combinations and keys are rotated and changed as required, user identification, removal and revalidation are also in place. These similar measured are used to ensure the proper users have access and those who have moved, changed jobs or otherwise have lost their clearance or need to know have had their access to the IS removed [14]. Additionally, each user's identification is revalidated at least yearly for those who still require access. Authenticators such as the keys, passwords and smartcards are protected at the highest level of classified information used in the system. Users are not authorized to share, loan out or otherwise give to others and logons are audited for proper use.

Passwords

Passwords should be protected at the highest level of classification found on data stored or processed by the IS. If an IS is configured to process data classified at the SECRET level, then the password is classified at SECRET. It cannot be stored in a phone, personal data assistant or otherwise written down and must be protected and stored in a security container. The passwords should be at least eight characters long and generated based on length of password, structure and size of password space as described in the ISSM's system security plan (SSP). The passwords should be changed every year and factory installed passwords in software and operating systems should be replaced prior to giving users access to the IS [15].

Maintenance of IS

If maintenance cannot be conducted by an authorized cleared employee, uncleared maintenance personnel may be authorized to repair IS with constant escort. The escort or other cleared employee should conduct all login and logoff procedures as well as have a keystroke monitoring system in place [16]. All classified data and media should be removed to deny access to the unauthorized repair persons. These controls prevent the uncleared persons from gaining access to passwords, authentications and classified data. They are only allowed to work on the system after system access is granted. This scenario is similar to opening a combination and removing contents of a security container prior to granting authorization for an uncleared locksmith to make repairs.

If information cannot be removed from the IS, the ISSM should have a backup plan to protect classified information. Such plans include ensuring that a knowledgeable person escorts a repair person so that they do not access classified information.

Personnel and Physical Security Measures

Physical and personnel security systems play an important role in the protection of classified information. Information systems should be protected with hardware, software, identification, authentication and other security measures to prevent unauthorized access, manipulation, and destruction of classified data. Additionally, personnel and physical security provide in depth protection of classified data and IS where it is stored and processed. The ISSM/ISSO can take advantage of well informed cleared employees and use them as force multipliers, giving the security program added momentum and support.

Employees with security clearances and access provide oversight of the IS and ensure the confidentiality, integrity and availability. Users play a prominent security role by ensuring IS protects the data and that the IS provides the data whenever needed. Users should follow security procedures to detect and deter unauthorized access to the IS and its associated software and hardware. Just as a security container is constructed to detect and prevent intrusion, so are the procedures established in the security policies.

Those who process classified data on an IS should only do so in areas approved by DSS. Computer monitors and printers should be positioned to prevent unauthorized persons from casually viewing classified information printed out or shown on a monitor. Additionally, output should be reviewed using approved methods to determine the proper security level and to ensure the information and media is properly classified and marked.

Configuration Management

Configuration management (CM) is another tool with which the ISSM and DSS collaborate to ensure that safeguards associated with IS are functioning and implemented as approved [17]. Critical analysis and certification provide milestones designed to identify the health of the IS security measures as outlined by the ISSM. Without the validation, violations could occur as organizations operate classified IS without regard to the effectiveness of the security procedures or without adhering to agreed upon security procedures.

Configuration management is designed to identify and document IS specifics, the system connectivity (wireless and any type of communications devices) and the connection sensitivity (documenting the sensitivity level for the connection or port). Configuration management is dependent on a plan that covers the review and approval of security related hardware and software, management of all documentation, periodic testing and verification of the plan and process. The CM plan is the tool that ensures any variations of the IS or security measures outside of the agreed upon plan are not conducted without prior approval.

Protection Levels

Though integrity and availability of information is critical to meeting mission requirements, these IS qualities are not addressed in the NISPOM [18]. They are better delivered and addressed in contracts and performance specifications. The NISPOM is concerned with confidentiality and the ability to protect classified information against all threats. The IS security measures meet protection requirements to address the confidentiality level.

Information systems are further protected through the enforcement of protections levels (PL's) (Figure 8-2). The established PL's determine the type of processing on the system and the access that the users have. They are broken down into PL-1, PL-2, and PL-3 based on the user access requirements. This protection level uses technology capabilities and physical security to segregate and control the user's access to prevent the accidental release, spillage or otherwise unauthorized exposure of classified information.

PL 1, or Dedicated Security Mode, is performed when all users possess the same clearance and need to know. PL 1 provides formal access approval for all information on the system [19]. For example, consider a research and development oriented cleared contractor. Each cleared employee with access to the IS has a TOP SECRET clearance and all are working on the same project. Controls are in place to ensure that each person has the proper login and authentication for that level of procession.

PL 2 is used when the clearance level and access approvals for all users are the same, but everyone has different need to know [19]. Users are segregated by their varying need to know requirements. For example, consider that in addition to the requirement for the classified work as described above, new contractor personnel are brought in to perform on a different aspect of the contract. The group in the PL 1 situation has the same clearance, access requirements and need to know. However, additional personnel brought in are working on a small part of the project and do not have the need to know of other details. In this case this new group will authenticate and sign-in using different methods.

CONFIDENTIALITY PROTECTION LEVEL			
Requirements	PL 1	PL 2	PL 3
Audit Capability	Audit 1	Audit 2	Audit 3 and 4
Data Transmission	Trans 1	Trans 2	Trans 3
Access Control	Access 1	Access 2	Access 3
Identification and Authentication	I&A 1	I&A 2,3,4	I&A 2,4,5
Resource Control		ResrcCtrl 1	ResrcCtrl 1
Session Controls	SessCtrl 1	SessCtrl 2	SessCtrl 2
Security Documentation	Doc 1	Doc 1	Doc 1
Separation of Functions			Separation
System Recovery	SR 1	SR 1	SR 1
System Assurance	SysAssur 1	SysAssur 1	SysAssur 2
Security Testing	Test 1	Test 2	Test 3

Figure 8- 2 Protection Profile Table for Confidentiality.
Source: DoD 5220.22-M, National Industrial Security Program Operating Manual, February 28, 2006

Finally PL 3 is enforced when users have the same clearance levels but access is controlled to allow only those with enhanced need to know or other segregated approval for some of the information. Those employees who have no need to know certain information will be further removed. They may have the proper clearance, but are not permitted access to certain information [19].

The protection level corresponds with requirements necessary to protect the information at the appropriate level while on the IS. These parameters are categorized to reflect audit, transmission, access control, identification and authentication, resource control, session controls, security documentation, separation of functions, system recovery, system assurance and security testing [20]. These protection requirements are graded based on the confidentiality level. This confidentiality level is a milestone that can be tested, observed and provide feedback as to the accuracy and effectiveness of the IS protection.

Figure 8-2 demonstrates how the protection requirements are addressed per protection level. For example, PL 1 identifies an audit capability level of "Audit 1" and each requirement is identified on the protection profile table. At this point we will identify the definitions of each requirement and provide examples of their application. This chapter will only define the levels necessary as identified in the table. Additional details and information is available in the NISPOM.

Audit capability

Audit reports provide an accountability of user access to the IS. When all users have the same access and need to know Audit 1 applies, requiring an automated audit trail. The accountability provides enough information or computer forensics to reconstruct a documented history of IS misuse, compromise or damage. The audit trail provides the identity of the user and date and time of access including successful and unsuccessful login attempts and changes in user authentication. The audit trail also provides information about overall user activity including attempts to bypass, modify or disregard established IS security measures [21].

When all users have the same clearance, but different need to know, Audit 2 applies. Audit 2 requires the capabilities of Audit 1 with the addition of the ability to identify unique users such as an individual or group logon [21]. This allows the ISSO or ISSM to view the activities of each identified and authorized user and ensures each user can only access information according to their need to know. The ISSO or ISSM is required to test the IS security effectiveness.

When all users do not possess the same clearance levels, Audit 3 and Audit 4 apply. Audit 3 requires the scheduling of analysis and reporting using automated tools. This control in place to ensure the security parameters are working. It also identifies any efforts of users to gain unauthorized access beyond their clearance levels [21].

Audit 4 establishes the recording of changes to user formal access permissions [21]. When users with different clearance levels access the same machine, identification and authentication procedures allow access to information at their level of clearance or lower. Any attempt to change permission levels or otherwise gain unauthorized access to classified data is recorded and can be acted upon properly and in a timely manner.

Data Backup

IS data backup ensures information is available when needed. Backup systems should be checked regularly to verify they are working as expected. Without backup, information could be lost and no longer accessible. Backup 1 confirms that the ISSM is performing procedures requiring the backup of data, software and settings that protect classified IS. The ISSM also designates the backup frequency [22].

In addition to Backup 1 requirements, Backup 2 requires an alternate storage site for backup information. This storage must be cleared at the same level or higher as the classified information being backed up. This could be in another part of the enterprise or off site. The backup procedures should be documented. There are cleared companies available to perform this service. Backup 3 requires the same as Backup 1 and 2 with the addition of annual testing of the ability to restore backed up material onto an IS [22].

Data Transmission

Just as classified products are double wrapped and mailed, delivered or escorted according to approved methods; electronic data is afforded equal protection. Regardless of protection level, classified data is protected at Trans 1, meaning it cannot be introduced outside of a closed or cleared area without the proper precautions. To prevent unauthorized access to classified information, distribution can only occur in the following instances [23]:

Area approved for open storage-A closed area where classified information is stored outside of the GSA approved container and is protected via multiple layers of security. For example, a closed area is inside of an access controlled facility where a receptionist greets all visitors and employees. The closed area is constructed as outlined in the NISPOM or Director of Central Intelligence Directive 6/9, "Manual for Physical Security Standards for SCI Facilities," and employs user identification and verification access control. At night the room is safeguarded with an approved lock and monitored alarm system.

Approved protected distribution system-Protected Distribution System (PDS) is a system used to move unencrypted classified information through an area that is not controlled nor approved for storing classified material at the same level. However, since the information is unencrypted, it is vulnerable to exploitation, thus the PDS should be equipped to detect attempted unauthorized entry through the protected distribution system.

National Security Agency approved encryption machines-These encryption devices are controlled by NSA and are approved for processing classified information. Designated communications security (COMSEC) custodian account for and track COMSEC equipment and set up accounts with the NSA.

Access Controls

Access controls are installed to protect the classified information systems from access by unauthorized persons. This system only allows users to have access based on authorization. When all users have the same access and need to know, Access 1 applies. Access 1 requires the ability to physically prevent unauthorized persons from gaining access. Unauthorized persons who need access should be escorted at all times [24].

When all users have the same security clearance level, but different levels of need to know, Access 2 applies [24]. Access 2 requires the capabilities of Access 1 including the ability to distinguish between users and grant access to the appropriately authorized information. Consider an IS designated for classified processing at the secret level. There are five separate files, each requiring different levels of need to know. Five cleared users are authorized to access the computer, but each cleared user is only authorized one file each. The access control recognizes the authorized user and based on logon information, provides access to the appropriate file.

When all users do not possess the same clearance levels, Access 3 applies [24]. Access 3 has the same requirements as Access 1 and 2 with the addition of two measures which allow users to designate others and determine how entry to IS will be permitted. They also identify the vulnerability of the information.

Identification and Authentication (I&A)

When all users have the same access and need to know, I&A 1 applies. I&A 1 provides protection by allowing access to only those with proper identification and authentication. These are applied at the entry to the secure area or in the information system [25]. When all users have the same clearance, but different need to know, I&A 2, 3 and 4 are put in place. The requirements of I&A 2 include those of I&A 1 with the addition of the user being assigned a unique logon. The authorized user's actions are also audited and recorded. Requirements include having users logon as individuals prior to logon as a member of a group.

The requirements of I&A 3 are the same as I&A 1 and 2, with the addition of more stringent authentication. In I&A 3 the cleared user is outside of IS secure area or where lines of transmission leave the secure area. I&A 4 includes the addition of approved tools to validate the strength of passwords [25].

When all users do not possess the same clearance levels, I&A 2, 4 and 5 applies. I&A 5 requires the use of strong authentication when users connect remotely to the IS [25]. To protect the IS and data at the required level, a device is used to generate an authentication that is strong enough to prevent easy access

Resource Controls

Resource Control ensures that all data has been removed from an IS when no longer needed. This helps prevent the threat of purposeful or accidental unauthorized logon and exploitation of classified information. Protection levels require measures to verify that no data is left over on IS or components prior to reassigning them to new users. The media is sanitized or cleared according whether or not it will be reissued in an environment of the same level of security classification [26].

Session Controls

Session Controls-are measures to limit the user's experience while logged on. These controls include warning banners, logon attempts, system entry granting, and logon notification [27]. Session controls notify the user that the IS is constantly monitored and recorded. This strengthens accountability and reporting capabilities due to approved technology implementation.

When all users have the same access and need to know, SessCtrl 1 applies. SessCtrl 1 notifies that access to the system represents their consent to monitoring and recording and that unauthorized use could result in civil and criminal penalties. An approved warning banner is displayed promptly on the monitor prior to the user logging on [27]. This notification provides incentives for users to conduct their sessions responsibly thus strengthening the security posture. When penalties are enforced, the possibilities of data theft, destruction, compromise or introduction of malicious code are significantly reduced. This method requires follow-up and enforcement. Without such enforcement, the warnings could appear to be just a formality and are prone to be ignored.

Logon attempts should be recorded and controlled. Users who enter the wrong password over five times should be denied access [27]. An example of logon controls is evident while gaining access to some government websites, online banks and other e-commerce websites. These sites require users to contact the administrator to have their passwords reset.

When all users have the same clearance, but different need to know or when all users do not possess the same clearance levels, SessCtrl 2 applies [27]. The requirements of SessCtrl 2 include those of SessCtrl 1 but limit the number of logon sessions. When users are not making mouse or keyboard input or the system recognizes user inactivity, the user will have to re-authenticate. These instructions are included in the SSP for approval [27]. This control prevents unauthorized persons from accessing the IS in the event an authorized user leaves the area without logging off the system.

When applicable, the system should be configured to notify the user of the last successful log on [26]. This detailed notification is given after a successful log on and requires users to verify that they last logged on during the time period reported on the banner. If there are discrepancies, they must notify the ISSM for further research into possible compromise.

Security Documentation

This information is the proof that the system configuration and all security software, procedures and plans are in place and have been approved. The primary document is the SSP and serves the lifetime of the system [28].

All three protection levels require Doc 1 application. The Doc 1 protection requires the submission of an approved SSP and the related documentation [28]. The SSP identifies the system and components, configuration, connections, security support and IS mission. Names, locations and contact phone numbers of the system owner, agency point of contact, ISSM and if applicable the ISSO are provided for accountability. The SSP also identifies the sensitivity and classification levels including user need to know, the identified protection measures and approvals for variations in the protective measures. A risk assessment is made and any identified risks and vulnerabilities are assessed and countermeasures put in place to reduce the effects or mitigate the vulnerabilities.

Finally, Doc 1 requires the recording of certification and accreditation [28]. This includes security testing and reporting and is posted in the SPP. The ISSM signs the certification verifying that the IS is in compliance with the protection levels and levels of concern and sends it to the approving agency.

Separation of Function

This is necessary during PL 3 operations. When users have different security clearances, the ISSO and system manager duties cannot be performed by the same individual [29].

System Recovery

All protection levels require that when and if the system fails, the system security functions are working or the system shuts down. SR 1 requires that when the IS security is not functioning properly, then the operations are suspended or functions are limited to those monitored by the ISSO [30].

System Assurance

This is the identification of IS components that are necessary for maintaining the IS security policies [31]. When all users have the same access and need to know SysAssur 1 applies. With SysAssur 1, only authorized persons shall have access to the identified IS protection components. This includes software, hardware, firmware, etc where the security policies are committed.

When all users do not possess the same clearance levels, SysAssur 2 applies [31]. The SysAssur 2 requires the documentation of the protection measures to be in place as well as validation that the system security measures are operating correctly.

Security Testing

Testing is conducted to ensure all components are operating properly. When all users have the same access and need to know, Test 1 applies. Test 1 requires that the approval agency verify that the system has been tested and operates as outlined in the SSP [32].

When all users have the same clearance, but different need to know, Test 2 applies [32]. Test 2 requires the capabilities of the written verification as identified in Test 1 with the addition of applied discretionary access controls. Discretionary access controls ensure those who create files also create access policies to those files. For example, suppose three users of an IS have the same clearances but work on different projects. They do not have need to know of the classified information of each other's project. With discretionary access control, each employee can create files that none of the others can access. Employee C would create files that would deny access to employees A and B and employees A and B would also limit access to their files. Test 2 would verify that the files are successfully segregated.

When all users do not possess the same clearance levels, Test 3 applies [32]. Test 3 requires the development of testing and functionality assurance. This is accomplished with descriptions of a test plan and the verification that the assurance for the protection levels are working as they should. For example, employee A has a CONFIDENTIAL clearance, employee B has a SECRET clearance and C has TOP SECRET. Employee C would create files that would deny access to employees A and B and employee B could deny access to employee A. Test 3 would verify that the files are successfully segregated.

Summary

A contractor appoints a cleared employee as an ISSM to manage classified IS processing. In some cases an ISSO is also appointed to help with the workload. Prior to establishing classified information processing, the ISSM establishes the requirements for safeguarding both the information systems and the classified data. Controls are identified and established to ensure classified information is not disclosed to unauthorized persons, prevent introduction of mal-ware or otherwise manipulate data. Protection measures include physical and administrative barriers denying access to unauthorized persons. These security measures protect the physical location of the IS as well as provide authentication for logon.

Just as combinations and keys to classified security containers are protected, so are the passwords and authenticators to information systems. This chapter addressed how to properly protect IS provide proper validation and certification to the ODAA for approval. The certification packet includes documentation and the SSP providing required personnel positions, risk assessment, reports, certifications and authorizations, access controls, how to protect data according to classification level, password and authentication requirements. Once the ODAA receives the certification packet, they review the documentation and provide authentication or authority to operate classified IS.

Questions

1. Accredited systems demonstrate that the approval authority has considered what would happen should a loss of any three critical system capabilities occur. What are three critical capabilities and what their definitions?

2. Session controls are used to control what the user does on an IS. Controls provide statements and actions to warn and prevent unauthorized users and unauthorized activities. Name the controls that the ISSM can establish on an IS.

3. There are two types of users an ISSM can establish on an IS. These users have varying levels of access and permissions. Name the two types of users and the level of activity they are allowed on an IS.

4. A cleared employee is currently in the middle of classified work. Everyone on the program has to access the same information; they all have the same clearance and need to know. Each person has a TOP SECRET clearance and all are working on the same project. Controls are in place to ensure that each person has the proper login and authentication for that level of procession. Which Protection Level does this situation refer to?

RESOURCES

1. Intelligence Community Directive Number 503, Intelligence Community Information Technology Systems Security Risk Management, Certification and Accreditation, 15 September 2008, downloaded on 2 Feb 2011. http://www.dni.gov/electronic_reading_room/ICD_503.pdf

2. Department of Defense, DoD 5220.22-M, National Industrial Security Operating Manual, section 8-103, February 2006

3. Department of Defense, DoD 5220.22-M, National Industrial Security Operating Manual, section 8-202, February 2006

4. Department of Defense, DoD 5220.22-M, National Industrial Security Operating Manual, section 8-403, February 2006

5. Department of Defense, DoD 5220.22-M, National Industrial Security Operating Manual, section 8-201, February 2006

6. Department of Defense, DoD 5220.22-M, National Industrial Security Operating Manual, section 8-101a, February 2006

7. Department of Defense, DoD 5220.22-M, National Industrial Security Operating Manual, section 8-101b, February 2006

8. Department of Defense, DoD 5220.22-M, National Industrial Security Operating Manual, section 8-103 February 2006

9. Department of Defense, DoD 5220.22-M, National Industrial Security Operating Manual, section 8-105, February 2006

10. Department of Defense, DoD 5220.22-M, National Industrial Security Operating Manual, section 8-303, February 2006

11. Department of Defense, DoD 5220.22-M, National Industrial Security Operating Manual, section 8-301, February 2006

12. Department of Defense, DoD 5220.22-M, National Industrial Security Operating Manual, section 8-502e, February 2006
13. Department of Defense, DoD 5220.22-M, National Industrial Security Operating Manual, section 8-602, February 2006
14. Department of Defense, DoD 5220.22-M, National Industrial Security Operating Manual, section 8-303f, February 2006
15. Department of Defense, DoD 5220.22-M, National Industrial Security Operating Manual, section 8-303i, February 2006
16. Department of Defense, DoD 5220.22-M, National Industrial Security Operating Manual, section 8-304b, February 2006
17. Department of Defense, DoD 5220.22-M, National Industrial Security Operating Manual, section 8-311, February 2006
18. Department of Defense, DoD 5220.22-M, National Industrial Security Operating Manual, section 8-400, February 2006
19. Department of Defense, DoD 5220.22-M, National Industrial Security Operating Manual, section 8-402, February 2006
20. Department of Defense, DoD 5220.22-M, National Industrial Security Operating Manual, chapter 8, table 5, February 2006
21. Department of Defense, DoD 5220.22-M, National Industrial Security Operating Manual, section 8-602, February 2006
22. Department of Defense, DoD 5220.22-M, National Industrial Security Operating Manual, section 8-603, February 2006
23. Department of Defense, DoD 5220.22-M, National Industrial Security Operating Manual, section 8-605, February 2006

24. Department of Defense, DoD 5220.22-M, National Industrial Security Operating Manual, section 8-606, February 2006

25. Department of Defense, DoD 5220.22-M, National Industrial Security Operating Manual, section 8-607, February 2006

26. Department of Defense, DoD 5220.22-M, National Industrial Security Operating Manual, section 8-608, February 2006

27. Department of Defense, DoD 5220.22-M, National Industrial Security Operating Manual, section 8-609, February 2006

28. Department of Defense, DoD 5220.22-M, National Industrial Security Operating Manual, section 8-610, February 2006

29. Department of Defense, DoD 5220.22-M, National Industrial Security Operating Manual, section 8-611, February 2006

30. Department of Defense, DoD 5220.22-M, National Industrial Security Operating Manual, section 8-612, February 2006

31. Department of Defense, DoD 5220.22-M, National Industrial Security Operating Manual, section 8-613, February 2006

32. Department of Defense, DoD 5220.22-M, National Industrial Security Operating Manual, section 8-614, February 2006

HELPFUL WEBSITES

DSS Office of Designated Approval Authority (ODAA)
https://www.dss.mil/GW/portlets/AutonomyRetrieval/Autono-
myRetrieval.jsp
NISPOM
http://www.dss.mil
http://www.redbikepublishing.com
NSTISS National Security Telecommunications And Information
Systems Security No.7003, 13 December 1996 Protective Distribution Systems(PDS)
http://www.cnss.gov/Assets/pdf/nstissi_7003.pdf

CHAPTER 9 REMOVING CLASSIFIED MATERIAL

Introduction

The NISPOM requires accountability of TOP SECRET items, but accountability is not required for classified information at SECRET and below [1]. Additionally, CONFIDENTIAL information does not require receipting action when transferred between cleared facilities as does SECRET and TOP SECRET [3]. Where accountability and receipting is not specifically required, the NISPOM states that cleared facilities should be able to retrieve classified information during a reasonable amount of time using an IMS [2].

This chapter will demonstrate ways to properly track, disseminate and destroy classified material and applies to both possessing and non-possessing facilities. Possessing facilities are not the only places where classified information can be used. A non-possessing facility can possibly disseminate, destroy or release classified information during a classified visit, meeting or presentation where classified information is discussed.

This chapter also provides recommendations on how to use an IMS to meet the cleared facility needs. Other topics include structuring the organization to ensure only cleared personnel perform the dissemination functions. This proper removal of classified information from a cleared facility is authorized in the following situations:

- Mail-Send properly wrapped and documented classified media via the United States Postal Service (USPS)
- Hand Delivery – Authorize cleared employees to personally deliver classified material via air, land and sea transportation
- Courier –Deliver classified information via approved escort

services
- Electronic Transmission – Use computers, email, internet and other approved means to send classified information
- Destruction –obliterate classified material no longer needed by the GCA
- Retention of Classified Material – Request permission to maintain classified material beyond the contract expiration date

ACCOUNTABILITY

According to the 32 CFR Parts 2001 and 2004, Classified National Security Information (Directive No. 1); Final Rule, classified information should be transmitted and received with proper accountability [3]. The IMS mentioned in NISPOM for SECRET and below and the separate accountability system required for TOP SECRET provides such a solution for defense contractors. Additionally, classified material should be transmitted in such a way as to prevent accidental opening, detect tampering and ensure expedient delivery. Persons sending classified material should ensure that the recipients have the proper clearance and need to know [4].

Protection not only addresses classified material within a cleared facility but extends to classified movement from the cleared facility. The organization disseminating classified material by any of the approved methods has the responsibility of doing so in such a manner that prevents and detects attempts by unauthorized persons from gaining access at anytime. Preventive measures include proper wrapping, getting approval for and selecting the transmission methods, coordinating and arranging pickup and delivery, and surveillance of the classified material while in transit.

CLASSIFIED INFORMATION DISSEMINATION PROCESS

Prior to removing classified material from a cleared facility, FSOs should verify that the action is absolutely necessary. Because of inherent risks with air, land, rail and sea movement, removing classified material should be a last resort. The shipper or receiver cannot control the

environment but must rely on services provided. The person disseminating classified information should perform due diligence and understand the risks and available countermeasures. These measures include
removing the items from the cleared facility's IMS, proper preparation
of the item for delivery and documenting the authorized receiver's ac-
knowledgment of receipt.

When a contractor needs to transfer classified information, the
FSO should verify that the recipient is authorized to receive the classified information. Verification is performed through the DSS's Industrial Security Facility Database (ISFD). This database lists facility contact
information, address, phone number, CAGE code, facility clearance
and classified storage capability if applicable.

Once verified, the FSO should update the classified information's
status in the IMS. This action serves as a reminder during document
inventories and annual inspections that the classified items are no longer in the facility. After removing the classified item from accountability and generating a receipt, the FSO should wrap the item for shipment. Nothing on the final preparation (container, box, envelop and
etc) should indicate that the item is classified. Additionally any attempts to gain access to the classified information should be detectable
at some point during transit or identified upon receipt at the destination. Other than the tracking process or physical controls, the package
should look like every other package.

Recall that CONFIDENTIAL classified information does not require a receipt. However, a good practice is to always generate a receipt and request signature. This provides a close out or evidence that
the items arrived and were received. Once properly transferred, the receipts should be signed by the receiving FSO and returned to the sending security office. The IMS process begins with the receipt of the classified document. The sending industrial security office receives the
signed receipts and closes out their responsibility and tracking process
for that classified material.

Classified Material Preparation for Shipment

The classification level should be the first consideration when determining how to disseminate classified information. Dissemination of TOP SECRET has more restrictions than does SECRET and CONFIDENTIAL. Likewise SECRET has more restrictions than CONFIDENTIAL. According to the NISPOM, classified information should be wrapped with opaque durable material such as cardboard, envelopes, or boxes. It should be transmitted in a way to prevent accidental and unauthorized disclosure and detect tamper.

Figure 9-1 Classified information is prepared in two layers. Notice that the inner layer is wrapped with rip proof tape and is marked with the classification level on the top, bottom and all sides.

Inner Layer

The NISPOM does not address seams of packages, but a good practice is to cover seams with rip-proof opaque tape or other similar material. Next, the FSO should mark the package on the top and bottom of all sides with the proper classification level (Figure 9-1). They should then add the "to" and "from" with two copies of receipts either attached to the first layer or inside the first layer [5]. Internal contents that come in contact with the wrapper could be imaged or observed in certain situations. To prevent this, the preparer can place wrapping paper, patterned paper, receipts or fold the documents in such a way that they cannot be read through the wrapping.

Outer Layer

The outer wrapper is the second line of defense for the classified information. Once the classified information leaves the cleared facility, the level of protection is severely reduced. The wrapping requirements are similar to those of the inner wrapper and should be the same size to prevent looseness or movement that could fray or damage the inner wrapping's seams. The outside label should not identify the recipient by name. Office numbers or symbols should be used to prevent associating a classified package with a particular person. When addressing shipment labels to contractors, the outer label should be addressed to "FSO" or "Security". When addressing shipment labels to military agencies, the outer package labels should be "Commander". Additionally, addressing deliveries to an authorized department ensures the package is received by authorized persons. Providing a person's name on the outside label could cause problems if they are not around to receive it and could result in returned packages.

The inner layer identifies that contents are classified. The intent is to provide warning against further unauthorized opening. For example, suppose a carrier truck overturns and the contents of the carrier are strewn over a large area. Clean up efforts ensue and all packages and containers are recovered. If a classified package is recovered with no damage, it can continue to its destination. If the outer wrapper is torn or destroyed, the package can be properly controlled to ensure it does not fall into unauthorized hands.

A good practice is to use strong, durable wrapping material readily available at postal or office supply stores. A good rip proof tape is heavy lined with string and is somewhat difficult to rip, remove or cut without leaving evidence. The protection level can be strengthened with the addition of tamper resistant and detecting seals. The seals are numbered and can be logged in a record. If tamper occurs the seal will stretch out of shape or break thus preventing re-application. When the classified shipment arrives, the receiver can compare the seal with a shipping document or receipt. If a new seal has been applied or the existing seal indicates tamper, the receiver can report the suspected compromise. Together the wrapping material and seals can prevent and detect unauthorized persons from accessing the classified material without leaving traces of the attempts.

The following scenario provides an example of how classified material can be prepared for shipment. A cleared employee approaches the FSO with a request to mail a package to their government customer. He identifies the item, recipient, date needed, and preferred method of delivery. The FSO pulls the document and consults the security classification guide and the DD Form 254 to determine whether or not classified items can be mailed and the approved delivery methods. The FSO then accesses ISFD for the proper mailing address.

She enters the document transaction in the IMS to indicate removal of the classified information. She prints two receipts identifying the document title, where it is going and method of delivery. Then she puts the receipt copies in the package and marks the calendar to remind her that a signed receipt is due back within 30 days.

To help with proper wrapping procedures, the FSO consults an internally produced classified package wrapping guide (Figure 9-2). The FSO places the classified document and the two receipts on the wrapping table. She wraps the items and marks the package as SECRET, according to the classification of the document and affixes the address label. Next, she applies the outer wrapping and label, but does not apply the classification level (Figure 9-3). The package is now ready to be delivered through the mail, hand carry, overnight, courier, or whatever approved means desired by the customer.

Alternate wrappings

Large sizes, bulk, weight, mission requirements or other structural make up could prevent transmission of items by traditional means. These could be machines, vehicles, aircraft, missiles, or other cumbersome, odd shaped, heavy or odd sized items. Brief cases, canvas courier bags, hard cases, shipping crates, large tarps and other types of containers can serve as proper wrapping provided they are approved by DSS [5]. The containers are a part of the process to provide multiple layers of protection, deny accidental access, detect tampering and ensure expedited transport.

CLASSIFIED PACKAGE WRAPPING CHECKLIST

INNER WRAPPING:

1. Mark opaque envelop with highest classification
2. Label with recipient company name and address, ATTN: Recipient's name, section, mail stop, etc.
3. Seal all seams with opaque tamper-proof tape

OUTER WRAPPING:

1. Label opaque envelop with company name, address, ATTN: Facility Security Officer
2. Seal with opaque tamper-proof tape covering all seams.
3. Include two copies of receipt inside or attached to inner opaque envelop

Classification or other restrictive markings are not annotated on outer wrapper*

Figure 9-2 A classified package wrapping checklist serves as a reminder of how to prepare classified information for delivery. Improperly packaged classified material could lead to loss or compromise of classified information.

Figure 9-3 The classified document outer wrapper does not have classification markings, but does have the rip proof tape.

TRANSMITTING MATERIAL BY CLASSIFICATION LEVEL WITHIN THE U.S. AND TERRITORIES-OVERVIEW

TOP SECRET

Contractors can only transfer outside of a cleared facility with the approval of the Government Contracting Activity (GCA). Only Federal agencies authorize the transfer of TOP SECRET material within their agency control. The approved methods for dissemination of TOP SECRET within the US and territories follow [6] (Note that USPS shipments are not authorized for TOP SECRET):

- NSA approved or designed cryptographic means
- Defense Courier Service when authorized
- Appropriately cleared and approved DoD courier or escort (courier orders (Figure 9-4)) on approved commercial air or ground transportation

SECRET

- Any means as authorized for TOP SECRET [7]
- United States Postal Service Registered and Express Mail [7]
- Cleared commercial carriers [7]
- GSA approved overnight delivery services [7]
- Cleared local messenger service [7]
- Other methods as approved by the GCA [7]

CONFIDENTIAL

- Any means as authorized for SECRET and TOP SECRET [8]
- Commercial carriers do not have to be "cleared" as long as they provide a Constant Surveillance Service (CSS) [9]
- USPS Certified Mail [8]

Transmitting material within the U.S. and Territories In Detail

TOP SECRET
National Security Agency approved or designed cryptographic means

The largest threat facing the United States is economic espionage. Billions of dollars worth of damage occurs monthly as companies lose their valuable technological edge. Though other nations and enterprises seek to steal technology, much of it is released because employees do not understand how to protect their company and privacy information. Unencrypted Email, facsimile machines, and telephones are not secure. They are portals open to scrutiny and intercept. Organizations that regularly send sensitive information through open channels may lose their propriety and technology lead.

The threat is similar for classified information. Cleared employees must understand their roles in protecting classified information from receipt to dissemination. To prevent inadvertent release via electronic transmission the federal government requires the use of encryption and decryption devices. Those who use encryption devices designate a communications security (COMSEC) custodian to account for COMSEC equipment [10]. This system involves setting up an account with the NSA and using secure telephone and facsimile machines. Classified information should never be sent over unapproved telephone or facsimile machines.

Defense Courier Service (DCS)

The DCS is an organization reporting directly to the Commander In Chief Transportation Command 11. The DCS is a network of professionals with the mission of providing international support and distribution of sensitive and classified information. This service is available to qualifying military, government and defense contractor organizations and provides continuous surveillance of the classified material aboard U.S. flagged carriers or when not available, authorized.

Appropriately cleared and approved DoD courier or escort on approved commercial air or ground transportation

TOP SECRET information can be transmitted by courier or escort when approved. TOP SECRET information should only be hand carried or escorted as a last resort and only if the information is not otherwise available or it is critical to fulfilling the contract.

SECRET

SECRET information can be disseminated using the same methods as TOP SECRET. However, they can also be disseminated by the means listed below:

United States Postal Service Registered and Express Mail (within the United States and territories)

Registered and Express Mail within the US and territories is approved for SECRET. Registered mail uses a system of receipts and monitoring throughout the journey to provide the most secure method the USPS offers. With today's technology, the sender can verify a signed delivery almost immediately by logging onto the USPS website and entering the tracking number. Once delivery is confirmed with the appropriate signature, the FSO can verify with the receiver and print and file the confirmation.

Express mail can also be used for secure overnight delivery. The USPS guarantees overnight delivery where available at all times of day and night. However, the sending organization should only use USPS Express service after delivery is coordinated and the recipient is available to sign for and receive the classified delivery. When using USPS Express service, the FSO should schedule either a pickup or delivery to a USPS facility. Depositing classified material in a drop box is not authorized and provides no protection against theft, accidental loss or exposure of classified information. Also, the sender should make arrangements to deliver only to an office where an authorized person can sign for the item. According to the NISPOM "The 'Waiver of Signature and Indemnity' block on the U.S. Postal Service express mail label 11–B, will not be executed under any circumstances." The required signature ensures the item is received by a cleared person [10].

Cleared Commercial Carriers

Department of Defense contractors can use government approved commercial carriers to transport SECRET and below. The deliveries are not authorized for international travel and can only be made within the continental US or within Alaska, Hawaii and each territory with GCA providing routing information.

Commercial carrier shipments should be protected using hardened containers or other material authorized by the GCA [12]. Additionally boxes, cars, compartments and sections should be protected with numbered seals. The numbers can help determine whether or not the containers or equipment has been opened or an attempt made to open them.

When seals are used, the following statement applies: "Do not break seals except in case of emergency or upon prior authority of the consignor or consignee. If found broken or if broken for emergency reasons, apply carrier's seals as soon as possible and immediately notify both the consignor and the consignee." [12]. The bill of lading should contain the statement to the effect that Protective Security Service is required. Upon delivery, the receiver should inspect the bill of lading against the container and seals and report discrepancies immediately to the FSO.

When requesting commercial carrier support, the contractor should notify the GCA of the proposed classified material to be shipped, the point of origin and the destination [12]. Once approved, they should notify the consignee and the shipping activity of the shipment and provide details of the type of shipment, number of seals, and projected time of arrival. The FSO notifies the intended recipient to expect the delivery of classified material. If the shipment does not arrive within 48 hours the receiver should notify the sender.

GSA Approved Overnight Delivery Service

SECRET and CONFIDENTIAL material can be sent using GSA approved companies. A list of these companies is available at http://www.gsa.gov. These services should not be used without DSS approval. When using an overnight delivery service, the FSO of the sending organization should alert the receiving organization that classified information will be arriving via overnight service. Though overnight carriers are approved through the GSA, the carrier companies do not need to hold a facility security clearance. The carriers are only required to meet requirements of tracking shipments [7].

Every precaution should be made to ensure that the overnight delivery will not arrive during a holiday or scheduled day off. The best method is to not deliver the day prior to a weekend or federal holiday unless the receiver is operating a mail room with cleared persons and the proper storage capability.

Cleared Local Messenger Service

Cleared commercial messenger services can hand deliver classified information provided they have a facility clearance and cleared messengers. Once the cleared messenger service has been authorized and verified in the ISFD, the FSO should coordinate the delivery with the service and the receiver. The cleared messenger should sign for a receipt when they pick up the classified package. They then require the receiver to sign a receipt acknowledging taking the classified material into their accountability.

CONFIDENTIAL

CONFIDENTIAL information can be disseminated using the same methods as SECRET and TOP SECRET. However, they can also be disseminated by the means listed below:

USPS (within the US and territories)

Confidential material can be transmitted the same as SECRET

when using USPS. However, in most cases classified material can be sent using Certified Mail. The USPS Certified Mail service provides a level of security which includes tracking and delivery confirmation. As with USPS Registered Mail, the cleared facility mailing the classified items is issued a receipt and tracking number. The sender has the opportunity to verify a signed delivery almost immediately by logging onto the USPS website and entering the tracking number. Once delivery is confirmed with the appropriate signature, the confirmation can be printed and filed.

Commercial Carriers

The commercial carrier does not need to maintain a facility security clearance to transport CONFIDENTIAL material. However, the DSS or GCA must approve the shipment [9]. These commercial carriers can be hired as long as they are within US boundaries and provide a Constant Surveillance Service (CSS). In other words, the carriers be alert and document visual inspection of the classified material while en route.

Transmitting Classified Information with Couriers/Escorts

Couriers hand carry classified information during all stages of travel. Escorts accompany classified information during travel but may not be physically in the same area. While an escort may be in a passenger area, the classified information will be in a cargo area. When authorized, defense contractors can transmit classified information using cleared employees with a courier briefing. Hand carrying should be a last resort as more risks are involved and should not be used as a matter of convenience. Prior to using cleared employees, the FSO should ensure the cleared employees protect the classified material at the proper level. Prior to hand carrying classified information the security manager verifies the following requirements [13]:

- The classified material does not exist at the destination and is necessary to meet a contractual requirement
- The material cannot be sent via facsimile, other electronic

means or the United States Postal Service

- Hand carrying is authorized by GCA or appropriate official
- Classified information is in control of escort at all times. Arrangements are made for security storage for overnight stops (not hotel rooms or homes)
- Receipts are exchanged at the destination and forwarded to the sending security office

If none of the above can be verified, the shipper should designate alternate methods of movement or consider not moving the classified material at all. The USPS and electronic dissemination methods provide more security during movement.

An authorized courier has a security clearance and need to know. After the classified material is properly packaged, the FSO should brief the cleared employee on their responsibilities to protect the classified material in their possession. The courier should understand that they are responsible for the classified information under their care and planning should cover pre-trip, en route, and after trip preparations.

Pre-Trip

Courier should have tickets, a travel plan, a courier letter and coordination made with involved parties. They should also inspect the classified package and ensure receipts are included, and written authorization is provided and picture identification is available [13]. A good practice is to issue courier papers that identify the cleared employee as authorized to hand carry classified material from their cleared facilities. The courier credentials should be issued only after the cleared employee has acknowledged their understanding of training. Practice runs, hands on training or using couriers with more experience is always a good practice and confidence, experience and education combine to prevent security violations.

En route

Courier should adhere to the planned route and not make deviations. If stops are necessary, they should be part of a plan with approved locations to store the classified information. The classified information must remain with the courier and should not be opened by unauthorized persons or contents discussed openly. The classified package is never to be left unattended and the courier should not allow themselves to be distracted from protecting the classified material.

If the trip involves an overnight stay, a stop should be scheduled and arrangements made for approved storage [13]. Plans should also include what to do in case of emergencies such as unintended layovers, breakdowns or other unplanned events. This approved storage should be coordinated with the GCA or DSS. Authorized overnight storage locations include federal and government installations and other defense contractor facilities with approved classified storage capacity at the same level as or higher than the transported package. The briefing should also include delivering the classified material only to authorized persons and at the approved facilities. The courier should not store classified information in lockers, private homes, automobile trunks, hotel safes or other unauthorized areas.

A government customer may require a defense contractor to attend a classified visit or meeting at another defense contractor's cleared facility. When such arrangements are made, a contractor could also escort classified information to the meeting. Prior to departure, an inventory of the classified material should be conducted [13]. The cleared facilities where the meeting occurs may authorize the courier to report directly to the meeting without additional processing. However, the courier should be prepared to introduce the classified information according to the cleared facility's policies or per instruction from the government sponsor. Prior arrangements and coordination will prevent any delays or surprises.

After Trip

The courier should be prepared to receive a receipt from the recipient of the classified information. If they will be returning with a classified package, they should again ensure that it is properly prepared for delivery.

Modes of Travel

Hundreds of thousands of tons of cargo travel our roads, rails, and airspace daily. America depends on transportation to get products to customers safely and on time. When products are lost or damaged, carrier insurance will reimburse either the shipper or receiver. However, there is no insurance for damage to national security. Classified items lost, stolen or exposed during shipment pose a threat. No matter how dependable a carrier's track record, the shipper should do everything possible to transport classified information while mitigating any risk of loss or compromise.

The volume of material transported on any given day is staggering. Transportation by any means is reliable but not risk free. Vehicle accidents, traffic jams, break downs or any number of problems with land, air, rail and sea transportation can threaten the security of the classified product. Natural disasters and mechanical failure can cause delays in the reliable movement of items. Air travel also has inherent risks including: late gate departures and arrivals, crowded terminals, and maintenance problems significantly threaten the ability of an escort to keep a close eye on the cargo hold. Those escorting classified material via trains, over the road vehicles, and air carriers should be aware of inconsistencies or events during the shipment that could negatively impact the security of the item. When any event happens to cause an unscheduled delay, the escort should immediately notify the shipper

Rail

When shipping classified information by train the escort should ride in the same car, keep the package under constant surveillance and remain vigilant during stops and layovers. Experienced travelers understand the frustrations involved when others have retrieved the wrong baggage. Escorts should ensure they maintain their receipts and watch their package to prevent such mistakes from occurring as well as other attempts to pilfer or steal. Shipping classified material in a separate car poses a more difficult challenge. Coordination with railroad employees will significantly reduce the challenges while helping to strengthen security. When freight cars and passenger cars are separated, the FSO should arrange with the railroad for the freight car to be positioned immediately in front of the escort's car [14]. The biggest threat occurs during stops. When time permits, escorts should leave the train at all stops and perform a physical inspection of the protective measures (seals, locks, etc) applied to the classified items on the shipment cars.

Highway

Overnight escorts should remain alert for security violations, theft, piracy, pilferage, hi-jacking, damage or other incidences that could jeopardize the shipment and compromise the classified information [15]. Rest and overnight stops, regulated driving hours and refueling pose additional risks to the voyage. At every stop the escort should keep the vehicle in view and remains alert to threatening actions. Highly sensitive items, urgency and threat may require a carrier to provide enough escorts to work around the clock shifts.

Air

Airlines also offer unique challenges to transporting classified material. Air carriers are experienced in flying various types of cargo to worldwide locations. Federal marshals fly prisoners, zoo keepers ship exotic animals, and doctors transport donor organs. Those transporting classified materials are also limited to the type of cargo the Federal Aviation Administration and the National Transportation Safety Board authorizes. Prior arrangements with the air carrier help them understand the unique requirements for shipping classified material and will better meet the requests of the consignor.

Passenger travel is a choreographed event. Passengers board when invited, remain in their seats during takeoff and landing and deplane when instructed. When transporting classified material, the escort should request boarding and deplaning services outside of normal operations. When layovers are expected, the escort should be the first off the plane and wait in an area where they can observe activities on and around the cargo access door. If the cargo is transshipped using another airplane, the escort should observe the process. When the plane is ready to continue the journey the escort is again the last to board. Upon reaching the final destination, the escort becomes the first to deplane.

Cleared employees traveling by commercial aircraft should conduct extensive pre planning. In addition to identification, a courier briefing, and notification to maintain accountability of the classified material at all times, should be coordinated with the Transportation Security Administration (TSA). For example, while traveling by automobile, the courier may only need to drive to the final destination without having to speak to anyone. The route is often direct to the destination with no interruptions. However more vigilance is needed when traveling to and through an airport terminal.

Prior to a cleared employee traveling with classified information on commercial airlines the FSOs should coordinate with the TSA. TSA can help the courier or escort transition security with the least amount of interruption or intrusion for both the courier and TSA agents. TSA agents might examine the classified package with x-ray equipment. Depending on the size of the airport, urgency and threat level, the arrangements and coordination made with TSA can help make negotiating through to the secure area easier.

A good working relationship between the FSO and TSA helps both parties understand the importance of the courier remaining with the classified package at all times. When it is necessary to send the classified material through the x-ray machine, the courier must remain vigilant and know where the item is at all times [15].

Classified material should never be opened in transit [15]. Such a contingency should be planned with the FSO during the courier briefing. In the briefing and planning stage, the courier and FSO should understand that TSA may need to open the packaging to verify that the item is indeed a document as identified in the courier letter. If TSA requests to open the package, the courier should request to see the senior agent to quietly explain the situation. They should produce the courier paperwork and permit inspecting the package privately while not bringing attention to the fact the contents are classified.

There may be occasion to escort large, heavy, bulky or other classified material. Some classified packages cannot otherwise be inspected

XYZ CONTRACTOR
123 Bramlet Drive
Huntsville Alabama 35802

1. John Alfred Brown an employee of XYZ Contractor is authorized to hand carry classified material aboard commercial air carrier. Mr. Brown's description is as follows:

Born: January 7 1952
Ht: 5'8"
Wt: 165 lbs

2. Mr. Brown will hand carry a brown package approximately 13" x 15". XYZ Contractor requests that this package not be opened during any part of the trip. Mr. Browns itinerary follows:

Depart 7:30 am from Huntsville International Airport
Arrive at the William B. Hartsfield International Airport (ATL) at 8:30 am
Depart ATL at 10:30 am
Arrive at Baltimore Washington Airport at 12:00 pm.

3. If there are any questions, please contact the undersigned at 256.555.5555 or Defense Security Services, Defense Security Services, Xxx lane, Huntsville, Alabama 35824. 256.555.5567

Edward Parker   John Alfred Brown
FSO   Project Manager
XYZ Contractor   XYZ Contractor

Figure 9-4 Sample Authorization Letter, such documentation and coordination with the TSA makes the transportation of classified material a successful event.

with an x-ray machine or other visual means without causing compromise. In such cases prior arrangements are made with the TSA or the air carrier to accommodate conveying classified material by air.

Defense contractors traveling by air should also travel with a written authorization (9-4). This authorization identifies the traveler by full name, date of birth, height, weight, type of identification used and signature. The letter also describes the classified material, all relevant travel points, name, telephone and address of the FSO and the DSS office and expiration date of the letter. The authorization letter should provide authority for the special courier requests and the courier presents the authorization upon request.

DESTRUCTION OF CLASSIFIED MATERIAL

Unless permitted by the GCA, classified information must be destroyed or returned as soon as it has served its purpose. According to NISPOM section 5-701, classified information can only be retained for two years unless the GCA approves an extension. Cleared contractors should develop a system to evaluate the classified information in their possession for reduction. Classified information no longer needed should be returned to the GCA or destroyed using approved methods. The FSO should create a system to help prioritize which items to evaluate. The IMS or accountability system can be used in the process to manage classified holdings and help determine what is still useful and what can be removed. The objective is to maintain only the classified material necessary to execute the classified contract. Additionally, the FSO should be able to determine that the documents were actually destroyed or returned and not lost.

The IMS can also be used to help determine classified information by status. For example, the FSO can sort classified information by contract and see how many related documents and copies exist. Items can be prioritized for return or destruction based on expired contracts, duplicate copies or other criteria as identified in the IMS.

Approved Destruction Methods

Two people are required to destroy and document the destruction of TOP SECRET information. SECRET and CONFIDENTIAL only require one person. Records and receipt of destruction should be kept on hand for two years when TOP SECRET is destroyed. However, records should also be maintained for SECRET and CONFIDENTIAL. This documentation helps determine the disposition of classified information during inspections and inventories.

Classified information can be destroyed by approved means based on its composition. For example, paper products can be shredded, burned, pulped or pulverized. The residue should be inspected to ensure that classified information is no longer legible. Shredding should only be accomplished using NSA approved equipment.

Commercial enterprises and vendors also provide destruction services. Burn facilities operate at temperatures hot enough to burn paper in bulk, computers and hard drives and other medial. However, approval through DSS should be acquired prior to using such services. Also, classified information should be destroyed the same day as it is removed from the cleared facility and should be prepared for transmission by the same methods as dissemination described earlier.

Summary

Classified information should only be removed from the protection of a cleared facility as a last resort and when otherwise authorized and absolutely necessary. Each time SECRET or TOP SECRET classified material is introduced or removed from a cleared facility, a receipting action should take place. When directed to send classified material to another cleared location the sender should protect it from attempts to tamper, steal, or otherwise gain unauthorized access.

Review Questions

1. You are an FSO for a large cleared contractor organization and have just been notified by your government customer to transfer a series of compact disks classified as SECRET to another

business under contractual agreement. The other business is across the country. Specific guidance is as follows: "The contractor needs the classified material at their facility to begin critical analysis and solve a pressing problem defining the success of the program."

a. Identify authorized methods of transporting classified material at the SECRET level.

b. Which resources will you consult for authorized methods of transmission based on your contract?

2. Your customer calls ten minutes later with a change. The contractor needs to begin work immediately.

a. Based on the request which resources are available for shipping classified information overnight?

b. DSS has provided written authorization to transport classified information using approved overnight carriers. Where would you go to find a list of approved overnight carriers?

3. How would you prepare the classified compact disks for dissemination to another location? In other words, describe the process for wrapping or preparing the classified information for delivery (layers of protection, address labels and classification markings).

4. Suppose overnight carriers were not authorized for the above scenario. What methods are available through USPS?

5. If the recipient is not available to sign for the package, should the classified material be forwarded? Why or why not?

Resources

1. Department of Defense, DoD 5220.22-M, National Industrial Security Operating Manual, section 5-201, February 2006
2. Department of Defense, DoD 5220.22-M, National Industrial Security Operating Manual, section 5-200, February 2006
3. PART IV, National Archives and Records Administration, Information Security Oversight Office, 32 CFR Parts 2001 and 2004 Classified National Security Information, (Directive No. 1); Final Rule

4. Executive Order 12968—Access to Classified Information, Federal Register, section 2.5, August 1995
5. Department of Defense, DoD 5220.22-M, National Industrial Security Operating Manual, section 5-401, February 2006
6. Department of Defense, DoD 5220.22-M, National Industrial Security Operating Manual, section 5-402, February 2006
7. Department of Defense, DoD 5220.22-M, National Industrial Security Operating Manual, section 5-403, February 2006
8. Department of Defense, DoD 5220.22-M, National Industrial Security Operating Manual, section 5-404, February 2006
9. Department of Defense, DoD 5220.22-M, National Industrial Security Operating Manual, section 5-409, February 2006
10. Department of Defense, DoD 5220.22-M, National Industrial Security Operating Manual, section 9-403, February 2006
11. DoD 5200.33-R, "Defense Courier Service Regulation", January 5, 1995 Assistant Secretary of Defense for Command, Control, Communication and Intelligence
12. Department of Defense, DoD 5220.22-M, National Industrial Security Operating Manual, section 5-408, February 2006
13. Department of Defense, DoD 5220.22-M, National Industrial Security Operating Manual, section 5-410, February 2006
14. Department of Defense, DoD 5220.22-M, National Industrial Security Operating Manual, section 5-413, February 2006
15. Department of Defense, DoD 5220.22-M, National Industrial Security Operating Manual, section 5-411, February 2006

CHAPTER 10 TRAINING AND REPORTING

INTRODUCTION

Developing relationships with cleared employees creates an environment of cooperation. This environment facilitates the recruitment of all employees to protect national security. Those working in the enterprise can be the eyes, ears and muscle, acting as force multipliers, and extending the effectiveness of the security department.

FSOs should conduct initial and refresher training and file reports as required by the NISPOM. Instead of conducting training just to be compliant, the training can be performed as an effective relationship building opportunity. This education increases a cleared employee's knowledge of responsibility to protect classified material; detect attempts at espionage and other security violations; and report incidents, violations and status changes affecting personnel and facility clearances.

This chapter provides information of training and reporting requirements as outlined in the NISPOM. The reader will have access to training ideas to create a synergistic program involving all employees. This enables robust security far exceeding the capabilities of a single department. This chapter will address the following issues:

- **Training All Employees for Effective Performance** – The NISPOM requires cleared employees to attend initial and refresher training [1]. The FSO should understand the requirements and how the training objectives relate to their industry. Any FSO can quote regulations, but a good one knows how to take this annual requirement and make it applicable to the organization.

- **Adverse Information** – A report of adverse information can indicate an employee's inability to protect classified information. However, only credible and factual adverse information should be reported. As with corporate fraud and other crimes, cases of espionage often occur over a longer duration than necessary. Traditionally, those who have stolen information from their organizations have demonstrated patterns and behavior that should have raised suspicion with coworkers much earlier. Too much time at the copier, working late when unnecessary, sudden unexplained wealth and other indicators have been reported to investigators after the fact. Timely reporting is a vital link between security and employees in the protection of classified information. Adverse information should be reported immediately [2]. Reluctance to report information on themselves could stem from FSOs not adequately communicated the objective of reporting.

- **Security Violations** – Security violations occur when classified information is not protected. When violations do occur they must be reported immediately. Relationships can develop while conducting training and other interaction opportunities could lead to more willingness to report minor incidents and major violations. Investigations and interviews should be conducted to find root causes and determine whether or not a loss, compromise or suspected compromise has occurred. The results are either handled in-house or sent to DSS depending on the findings.

TRAINING

DSS should give initial training and briefings to the FSO [3]. The FSO is then authorized to provide the training to the cleared employees. According to NISPOM, the FSO is also required to attend the DSS mandated FSO Program Management Course within one year of appointment [4]. DSS provides new courses designed for FSOs of possessing and non-possessing facilities. FSOs should coordinate with their

DSS representative to determine the training that's right for their situation. The training is designed to prepare the FSO to implement and direct a NISPOM based security program in their cleared contractor facility including, but not limited to the following topics:

- Protecting classified material – The proper receipt, accountability, storage, dissemination and destruction of classified material. The FSO learns how to protect classified information in a cleared contractor facility.
- Required training – This instruction helps the FSO establish an ongoing training program designed to create an environment of security conscious cleared employees. The FSO learns to present effective training to cleared employees, teaching them to properly protect the classified material and report questionable activity and violations.
- Personnel security clearances – The FSO gains an understanding of the personnel security clearance request procedure, briefing techniques and maintenance of personnel clearances.
- Facility clearance –The FSO learns how FCLs are established and which records and activities are required to maintain the FCL.
- Foreign Ownership Control and Influence (FOCI) - Organizations analyze foreign investments, sales and ownership on a regular basis using the Certificate Pertaining to Foreign Interests (SF 328). FSOs learn to interact with management and provide guidance and direction in preventing a foreign entity from unauthorized access to or controlling work involving classified and export controlled information [5].
- Exports compliance and international operations –FSOs receive instruction on how to prevent unauthorized disclosure of critical technology, classified and export controlled information. Companies can thrive in such an international environment provided they can execute Departments of State and Commerce licenses and agreements as required.
- Restricted areas –The restricted area is established to control temporary access to classified material. At the end of each work day, the classified material is returned to the approved

classified holding area.

- Closed areas – Space is approved to store and work with classified material. This involves approved construction and limited accesses controls to prevent unauthorized disclosure during and after work hours.
- Contract security classification specification (DD Form 254) – The cleared contractor is allowed access to classified contracts based on the DD Form 254. The FSO learns how the DD Form 254 is constructed and how to provide input to better meet security requirements.
- Security classification guides (SCG) – As the DD Form 254 provides authorization to execute a classified contract, the SCG provides the "how to" instruction. All employees performing classified work consult the guide to understand what is classified and how to provide the required protection.
- Security administration and records keeping – This teaches the maintenance of facility and personnel security clearance information as well as all other accountability and IMS. The FSO is expected to provide information on personnel clearances, original documentation of their facility clearance and demonstrate classified information accountability during the DSS annual security inspection.
- Sub contracting – When approved to subcontract classified work, the prime contractor will provide a DD Form 254 to the subcontractor. Other topics necessary to direct and implement a successful training program.

The FSO must attend the required training at either at DSS Academy or through a mobile training team. Once successfully trained, the academy issues a certificate which should be filed for presentation during security audits. The FSO training should not end with this course. Career enhancing training is available through various security and management courses. More in depth online and residence training is available in each above mentioned topic. Other agencies may offer more training certification in special access programs, COMSEC, and intelligence protection. Other training is available in colleges, professional organizations, vendor websites, through books like this and within the security community.

BRIEFINGS

Initial Security Briefings

The initial security briefing is designed to familiarize the cleared employee with the NISP as applied to the cleared facility. It also provides fundamental training of the classified work specific to the contracts under which the classified work is performed. All new cleared employees should attend this briefing regardless of whether they are receiving a clearance for the first time or bringing 30 years of related work experience [1]. As important as this initial orientation is, a truly successful program continues with on the job training.

The initial security briefing (Figure 10-1) reflects how the organization protects classified material according to Presidential Executive Order 13526. The EO directs training to ensure cleared persons know how to protect classified information and the possible penalties that they can be charged with if they contribute to unauthorized disclosure [6]. The NISPOM requires that an FSO provide training to cleared employees on the following topics [1]:

- Threat awareness briefing – this is designed to inform the employee of active threats attempting to gain access to sensitive information and methods used to collect it. The briefing should be tailored to address the immediate threat to classified information stored in a cleared facility as well as knowledge possessed by the cleared employees. The agency threat office, DSS and CSA can provide valuable training information.
- Defensive security briefing – provides information to cleared employee travel to other countries. Employees should understand how foreign intelligence services might target them for recruitment or espionage attempts. The State Department, DSS, FBI and other federal agency threat offices are good resources for training content.
- Overview of the security classification system – This information covers the levels of classification, marking, safeguarding and other tasks involved with protecting classified materials.

- Employee reporting obligations – employees are required to report suspicious contacts, adverse information, security violations and incidents. This briefing equips the cleared employee with what to report and who to report the information to.
- Security procedures and duties applicable to the cleared employee's job – contracts are as unique as the security programs. New employees should understand the organization specific policies as they apply to their jobs and tasks.
- Exit briefings – Employees should be made aware that security clearances are only issued when required and are not a right or a permanent status. Though an exit briefing is not part of the initial security briefing, the cleared employees should be aware that they will be given an exit briefings when they no longer require a clearance.

Cleared employees should be thoroughly briefed when they no longer require a clearance. A new job, loss of contract, termination, retirement and removal of access are situations where FSOs should explain the responsibility of continuing to protect the classified information. These employees should understand that they are not authorized to use the classified information they formerly had access to in future jobs, to put in resumes, for books, internet postings and etc. FSOs may be tempted to provide a canned briefing and have the employee sign the SF 312.

The exit briefing can be much more than the minimum required and conducted using information from the DD Form 254, scope of work and other contractual and job specific information to remind the employee of specifically what they had access to and that they can no longer use that information. When all individuals in the organization understand the security program and all information and tools are in place, the FSO should be able to create, implement and direct successful protection of classified information. Depending on time, resources and availability, organizations should attempt to structure this initial security briefing by experience level. For example, newly cleared employees require more in depth training than veteran security clearance holders recently hired at a defense contractor organization.

All newly cleared and all new cleared employees regardless of experience should receive initial refresher training before gaining access to classified information.

New Employees

Federal agencies may have separate regulations, but over-arching executive orders provide very similar initial security training requirements:

- Understand the nature of classified material and how to protect it

- Place cleared employees on notice of their responsibilities to protect classified information and the consequences of unauthorized disclosure

- Recognizing and protecting U.S. and foreign government classified material

- Criteria for authorizing access to classified information

- Responding to classified information released to the public

- Security chain of command and support structure for addressing problems

- Cleared employees on foreign travel

Figure 10-1 Initial Security Briefing Topics

FSOs should dedicate more security awareness training to new employees who will have a security clearance for the first time. This is because they will be newly introduced to classified material and how to work with it. The words CONFIDENTIAL, SECRET and TOP SECRET may require further explanation. The newly cleared employee may not understand how to dial a combination or determine who to allow access to classified material. Without proper training, the newly cleared employees may make honest mistakes leading to security violations.

As an example of preventable security violation, consider an FSO conducting a survey of the cleared facility's security program. She wants to get a good understanding of the security successes and challenges the company faces. She recognizes that the veteran engineers, program managers and other cleared employees have a good grasp on their responsibilities to safeguard classified material. All she has to do is provide training and resources to maintain their level of proficiency and communicate security goals and procedures on a regular basis.

Upon reviewing the security violations, the FSO noticed a trend with newly cleared employees. Though each newly cleared employee had signed a Classified Information Nondisclosure Agreement (SF 312) and an initial security briefing attendance roster, they contributed to the most incidents and violations. In one incident a newly cleared employee had failed to return a classified compact disk to the classified document holding at the end of the day. According to the preliminary investigation, the FSO attempted to contact the employee over a course of three hours. Finally at 8:00 p.m., the employee returned to work with the classified disk. His explanation involved attending a dinner and returning later to the office and finish his classified work. He had explained that as long as the disk was on his person, he had provided adequate safeguarding. Both the FSO and the employee's supervisor had assumed that the employee had understood how to protect classified information.

New Employees With Extensive Classified Work Experience

Cleared facilities with new employees who have already received security clearances still have a responsibility to provide the initial security briefing. The new employees may have experience protecting classified material, but there is no way to verify the type and strength of the experience. Unique contractual requirements may have specialized performance requirements. New employees, regardless of experience level, should receive reinforcement security training on the threat, how to recognize and protect classified information and reporting suspicious contacts or security violations. Those with experience protecting classified information should be provided an overview of the NISP with a more contract and organization oriented briefing. They do not always need the same in depth briefing as a newly cleared employee receives. However, they should have a clear understanding of implementing the NISP to contract specific classified work.

The FSO is the primary security awareness trainer for the cleared contractor and DSS provides required briefings to the FSO. Once trained, the FSO provides the training to cleared employees. The training of newly cleared employees begins with a briefing of their responsibilities to protect classified information and as outlined on the SF 312.

The SF 312 is an agreement between the cleared employee and the U.S. government outlining both parties' responsibilities to protect our nation's secrets. The FSO does not grant a newly cleared employee access to classified information or program until the employee is trained and signs the SF 312 and the employee should not be asked to sign the SF 312 until fully trained on the nature of the classified material and how to protect it. A common practice is to provide the initial security briefing prior to presenting the SF 312 for signature. Once the SF 312 is signed by all parties, the FSO will forward it to DSS.

However, the SF 312 is not required just because an employee begins a new job at a new company. If a new employee already possesses a clearance while employed at another defense contractor or federal agency, the FSO just records the training and assumes responsibility of the cleared employee in JPAS. They do not have to process another SF 312 unless there is not one on file required specifically by DSS. An FSO can verify whether or not a cleared employee has signed an SF 312 through JPAS.

Annual Refresher Training

In addition to the initial security briefing, the FSO should provide annual refresher training. This training should build upon the initial briefing and the on the job training. The training covers the same topics as the initial security briefing with the addition of any new changes in the NISP since the last training event. Though the requirement is for annual refresher training, the frequency is the minimum standard. A good security program might provide constant training on a recurring basis. Whatever the frequency, the training should be documented to demonstrate each cleared employee's participation.

The changes or additional topics included in the annual refresher training should include updates to security regulations at the national level. These changes occur anytime an executive order is amended, DSS updates regulations, or any other administrative or procedural updates affecting cleared facilities and employees. Closer to home, the additional subjects could include security requirements of new classified contracts, updated security hardware, software, alarms or procedures impacting the work force. The addition of newly constructed facilities; updated emergency procedures and local security policies and procedures; addition of classified computer processing or any other new classified work introduced to the organization are excellent topics for training [7].

Top Secret Control Official Training

Certain topics should be provided during initial security briefings and annual follow up training for those cleared employees with TOP SECRET clearances. After all, the higher certification lends to tougher standards and more accountability. Full and complete training will enhance national security by empowering the holder to protect information appropriately. The key to the training is the spelling out of the TSCO duties and how they support the other cleared employees.

Derivative Classifier Training

The NISPOM outlines requirements for derivative classification. Those performing derivative classification must be trained every two years. Before cleared employees can perform derivative classification, they must be trained. NISPOM lays out training requirements. The cleared contractor provides that training. Without the training, cleared employees won't know how to perform their jobs. Additionally, without training they aren't authorized to perform the derivative classification. This training will explain how derivative classifiers will write reports, design products, assemble end items, perform test, modeling and simulations involving information deemed classified by a classification authority. Cleared employees are not authorized to conduct derivative classification until they receive such training.

Performing Security Training

All training should be captured by date, topic and employee name and the information kept on file for DSS review. The many methods and opportunities are limitless, but some are provided below:

Special Briefings

Special programs, COMSEC, couriers, and intelligence are examples of classified work that requires briefings above and beyond the initial security briefing. The briefing should educate the indoctrinated cleared employees of additional security requirements and resources available for the protection of the classified material. Because of the special handling, caveats, inventory, accountability, control and storage requirements, cleared personnel should sign acknowledgement of the additional briefing. Once the additional required briefings are conducted, the cleared persons are permitted access. Such training should be incorporated into the annual security briefing as a refresher of security policy and procedure.

Presentations

The refresher briefing is often presented to large groups and with plenty of subject matter and may occur as a lecture. While providing a large amount of information in one sitting, there may not be much interaction. Therefore presentations are the least effective. If only provided once per year, this effectiveness decreases. However, presenting to large groups is not without benefits. The meeting can be captured on a calendar and scheduled, employees can be trained simultaneously and verification of training for large audiences can easily be captured electronically or on sign-in sheets. When combined with other methods like multimedia, games, interaction and with greater frequency, presentations become more effective and help to increase security awareness and anticipation of additional training

Computer Assisted Learning

Computers and email offer additional and inexpensive training opportunities. Affordable software provides interactive training in a professional medium. Vendors in many industries also have prepackaged training slides that can be augmented for specific training needs. The multi-media presentations are interactive and very effective. For companies with small budgets, employees with basic computer skills can generate effective slide presentations with software already installed. These presentations can be tracked to provide immediate feedback of completion. The FSO can hyperlink automatic training certificates or email notification at the end of the presentation for accountability and documentation purposes. They can send an updated presentation to the organization's company email list on a recurring basis.

Posters, Flyers And Banners

There are great resources for delivering pinpointed security messages. Companies can brand their security specifically to the organization or mission. Government agencies have websites with downloadable brochures and posters on many topics. FSOs have hosted poster contests where instead of relying on the security department to provide all the talent, cleared employees contribute. Organically produced posters can also use the company brand and carry on the company mission statement by having the security message reflect the organizational goals and values.

Videos/Skits

Informational and dramatic videos are increasing in popularity.

Many are available from government agencies while some organizations film speeches and presentations for broadcast to larger audiences. Others feature a rundown of security news and events in the Department of Defense. Mass produced videos offer a free or low cost method to provide alternate refresher security training for cleared employees.

If budget, time and talent permits, well made skits can provide a fun and entertaining message unique to the organization's mission. Using employees' talents and skills to write, act or direct provides a memorable training opportunity. The audience may be more apt to remember the message seeing familiar faces acting out situations depicting security related incidents. This method can be more enlightening than a group briefing or slide presentation. However, time, energy and resources dedicated to rehearsal, performance, cast and props add to overhead costs and lost manpower. A good and thorough return on investment (ROI) should be conducted prior to beginning any training project.

Organizations with a video department have combined live performance with their organic recording capabilities to produce high quality shows. These taped skits or plays require fewer actors and support at any given time than that of live performances. The performance can be recorded as quickly as necessary or spread out over as much time as needed. This flexibility facilitates filming with fewer work interruptions. Skits are written and performed without having large rehearsals or removing the cast from their primary jobs. The performances are made on a small scale, taped, edited and written to DVDs for dissemination or performance at a later date.

Newsletters

Newsletters provide an inexpensive form of education. Government websites, news organizations, and other media provide excellent sources for security articles. Additionally, vendors have subscription based industry specific security newsletters. Newsletters can also be locally written and emailed or printed and distributed to the entire organization. FSOs should also analyze national defense, crime and threat trends and statistics to provide real articles that relate directly to the organization's missions. For example, suppose a backlog of security clearance investigations is predicted to increase and the FSO is aware of the company's need to hire new employees for an upcoming contract. Additionally, several employees going through an investigation are eagerly waiting to be awarded a clearance. The FSO can publish the causes of the delays in an informative article and help the organization understand and adapt to the changes.

Caution: Newsletters should never be used as a primary source of communicating important news to management. Approved communication channels should be used to keep executives informed of security issues that will impact the organization's ability to perform classified work.

Department updates

Requests for bid, sub contracts, new contract awards, projects and mission changes affect the work requirements of federal and contractor cleared organizations. During the process of assigning a classified contract, government agencies and prime contractors analyze classified requirements. The analysis determines the type of classified work the contractor is expected to perform, the resources necessary to accomplish the mission, which part of the work is classified and how to properly protect the classified material from unauthorized disclosure and compromise.

Organic training resources

Defense contractors and subcontractors selected to perform on classified contracts should analyze the security requirements prior to beginning work. Those performing on the classified work receive the contract, DD form 254, security classification guide and interact with the Prime and Government customers. The cleared employees, management and the FSO identify necessary resources to receive, safeguard and perform the classified work. The analysis and dedication of resources and means to execute on classified contracts are intense and necessary form of security awareness training. Tasks associated with receiving and preparing for new classified work can be documented as security awareness training.

Reporting Security Violations

Providing required reports to the authorized persons or agency contributes to reducing the impact of the potential security violation, compromise or suspected compromise. Security incidents can be a minor infraction such as someone forgetting to sign an end of day checklist or as serious as a courier losing classified material. In either possible situation the involved cleared employees should understand to whom and what to report. The sooner the report is issued and the more details given, the more can be done to prevent or mitigate damage to national security.

Cleared employees should be trained to report events affecting the facility security clearance or personnel security clearances. These events include threats to the security of classified information or the fact that classified information has been lost or compromised. All cleared employees should know how to submit reportable information to the FSO. Additionally, FSOs have reporting channels through DSS and the Federal Bureau of Investigation (FBI).

Reports to the FBI

Defense contractors should report to the FBI when they become aware of any of the following occasions [8]:

- Espionage – Persons attempting to obtain national defense, proprietary or other sensitive information without the proper permission or clearance and need to know.
- Sabotage – Persons causing damage, diversion, destruction or other activity resulting in an opponent becoming less effective. Installing computer viruses, manipulating security systems or damaging property are examples of sabotage.
- Terrorism – These are acts to create havoc and shock in order to advance goals of ideology, money, or furtherance of political agendas. Terrorists target persons and groups and gain a psy-

chological advantage through shock and fear. Examples of terrorism and tactics abound from events of September 11, 2001, the bombings in Mumbai, India and across the world as innocent bystanders are targeted with extreme violence.

- Subversion – Acts to overthrow forms of authority. These attempts include unseating a government leader or those who aid, abet or provide relief for those who do. Subversion is exemplified through coups in other countries or through militant and paramilitary groups in the US. These groups work to overthrow the government and either cause chaos or install their own brand of authority.

The FBI is the proper agency trained and outfitted to address the above threats. Reports and follow-ups concerning the above issues should feed to the FBI. Written follow-ups should be reported to the DSS with the FBI's approval [8].

Reports to DSS

DSS is more able to address other issues impacting a contractor's facility and personnel security clearances. FSOs should train cleared employee to submit information that adversely impacts the ability of a person or facility to protect classified information. More specifically, reports submitted to DSS are [9]:

Adverse Information

Adverse information indicates that a contractor or federal cleared employee may not be able to properly protect classified information. Adverse information topics include criteria found in the investigation/adjudication process. Investigators research information about a subject based on 13 criteria [9]:

Once the investigation is complete, the results are adjudicated based on the whole person concept. After a clearance is granted, employees are expected to conduct themselves in a manner demonstrating continuous trustworthiness and the ability to safeguard classified material. Any activity demonstrating a violation of any of the 13 investigation criteria could define reportable adverse information. When cleared employees display any characteristics that could imply inability to protect classified material or make them vulnerable to recruitment, they should report that information. When a cleared employee observes such behavior in another employee, they should report that as well.

Suspicious Contacts

This is any attempt by any individual to obtain unauthorized access to classified information. This could include a coworker who attempts to gain unauthorized access to classified information. It could also include a foreign person attempting to recruit the services of a cleared employee to deliver classified material.

Change In Status

Agencies and contractors should report any changes in status of cleared employees. These reportable changes include: name, marital status, citizenship or termination of employment. Termination of employment involves removal of access until the employee is hired at another location requiring a security clearance. Finally, changes in citizenship and death will require removal of security clearance access and cleared employee records in JPAS.

Citizenship By Naturalization

When necessary, Non-U.S. employees can be granted Limited Access Authorization. In the event that these employees become naturalized U.S. Citizens, reports should be forwarded identifying the court and location where the naturalization occurred, the date naturalized, and the certificate number.

Refusal to sign the SF 312

Refusing the sign the SF 312 communicates lack of agreement to protect classified material or lack of training. Cleared employees desiring not to perform on classified work should be reported.

A Change Affecting The Contractor Facility Clearance

The defense contractor is granted a clearance based in part on their ability to safeguard classified information. As part of the procedure the company has demonstrated that it is US owned, conducting business in the US and in good standing. Changes in location, foreign control or influence, changes in key personnel status, and termination of business operations must be reported.

Changes In Storage Capability

Any changes in the storage capability must be reported. These changes include improvements or additions to the security program which raises the protection level or implement changes that deteriorate the protection level.

Inability To Protect Classified Material

Anything preventing a cleared facility from being able to protect classified information should be reported. These events include natural or man made disasters or other emergencies that could erode protection capability such as tornado, earthquake, fire, riot, or power loss. FSOs should also report vulnerabilities of security equipment such as those discovered in intrusion detection systems designed to detect and deter unauthorized access are reported.

Unauthorized Receipt Of Classified Material

Any classified information delivered from the cleared facility to an uncleared facility or person or classified information received without a contractual relationship should be reported.

Security Through Walking Around

An effective method of training and building rapport with other employees in the organization is to get out from behind a desk and meet them. When FSOs observe their environments they become more effective. While engaging in conversation with cleared employees, observing work habits and listening to issues, the FSO builds relationships and an understanding of how the security program is working.

Security through walking around requires a plan. A well designed and executed plan allows the FSO to enforce the security message as well as become familiar with the names and characteristics of employees, team members and executives. The FSO can simultaneously check on posters, restock pamphlets and security awareness flyers. Meeting employees also allows matching a face with the position and makes the FSO more accessible to the very people depended on to support the security programs.

The FSO should use a prioritized list of milestones that helps measure the program's effectiveness. This list could reveal effectiveness in matters of personnel, physical, IT, privacy, proprietary and, if applicable, classified information security. The FSO should build an agenda before walking through the areas. Understanding the policies in effect and the level of security success are vital to building and maintaining credibility. The FSO should know the organizational regulations and requirements and how they affect the business and team members. Answering policy questions with best guesses or flippant remarks, can contribute to the FSO losing credibility.

The FSO should anticipate feedback. There will be some who praise efforts and there will be some who criticize or question motives. Some may respond negatively to security implementing plans such as limiting access. These objections are perfect opportunities to talk about security concerns such as how access systems and door magnets prevent unwanted and unauthorized visitors while reducing energy costs. Other cleared employees may be upset with having to comply with NISPOM requirements that cause them inconvenience. This is also a great time to demonstrate how they impact the company and the benefits of compliance without quoting regulations. When faced with questions that require research, the FSO should be candid. "I don't know, but I'll get back with you," is a perfect response and the FSO should follow-up immediately.

The FSO should publicly offer praise and kudos to those deserving as soon as possible. FSOs should avoid criticism or wry comments directed toward or about an employee who expresses criticism of a program, has committed violations, or just doesn't understand security. Correcting behavior should be done in a professional manner and in private.

Investigating Security Violations

One of the tougher tasks of a security awareness program is teaching, establishing the reporting procedures and providing an environment where employees want to report activities affecting the cleared facility's or an employee's ability to protect classified material. Getting employees to understand security and report information about themselves or other employees is not easy.

The FSO is also charged with investigating security incidents. Security violations include: forgetting to set a combinations or alarms, losing classified items, receiving unauthorized classified information, transmitting classified material in an unauthorized manner, and etc. Each security incident should be investigated to determine whether or not loss, compromise or suspected compromise occurred. If loss, compromise or suspected compromise takes place, the FSO must notify DSS [10]. If the incident did not result in loss, compromise or suspected compromise, no report is forwarded, but an internal investigation should be conducted to find root causes and improve security performance.

FSOs should analyze and review all security incidents regardless of severity or impact. Finding root causes can provide basis for improvements in the security system and reduction of vulnerabilities. Additionally, DSS may ask to review any incidents and reports during the annual security inspection.

Anyone discovering a security violation or incident involving classified information should take positive action to protect the classified information. This protection could take the form of locking an open security container or vault, posting guard or standing by the classified material until relieved. The persons discovering the incident should report it to the FSO as soon as possible.

If an employee finds a security container or vault open or unsecured they should notify the FSO or someone identified as responsible for reacting to such violations. The person should remain in place until an authorized cleared employee relieves them. Next, the authorized cleared employee should perform an inspection of the security container to determine whether or not it has been tampered with. If there is evidence of tampering, the inspecting employee should stop the inspection and call for an authorized expert to determine the extent of the tampering. If there is no evidence of tampering or damage to the container or vault door, an exam of the contents should be conducted to determine whether or not all classified items are where they should be. The combination should be immediately changed to prevent unauthorized persons from having access if the combination has been compromised. If the security container contains combinations to other security containers then all the affected combinations must be changed.

An FSO should initiate a preliminary inquiry once they become aware of a security violation. This preliminary enquiry is used to determine whether or not loss, compromise or suspected compromise has occurred. The FSO or designated investigator should gather facts surrounding the incident in as much detail as possible to make the final determination. Investigations are best conducted using open ended questions to discover when, where and how the incident occurred, what happened, who was involved and why it happened. The preliminary investigation also records the specific classified items involved, the level of classification and the persons and all details contributing to the violation or incident.

When interviewing witnesses or the person committing the violations, questions are better phrased: "Who else was in the building when you noticed the security container unsecured?" Or "How did you discover the lock was not engaged?" These are better questions requiring detailed answers than the following: "Were you the only one in the building when you discovered the violation?" Or "Was the drawer left open?" Which result in a "yes" or "no" response.

The detailed information provides a picture of how the incident occurred. Contributing factors may include fatigue, rescheduled deadlines, a fire drill, forgetfulness, or internal and external pressures. These factors are not researched to provide an excuse, but can be used to implement process changes, re-training of offending employees or as material for analysis and education. The primary result is to discover whether or not classified information was released, determine what happened and prevent it from happening again.

The FSO should ensure follow-up reports are conducted until all the information is collected and the investigation is concluded. Once the investigation is complete a final report is written to determine loss, compromise or suspected compromise of classified material [10]. The final report includes additional information not found in earlier reports; name and identification information on the responsible employees to include records of prior loss, compromise or suspected compromise; corrective actions taken against the responsible parties and reasons for reaching the conclusion that loss, compromise or suspected compromise occurred. When the security violation determines that no loss, compromise or suspected compromise has occurred, the report is complete.

Depending on the severity of the violation, frequency of violations or attitude of the offending employee, graduating degrees of discipline is recommended based on company policy. The investigation should discover whether or not the violation occurred because of employee disregard of security policy, whether or not negligence was involved or whether or not the incident was deliberate. Corrective action should be taken to prevent a recurrence of the violation by the responsible employees and other employees learning from the experience. When a loss or compromise of classified material has occurred, the FSO should forward a report to DSS.

Summary

The successful FSO should understand the incredible contribution that interaction and education lends to a winning security program designed to protect classified information. The education should be continuous, informative and increase cleared employee awareness of company policy, how to identify classified information, responsibilities to protect classified information and report required information. This begins with the cleared employee's initial security briefing and continues throughout the lifetime of their security clearance. Those working in the enterprise can be the eyes, ears and muscle extending the effectiveness of the security department.

Problems

1. As an FSO, you have just given a new employee an initial security briefing and you provide a copy of the SF 312. She refuses to sign the agreement. What should you do?

2. Name three types of adverse information and a brief description of why that information should be reported.

3. You are an FSO walking the floor and assessing the state of security in your organization. You are looking at posters, restocking pamphlets and security awareness flyers and developing rapport with employees. You discover a closed area where classified work is performed. You use your badge to scan in and notice that nobody is around. You become alarmed as closed areas must be locked and alarms set when not occupied. You also notice that classified material is in the printer bin. A moment later an engineer enters. His face turns red as he notices you standing there and he sheepishly says, "I just went to the bathroom for a second. Sorry about leaving the door unlocked."

   a. What security violations have just occurred?

   b. What is your next step to address the violations?

4. The receptionist at the front door just calls. He is clearly agitated about the bomb threat he has just received. Luckily he had a cool head and collected some information about the caller and details about the bomb. Who would a defense contractor organization submit a bomb threat report to?

5. Security awareness training is conducted at least once per year and you maintain good records of those who attended and the subjects areas provided. However, you want to improve the training and add more intervals throughout the year. What are some training methods that you can use to increase the employee's understanding of protecting classified information?

REFERENCES

1. Department of Defense, DoD 5220.22-M, National Industrial Security Operating Manual, section 3-106, February 2006
2. Department of Defense, DoD 5220.22-M, National Industrial Security Operating Manual, section 1-302, February 2006
3. Department of Defense, DoD 5220.22-M, National Industrial Security Operating Manual, section 3-103, February 2006
4. Department of Defense, DoD 5220.22-M, National Industrial Security Operating Manual, section 3-102, February 2006
5. Department of Defense, DoD 5220.22-M, National Industrial Security Operating Manual, section 2-300, February 2006
6. The President, Executive Order 13526, Classified National Security Information—National Industrial Security Program, section 4.1(Federal Register, December 2009)
7. Department of Defense, DoD 5220.22-M, National Industrial Security Operating Manual, section 3-107, February 2006
8. Department of Defense, DoD 5220.22-M, National Industrial Security Operating Manual, section 1-301, February 2006
9. Department of Defense, DoD 5220.22-M, National Industrial Security Operating Manual, section 1-302, February 2006
10. Department of Defense, DoD 5220.22-M, National Industrial Security Operating Manual, section 1-304, February 2006

HELPFUL WEBSITES

NISPOM Training Topics Http://www.redbikepublishing.com
SF 312 Briefing Booklet Http://www.archives.gov/isoo/industry/index.html

CHAPTER 11 INTERNATIONAL OPERATIONS

INTRODUCTION

The United State's economy is increasingly global. Consequently, market success and failure in America impacts the markets overseas and Geopolitical events on one part of the world affect logistics and supply chain management in another. The most impacting events of the new century have involved outsourcing American jobs. Jobs such as computer services, factory work, chemical manufacturing, shipbuilding, help desks, and more have been sent to other countries where they are conducted with lower overall costs. Multinational job opportunities will continue to grow as the US seeks working partners from the international community with more and lower priced resources and services.

The US government wants US companies to be engaged in the international arena and has set goals toward that possibility. Other countries offer additional talent pools, resources and technology. While inviting US industry to compete overseas, the US Government does have regulations and guidance to ensure exports are executed with controlled technology transfer and with mitigated economic and intelligence threat.

This chapter addresses what every defense contractor should understand prior to undertaking international business opportunities. Regardless of whether or not classified work is conducted internationally, State Department, Commerce Department, GCA and DSS rules apply. Conducting classified and defense related business in an international environment requires extreme diligence.

EXPORT LICENSES

Many companies in America produce items for international export. American made products find their way into the markets of various countries demanding US resources, products, services and training. Some of these items are available for export with few limitations or controls. These items do not affect our national defense, technology lead or prevent our technological or economic advances. Details about their production are not protected but readily available in the public domain such as: newsstands, libraries, patent offices, meetings or conferences, or as provided in technical manuals.

However, some US technology is controlled critical military information and dual-use information that cannot be exported without a license or agreement approved by the US Government. A product does not have to be physically shipped to a foreign country to constitute an export as exports can occur within the US. Technical exchanges in conversation, viewing graphics, reading and any other methods of disclosing technical data are forms of exports. Exports can occur anytime a non-US person overhears a conversation or views a computer screen or printout containing export controlled technical data. This information should be protected from unauthorized disclosure or properly approved for export.

Because of the legal, ethical and civil implications associated with responsible exporting, defense contractors have assigned positions or additional duties to employees as Technology Control Officers (TCO), Exports Compliance Officers or similar titles. Employees in these positions are responsible for interpreting the International Traffic in Arms Regulation (ITAR) or the Export Administration Regulation (EAR) as it applies to the organization and the exporting mission. Defense contractors have assigned these positions internally or have hired consultants, trainers, lawyers and other professional organizations available to train and assist with export issues.

Determining Export Jurisdiction

The first step an organization should take when considering export is determining which agency has jurisdiction over the product. Depending on the technology involved, exports can fall under the jurisdiction of the State Department with the ITAR or the Commerce Department with the EAR. Defense articles are under the jurisdiction of State Department and dual use and commercial technologies fall under the Commerce Department. Other agencies exercising exports jurisdiction include the Department of Defense, Treasury, Homeland Security and Energy.

Manufacturers, exporters, and brokers of defense articles, defense services, or related technical data, as defined on the United States Munitions List (USML) (Part 121 of the ITAR) , are required to register with Director of Defense Trade Controls (DDTC). According to the DDTC website, companies desiring to export should consider which jurisdiction their product fall under [1]. If the export is certain to contain protected technology, the company should submit the products to DDTC to undergo a process to determine whether or not they fall under the guidance of ITAR, EAR or regulations of the other agencies. The affected organization is responsible for interpreting the regulations and applying the exports requirements related to their products.

Discovering jurisdiction is not always a clear task. Many jurisdictions blur as civil and military applications are not concrete and in many times overlap. When there is doubt as to whether or not the item applies to the USML, the organization can request a jurisdiction determination through the DDTC and will usually receive response within 65 days [1]. The process is used to discover the nature and function of the product to be exported and whether or not controls have been imposed by other countries. Throughout the process, the product may fall under the DDTC rules until the matter is resolved. Considerations while applying for jurisdiction determination include:

Items to export

The exporter should determine whether or not the article is commercial, dual-use or defense related. This requires a good analysis of the product and how it will be used.

Final Export Destination

The exporter should know where and how the product is to be used all the way to the final destination. If the article is to be exported to a third or fourth country, then the information must be put in the export license requests.

Final Export Customer

Businesses, countries and individuals have been excluded from export opportunities because of embargo actions or other sanctions. The contractor that wishes to export a product should determine whether or not sanctions are in place for the intended customer, organization or country. The Bureau of Industry and Security has such information on their website in the Denied Person's List http://www.bis.doc.gov/dpl/default.shtm.

The Intended Purpose Of The Product

How the product is to be used is extremely important in determining jurisdiction. Any product with a strictly military application will most likely go through State Department channels and dual use/commercial items will go through Commerce Department channels. There are other departments such as Transportation and Treasury that may be involved in the jurisdiction action.

Other Activities The Customer Is Involved In

Political activities, other types of business or other known practices are also important when considering jurisdiction. Exporting technical data to questionable entities could negatively affect national security.

State Department Jurisdiction

Defense Articles are made, designed, produced or modified exclusively for military purposes and do not have a predominant civil appli-

Category I—Firearms, Close Assault Weapons and Combat Shotguns

Category II—Guns and Armament

Category III—Ammunition/Ordnance

Category IV—Launch Vehicles, Guided Missiles, Ballistic Missiles, Rockets, Torpedoes, Bombs and Mines

Category V—Explosives and Energetic Materials, Propellants, Incendiary agents and their Constituents

Category VI—Vessels of War and Special Naval Equipment.

Category VII—Tanks and Military Vehicles

Category VIII—Aircraft and Associated Equipment

Category IX—Military Training Equipment and Training

Category X—Protective Personnel Equipment and Shelters

Category XI—Military Electronics

Category XII—Fire Control, Range Finder, Optical and Guidance and Control Equipment

Category XIII—Auxiliary Military Equipment

Category XIV—Toxicological Agents, Including Chemical Agents, Biological Agents, and Associated Equipment

Category XV—Spacecraft Systems and Associated Equipment

Category XVI—Nuclear Weapons, Design and Testing Related Items

Category XVII—Classified Articles, Technical Data and Defense Services Not Otherwise Enumerated

Category XVIII—Directed Energy Weapons

Category XIX [Reserved]

Category XX—Submersible Vessels, Oceanographic and Associated Equipment

Category XXI—Miscellaneous Articles

Figure 11-1 United States Munitions List

cation. Organizations that export defense articles, defense services or broker sales are required register with the DDTC. For example, a company making military weapons and demonstrates to others how to use the weapon system or provides the sale of such weapons systems is required to register [1]. One key component of the ITAR is the USML providing 21 categories of weapons, platforms and vessels falling under the control of exports (Figure 11-1) [2]. A defense contractor providing goods or services should review the USML to discover how their product applies. Find out more about State Department and exports at http://pmddtc.state.gov/

Commerce Department Jurisdiction

The Export Administration Regulations (EAR) addresses commercial exports and the Bureau of Industry and Security (BIS) has jurisdiction over commercial and dual use items. Companies falling under the EAR should demonstrate that their products do not impact national security and include dual use items; otherwise, they will fall under the jurisdiction of the State Department. Some items have both commercial and military application, meaning they are made for commercial use but can have military application. The Global Positioning System (GPS) and night vision technology are two examples of dual use technology. On the commercial side, millions of private cars or commercial vehicles benefit from GPS technology. Just punch in the address and the computer gives the directions. Also, GPS is vital to conducting rescue missions, finding lost hikers or locating aircraft, ships, cars and truck involved in accidents. The military also benefits from GPS technology as sophisticated sensors find exact locations or guide weapon systems and vehicles. Likewise, night vision technology is used extensively in the recreation industry. However, the military also uses the technology to fight at night.

Additionally, the EAR is made up of the Commerce Control List (CCL) (Figure 11-2). This list identifies 10 categories of dual use products, software or technologies that are export controlled. Each of the 10 categories has an Export Control Classification Number (ECCN). The EAR does not apply to items subject to other agencies or are otherwise available in the public domain (libraries, patent offices, etc). Discover more information about the EAR at http://www.access.gpo.gov/bis/index.html.

Plan Ahead

Regardless of jurisdiction, a company should always plan ahead as

0-Nuclear Materials, Facilities and Equipment and Miscellaneous
  1-Materials, Chemicals, "Microorganisms," and Toxins
  2-Materials Processing
  3-Electronics
  4-Computers
  5-Telecommunications and Information Security
  6-Lasers and Sensors
  7-Navigation and Avionics
  8-Marine
  9-Propulsion Systems, Space Vehicles and Related Equipment

Figure 11-2 Commercial Control List

an export license request can take months to process. For ITAR considerations, licenses and agreements allow the export or temporary import of a defense article or service. Licenses are used for one time exports, technical proposals, certain marketing materials and overseas purchases. The State Department also approves TAAs between US and foreign entities which permit technical services or disclosing technical data. The TAAs are used during ongoing transfers, design assistance, joint ventures and assembly, depot level maintenance and other training and service contracts [3].

Protecting Technology

Those providing defense items or services have the tremendous responsibility of keeping the technology out of the wrong hands. As identified in the ITAR, unauthorized release of technical information can affect the US military's fighting capability. Licenses and agreements provide a checks and balances between the US Government and the US Company desiring to export the technology. The company identifies the technology and application and submits export requests to the State Department. The State Department reviews the application and further researches military application and how the export could affect national defense.

Without such checks and balances, other countries could gain a technological advantage. Consider the GPS and night vision technology. No other nation has the abilities as the US does to operate at all times and in all weather. The US military's technological lead creates the ability to determine, where, when and how to fight. When other nations gain unauthorized technology, they can duplicate US products and either fight like the US military or degrade US military effectiveness.

According to the ITAR, organizations are required to have permission prior to exporting technology to non-US persons [4]. The organization is responsible for understanding the permissions required as well as the exemptions and the documentation necessary to ensure compliance. The ITAR governs defense technology exports and is a broad regulation subject to interpretation by the exporting organization.

An export is simply transferring controlled technology to a foreign person either inside or outside the US. The export or transfer is conducted in many different ways and the following is a list of examples:

- Hand carrying and transferring from a US to a foreign country or person
- Through conversation while conducting tours, briefings or performing conferences
- Performing a service or demonstration
- Reading blueprints, plans using software or other computer media
- Turning over ownership of vehicles, equipment or other items identified on the US Munitions List

Technology refers to specific information one would find necessary to reproduce, develop or use an item and can be classified or unclassified. Also, the technology can be a product such as a model, blueprint, or instruction book. Technology can also be a service, instruction or some type of training.

What is a US Person?

Citizenship designation is defined differently in the ITAR and NI-

SPOM. The ITAR addresses export of items with military application and NISPOM is concerned with protecting classified information. According to the ITAR, the definition of a US person includes those who have applied for citizenship to the US. This includes lawful permanent residents, lawful temporary residents, US citizens and nationals, and US organizations. These US persons may not be citizens, but are still authorized access to technical data without requiring export permissions [5]. However, the NISPOM requirements prevent such US persons from having a security clearance. When access to classified information is necessary, a Limited Access Authorization (LAA) may be awarded. US persons can access technology controlled items without a license, but only US citizens with a clearance and need to know can access classified information [6].

Technology Transfer

Anytime an employee travels abroad with a computer, they should expect to be liberated from their computer at the host country's customs. They should also expect to have the hard drive duplicated, files read and etc. These are the contingencies for which astute technology control officers, export compliance officers and FSOs plan. Sensitive, and protected technology should not be contained within computer and related media without proper permissions.

Foreign governments want US Technology and aggressively seek it and defense contractors should make the information very difficult to get. However, they may spend too many resources on actions that don't address the real threat. For example physical security efforts may focus on fortifying businesses with barriers, alarms, access control, cameras and etc. In reality technology is leaked through careless or malicious employee behavior or actions taken due to poorly understood responsibilities and security discipline.

Export compliance officers and FSOs should develop a culture within their organizations to prevent unauthorized disclosure of economic, classified or sensitive information. Such practices include destroying sensitive waste properly, locking all desk and cabinets drawers after work, putting classified items in a GSA approved container and using access control to keep employees, vendors and non-US persons from accessing unauthorized areas.

Foreign Travel

Some threats an employee can face while abroad are economic and intelligence related. Economic threat is the theft of technology and commerce. The agent may be after formulas, financial gain and etc. Foreign entities may target classified or company sensitive information to gain a competitive edge.

Prior to cleared employee travel anywhere, they should be given a defensive security briefing. A defensive security briefing is for cleared employees who travel overseas and may be vulnerable to foreign entity recruiting methods. They could also be tailored for protecting export controlled information and given to all employees who travel abroad. Briefings should be constructed to make the traveler aware of their responsibilities to protect employees, product, customers and those with which they do business.

If employees bring technical data and laptop computers, export controlled information not under license or TAAs should be removed from the computer. Some companies issue special travel computers with only the information needed to conduct business ensuring the information is authorized by license or agreement with the State or Commerce Department to prevent an exports violation.

Those conducting export operations should ensure that such actions are authorized with a license and or TAA before discussing technical data that falls under exports compliance. Employees should know the boundaries in advance before sharing any technical information with the foreign hosts. Additionally, a sanitized computer provides no threat of export violations or theft of economic or corporate data. An organization's information technology department or equivalent could provide a sanitized computer for the traveler's administrative needs. Travelers should keep technical information close at hand and prevent unauthorized disclosure of anything that could lead to export violations or the release of proprietary data.

When making corporate travel plans, a trigger mechanism should be in place to notify the FSO of an employee's need to travel on international business or pleasure. This includes plans for Canada, Mexico and Caribbean Countries. The FSO can then construct a defense briefing for the specific area after researching the area to be traveled. The State Department has a great website which can inform the business and the traveler on all necessary travel documentation and what to expect while abroad (www.state.gov).

CLASSIFIED INFORMATION DISCLOSURE

Classified information should be properly transferred through Government to Government channels 7. In some situations, exports of technical data related to the agreements may be excluded from ITAR licensing agreements. It's up to the cleared contractor to ensure whether or not exemptions or licenses apply. In the case of exemptions, the contractor must ensure exemptions are made in writing by an Authorized Exemption Official or an Exemption Certifying Official.

In the Government Security Agreement, countries sharing classified material should provide the amount of security required and identified by the owning country. For example, suppose that XYZ Contractor is working on a project and is using information that a foreign country classified as SECRET. The US government is expected to protect the classified information in the same manner as it would protect US SECRET information. Defense contractors are expected to honor the government's agreement.

The Government Security Agreement is not meant to authorize the release of classified information or guarantee that classified information is transferred. It is created to identify protection measures and limit the use of classified information if it is transferred. The NISPOM requires these security agreements to be in place prior to the transfer of classified information.

In the agreement, one government agrees to provide the classified material and instructions on marking and safeguarding the classified material and the receiving Government agrees to protect it according to the classification markings. The governments also agree to limit the use of classified products and information to what is necessary and efficient. The governments are limited with whom they can share the classified material and who has rights to the proprietary data [7].

WHEN CLASSIFIED TRANSFER IS AUTHORIZED

Contractors do not authorize the transfer of classified material but can provide classified information as allowed by the US government. Classified and unclassified technical transfers should be provided by license, and use of foreign classified information, and through government to government transfer. When a defense contractor works on a contract involving foreign government classified information, the US Government agency provides an Industrial Security Agreement in an Annex of the General Security Agreement [7].

Contractors should transfer classified information only after approved by the US government. There are several ways that classified information can be transferred to foreign persons or released to foreign countries. The GCA provides classified information and the State Department provides the authorization. Unless exemptions apply, the authorization is granted through licensing, technical assistance agreements, and other means of permission including exemptions. Once permission is granted, the transfer can take place.

DSS is responsible for ensuring that the contractor is providing the right level of protection, releasing the classified information in a proper and approved manner, and accounting for the process with the correct receipting methods. Once agreements and permissions are received, the defense contractor can release information. Unless exempted, the transfer should be executed with licenses and agreements through the State Department with input from the GCA and oversight of DSS.

The contractor can then move appropriately to provide contractually identified classified information. Aside from government to government agreements, other methods of transfer include, but are not limited to the following venues:

- Approved classified gatherings
- Foreign visits
- Temporary exports during demonstrations
- Commercial agreements

Approved classified gatherings

The government agency owning the classified contract information approves meetings, conferences, seminars, exhibitions, and etc where the classified information will be disclosed. The foreign visitors should be appropriately cleared, have a need to know and are approved to receive the classified information. The defense contractors involved in these events are allowed to provide the classified information at the direction of the agency, when licenses are provided the State Department and under the oversight of DSS.

When the defense contractor provides classified information based on a contract, they should forward a copy of the contract and the security provisions set in place to DSS. Additionally, the cleared contractor should maintain records identifying source of classified information involved in the contract.

Visits by Non-US Persons

The defense contractor is permitted to only disclose classified and other technical information as provided by terms of licenses and agreements unless exempted. The affected contractors should make every effort to prevent foreign persons from gaining access to any other contract, technical or classified information not identified in the agreements and permissions. Some measures include locking classified information in a security container and technical or export controlled information in desks or cabinets when not attended, using access control, and segregating work areas from foreign persons. Prior to a foreign person having access to classified information, the contractor should provide a DSS approved technology control plan (TCP) [8]. The TCP is a document demonstrating how the foreign person will be accommodated while being denied access to unauthorized information.

Temporary Exports

In the event classified material is exported to a foreign country for demonstration purposes, permission may be granted based on a temporary export. When a temporary export license is used, the classified information should remain under the complete control of the US person. Prior to gaining approval, the request should describe the nature of the demonstration, the items used during the demonstration, and how the items will be protected and stored under US government control. For example, a US person travels overseas on an approved display of a classified weapon system. While there, she will provide a live fire demonstration how the weapon performs. When the demonstration is complete, she will store the weapon at an approved location such as the US Embassy or US military facility.

Commercial Arrangements

There may be times or opportunities when a contractor can supply a classified product to a foreign country through commercial sales. These commercial sales are possible in support of a contract, international agreement or procurement requirement. However, before pursuing a foreign commercial sales opportunity, the contractor must coordinate with the GCA. Also, the defense contractor may need to obtain export permissions prior to engaging in dialog with a foreign representative that could lead to a contract involving classified information.

Subcontracting

Contractors that enter into agreement to subcontract a classified work to a foreign country can only do so with approval from the government agency owning the classified information, the State Department and with coordination with DSS. These permissions are the same as with unclassified exports authorizations; using technical assistance agreements, manufacturing licenses or some direct sales [9]. When classified information is involved, the contractor should provide contract security classification specifications (DD Form 254) as with subcontracting with a US organization. The contractor ensures that the export is permitted, the owning agency approves the transfer and DSS has records of the transfer and an understanding of how the classified information is to be protected and the transfer documented.

The defense contractor should maintain proper accountability of classified information transferred to foreign organizations and record which agency originated the classified information. Additionally, the contractor should provide detailed security specifications and the foreign entity should agree to only use the classified information as written in the contract. The US government owns and controls the classified information and approves the export. The foreign organization should only release, sub contract, or otherwise turn over classified information to a third party or foreign entity upon approved request or as directed by the contract. The foreign government should also re-mark the classified information with their own equivalent markings. This includes any classified information generated as required in the contract.

The foreign government should agree to report all loss and compromise of US classified information if it occurs. They also should agree to return all classified information upon termination of the contract. All of these provisions should be provided with detailed contract language in the contract and DD Form 254.

International Transfer

International transfer of classified information should be conducted as agreed upon by all countries involved. This level of protection begins with removing the classified item from US accountability and continues through the transportation and hand-off process. Written agreements are required per NISPOM prior to any transfer. For commercial endeavors the cleared contractor is required to write the agreement. For Government actions, the GCA is required to provide the agreement and provide copies to the contractor involved.

DSS plays a big role as they advise the contractor on the action as well as approves the written agreements whether provided by the contractor or the GCA. DSS appoints the US Designated Government Representative (DGR) as well as identifies the foreign DGR. They also ensure that transportation plan is adequate to protect the classified information.

A written transportation plan is required for all classified transfers and the GCA provides the plan in support of a government action.

They then provide the plans to the cleared contractor and DSS. The cleared contractor writes transportation plans for commercial actions and DSS approves them. Prior to any transfer of classified information, the cleared contractor should ensure a DSP-83 Non Transfer and Use Certificate is completed.

Hand Carry

A GCA can authorize a US contractor cleared employee to hand carry classified information to a foreign government representative [10]. The contractor is authorized to transfer only classified information marked at the SECRET level and below. The size and shape of the classified information should be in the courier's complete control at all times. Carrying packages too large or bulky could cause the courier to lose control of or become separated from the classified package and should be avoided. The cleared contractor should give DSS a 5 working day notice prior to transferring classified information. DSS should ensure that a good plan is in place. This plan includes checking that the GCA has provided written guidance for any contract or agreements with foreign governments. DSS also makes sure that the contractor is coordinating with the transportation security administration, foreign security agencies and customs officials for the smooth transition and any other arrangements.

Prior to departing, the cleared contractor employee should be briefed, sign a one time use courier certificate and prepare a properly wrapped package [10]. Additionally, the classified information should be inspected by a government representative and three receipts printed. The classified information should be double wrapped, properly marked and addressed. The contractor should also provide 24 hour notice to the recipient that the classified information will be sent. The FSO should begin a tracking system to ensure they receive documentation of the classified information's arrival. This begins when they receive a signed receipt when the courier accepts the package, and ends with a receipt when the package reaches its destination. If the FSO does not receive a final receipt within 45 days, they should notify DSS.

While on the journey, the courier should never relinquish control during transport, layovers, and meals or at any other time. Upon arrival in the foreign country every effort should be made to ensure the classified package is not opened or inspected. However, if an inspection cannot be prevented the courier requests a written and signed explanation of such action signed by the government official. They should then report the incident to their FSO [10]. The FSO will notify the GCA and DSS with details of the compromise included whether or not the government officials inspecting the items were from the country to which the materials are being transferred.

Though a customs officer may require an inspection, the courier should never release the package to their ultimate control. A customs search of classified material may be inevitable, but control should not be relinquished. The classified information should be turned over only to the designated foreign government representative identified on the receipts. The security manager ensures that the courier retains receipts anytime the classified material is transferred to another entity while in transit and at the final destination. Typically, the receiving government representative will inspect the classified package, compare contents with the receipt and sign a receipt for the courier.

Commercial Transfer

Prior to transferring classified information on a commercial contract, the US contractor organization should prepare a transportation plan [11]. This plan should identify how the classified information will be transported, the names of government representatives, and identified escorts. The plan should also provide information describing how the shipment will be protected from unauthorized access throughout the journey. The plan should be turned over to DSS for review and approval then delivered to the foreign government for review and their security implementation.

Foreign Government Information

A US contractor also has the opportunity to receive classified information when entering into a contract with a foreign organization.

When a US contractor enters into agreements with a foreign organization to receive classified information, DSS assumes oversight responsibility [12]. DSS will review the contract and work with the defense contractor to provide the correct protective measures of the foreign government information. Then they evaluate the contractor's ability to protect the classified information.

As with a US contract, the foreign entity should describe the classified information, classification level, markings, and how to protect the classified information in their contract security classification specification. When such information is not provided, the contractor can report it to DSS for a solution or documentation. Once the contractor receives the classified material and instructions, they assume the responsibility of protecting it at the proper level. Therefore, instructions should be understood both by both DSS the contractor [12].

The FSO should bring the FGI into the information management system. The accountability process includes inspecting the packages, signing the proper receipts, documenting and bringing the classified information into the inventory log, and either maintain the original markings or re-mark the classification markings with US equivalent markings. Either is fine as long as everyone working with the classified material understands the proper level to store and safeguard the information. However, the front and back cover should be marked appropriately with the overall US classification and the country of origin. The proper markings should either be annotated: "THIS DOCUMENT CONTAINS (NAME OF COUNTRY) INFORMATION" when the originating country agrees to be identified. When the originating country is concealed the marking is: "THIS DOCUMENT CONTAINS FOREIGN GOVERNMENT INFORMATION" Additionally, when the defense contractor provides classified information to a foreign government, they should ensure that they are marked with "THIS DOCUMENT CONTAINS UNITED STATES CLASSIFIED INFORMATION". [12].

The document is then ready for storage. The contractor should protect the document at the highest level indicated in the classification marking and as described in the agreed upon classification specification. The foreign government classified items should be stored in a manner that prevents getting them mixed up with US classified information [13]. This can be done with using separate drawers of a security container or separate shelves or rooms when open storage is authorized.

Depending on the contract, classified information could easily be generated or documents could be created with derivative information. Documents should be marked to identify that they contain FGI as well as where the information originated if derived. The contractor can only use the classified items as specified in the contract. If the contractor desires to use the information in any other manner than specified, they should get approval. Contracts with third parties or other foreign entities involving the foreign country information should be requested through the GCA and DSS. If the classified information or other technical items or services are approved for export, State Department authorization is required.

The FGI and all derivative classified information stored in US contractor facilities should be treated as US owned classified material. When moving foreign government classified information out of the facility, the security manager should transfer it using the same approved methods as apply to US classified information. For example, duplicating TOP SECRET information requires written permission from the originating government [14]. Finally, all security incidents, unauthorized disclosure, compromise and suspected compromise of foreign government classified information should be investigated and reported to DSS immediately.

CLASSIFIED VISITS

In the course of business, it is not unusual for a foreign entity to request a visit to a US company. Foreign business employees may desire to visit a US contractor in furtherance of a contract. When the business is related to a classified contract, involves classified information or relates to a government to government agreed upon plant visit, the foreign entity requests the visit through their embassy. Unclassified visit requests should be sent through commercial channels and are executed through licenses with the State Department or the Commerce Department.

According to NISPOM, Government approved visits constitute an ITAR exemption. However, the cleared contractor should understand exactly what is to be released and exactly how. It is the defense contractor's responsibility to determine what constitutes the exemption and what release requires a license. The cleared contractor should maintain records of the foreign visit involving the release of classified information for one year. However, where visits are covered by ITAR licensees or agreements, records should be kept for three years.

Visit requests submitted by a foreign entity pass through their government channels to the US government for approval (Figure 11-3) [15]. The US government agency having jurisdiction over the classified contract submits the request to the US contractor for their approval. The request also includes guidance and limitations of the information and items the foreign national will be allowed to access. The contractor should review the limitations and determine whether or not they concur with the request and has the final say of whether or not the foreign national will access their facility.

International Classified Contract Visit Request Process

1. Foreign Entity Submits Visit Request to Their Government
2. Foreign Government Submits Request to U.S. Government
3. Pentagon (Foreign Visit Section) Determines Approval
4. Pentagon Notifies Contractor of Request and Approval
5. Contractor Determines Whether or Not to Accept Request

Figure 11-3 Visit request process

For example, Country A has a contractual relationship with XYZ Contractor through the US government. Country A is able to produce sensitive electronics for a missile guidance system that XYZ Contractor is contracted to perform on. Country A draws up a visit request and submits it to their embassy for routing to the US Government channels. The US Government reviews the request and decides whether or not to grant the visit. The US Government can deny the visit, and if so, will notify the government representatives of the requesting foreign entity. If the US Government approves the request, they should provide details and access requirements specifically for Country A's visit to XYZ Contractor.

Continuing the scenario, XYZ Contractor receives the request. The program manager for the project calls a meeting with team players and includes representatives from key business units. The FSO, program manager and the contracts manager review the request. The foreign national from Country A is to be given access to only classified information related to the guidance system as contracted with the US Government. Access to other classified information and material is not authorized and XYZ Contractor should ensure that the foreign person is prevented from accessing unclassified information related to other contracts.

The FSO explains the use of the Technology Control Plan (TCP) as the required tool to prevent the visitor from seeing classified information. The advantages of the TCP includes protection of other sensitive, proprietary or privileged information in the form of blueprints, slide shows, memorandums, and classified material in conversations, computer screens or other sources. When a contractor accepts an international visit request, they assume the responsibility to protect national secrets, the company's technology and all export controlled items. The TCP controls the movement of the foreign national within the facility.

A TCP is a valuable tool written by the contractor and approved by DSS. The contents of the TCP should be enough to ensure every employee participating in the visit understands their role in protecting the information. Additionally, the foreign person should also be alerted to their duties to protect the information as well as their responsibilities not to attempt to gain access to unauthorized information. Both employees and the foreign visitors should sign the agreements of understanding.

SUMMARY

As part of the global market, US owned technology, defense articles, and commercial items can be exported with licenses and agreements. The State Department controls the export of defense articles and services, while Commerce Department governs articles with civil or dual-use application. It is up to the defense contractor or business entity to determine the jurisdiction of an item to be exported. When jurisdiction is not easily determined, they can submit a request for determination.

Classified information can be exported to another country based on a Government to Government agreement. A defense contractor should only export classified information when approved by the GCA or other US Government entity. Defense contractors may be required to store FGI information on site. If so, they should protect it at the same US equivalent level.

PROBLEMS

1. The vice president of business development has just brought up the wonderful opportunity of selling an all weather capability the company produces for medical evacuation flights to a foreign owned company.

   a. Suppose this item needs a license prior to export. Describe the first step an organization would take in consideration of a possible export.

   b. If the item is to be delivered to a foreign company just down the street, will export requirements still apply?

2. You are travelling as an authorized courier to deliver a package that contains classified information at the CONFIDENTIAL level. Upon arrival, the foreign government customs agent wants to take custody of the package. You present your credentials and attempt to talk her out of the idea. She informs you that as a representative of the foreign government, she is authorized to accept the delivery. Is she correct? Why or why not?

3. As an FSO, you have many responsibilities including approving classified visits. A program manager enters your office and informs you that his foreign customer wants to send an employee to perform at your location on a classified project. The program manager requests that you draw up a sample visit request form that the foreign company can use to submit a visit

request. Is this the proper request procedure? Why or why not?

4. In the same situation as question three, the visit has been authorized through appropriate channels. Since your cleared facility handles many classified contracts, you want to ensure the visitor does not gain access to classified and unclassified items not authorized for export. What will you produce to ensure the visitor and company employees remain in compliance with export laws?

5. Which agency has jurisdiction over commercial and dual-use items?

6. Which regulation covers commercial and dual-use items?

7. Which regulation governs the export of defense articles?

8. Your organization has an opportunity to perform a modification of a foreign government weapons platform. You will not be selling an item, but modifying the platform for a radio mount. If awarded the contract, your company will send a team to the foreign country to perform the services over the next few years. What type of request will you submit? Who is the approving agency?

RESOURCES

1. Guidelines For Preparing Commodity Jurisdiction (CJ) Requests, DDTC Response Team, Downloaded Jan 2010, http://www.pmddtc.state.gov/commodity_jurisdiction/documents/cj_guidelines.pdf

2. International Traffic In Arms Regulation, 22 C.F.R Chapter I, Subchapter M Parts 120-130, Part 121.1, http://pmddtc.state.gov

3. International Traffic In Arms Regulation, 22 C.F.R Chapter I, Subchapter M Parts 120-130, Part 120.22, http://pmddtc.state.gov,

4. International Traffic In Arms Regulation, 22 C.F.R Chapter I, Subchapter M Parts 120-130, Part 120.1, http://www.redbike-publishing.com/book/itar/

5. International Traffic In Arms Regulation, 22 C.F.R Chapter I, Subchapter M Parts 120-130, Part 120.15, http://pmddtc.state.

gov

6. Department of Defense, DoD 5220.22-M, National Industrial Security Operating Manual, section 2-209, February 2006

7. Department of Defense, DoD 5220.22-M, National Industrial Security Operating Manual, section 10-102, February 2006

8. Department of Defense, DoD 5220.22-M, National Industrial Security Operating Manual, section 10-508, February 2006

9. Department of Defense, DoD 5220.22-M, National Industrial Security Operating Manual, section 10-202, February 2006

10. Department of Defense, DoD 5220.22-M, National Industrial Security Operating Manual, section 10-405, February 2006

11. Department of Defense, DoD 5220.22-M, National Industrial Security Operating Manual, section 10-402, February 2006

12. Department of Defense, DoD 5220.22-M, National Industrial Security Operating Manual, section 10-300, February 2006

13. Department of Defense, DoD 5220.22-M, National Industrial Security Operating Manual, section 10-306, February 2006

14. Department of Defense, DoD 5220.22-M, National Industrial Security Operating Manual, section 10-309, February 2006

15. Department of Defense, DoD 5220.22-M, National Industrial Security Operating Manual, section 10-507, February 2006

Helpful Websites

Denied Person's List

Http://www.bis.doc.gov/dpl/default.shtm

Directorate of Defense Trade Controls

Http://www.pmddtc.state.gov/index.html

EAR

Http://www.access.gpo.gov/bis/index.html

ITAR

Http://www.pmddtc.state.gov/index.html

Http://www.redbikepublishing.com

State Department

Http://www.state.gov

NISPOM

http://www.redbikepublishing.com

CHAPTER 12 PUTTING IT ALL TOGETHER

INTRODUCTION

To better position security for influence and effectiveness, FSOs should understand the NISPOM and the cleared contractor's business. The FSO's ability to understand the nature of their business as it relates to the organization separates a professional from a technician. This chapter provides information on the skill set the FSO should possess to gain credibility within their organizations. Understanding how security fits into the organizational scheme helps the FSO better implement the security program.

FSO QUALITIES

The defense contractor's cleared senior official should understand the importance of appointing the proper person as FSO. In many circumstances defense contractors become aware of the requirement of the FSO appointment upon receiving a classified contract or at some point during the process. The NISPOM directs that the appointed FSO only meet two requirements, US Citizenship and a security cleared as part of the FCL [1]. However, unless the most senior officer in the cleared facility appreciates the impact of a qualified FSO, they might appoint an employee based on administrative skill and not their ability to influence a good security program. Miscalculating the role of an FSO as only an administrative position could result in appointing the person with the wrong skill set, leading to a weak and ineffective security program.

There are approximately 12,000 cleared facilities with just as many appointed FSOs. Though there are large companies with tens of thousands of employees and a mature culture, many are small enterprises with less than 50 employees. In some cases employees are appointed as FSO in addition to their primary job. This works fine when the position is held by someone who is used to the challenges of leadership. They are able to influence the culture by pushing security from the top down. Where an influential, cleared management employee is appointed as FSO, the rest of the organization suddenly becomes interested in following security procedure. The opposite results arise from the appointment of a cleared employee with limited influence. The cleared contractor should be aware of the implied tasks involved with running a compliance unit.

Appointing The Wrong FSO

A lower level employee appointed as FSO may be fine when the contractor is a small organization, there are few employees and the environment is informal. However, the FSO's effectiveness may deteriorate as the company grows, more executives and managers are hired and additional business units are developed. Companies that have grown in this scenario have increased the FSO job requirements and the position has outgrown the current FSOs skill level. This could make communicating security and compliance issues challenging for the FSO.

The FSOs in the above situation are technically proficient and understand their jobs very well. However, they may not possess the skills to develop healthy business relationships and communicate with other managers. This may leave them ineffective as compliance officers. Additionally, the organization charts may show the FSOs reporting to managers in non-program business units that do not understand contracting or how to manage a security program. These managers could be in overhead business units such as: safety, accounting, contracting or other administrative overhead position several levels away from program managers, engineers and classified contract based organizations the FSO supports. The FSOs could end up assigned to overhead divisions and away from those performing classified work. This could present a problem for the company as the FSO might have to address security issues through several filters before finally getting the message to the executive level.

Management should work with the FSO to keep the company in a position to maintain the facility and employee personnel security clearances. An ineffective FSO or one who is out of the decision making loop may fail in their responsibilities. Expectations for good security programs become unrealistic in this scenario as the FSOs have no input for planning or execution. Being outside of the circle of influence or decision making, the FSOs often play catch up when the company wins new contracts with increasing or new security requirements. The organization's senior officer should take into account the compliance issues of exporting technology, protecting classified information, seeking new classified contracts, maintaining an effective security environment, and the enterprise's growth potential prior to writing a job description for the appointed FSO.

Appointing the Right FSO

Primarily, the FSO should understand how to protect classified information as it relates to the cleared contract, organizational growth, enterprise goals, and NISPOM guidance. The FSO should be able to conduct a risk analysis, express the cost, benefits and impact of supporting a classified contract under the NISPOM requirements and sustain an environment of cooperation and compliance within the enterprise. Finally, they must be able to influence and compel the senior leaders to make good decisions, support compliance and integrate security into the corporate culture. After all, security violations not only cause damage to national security, but could also impact the organization with loss of contracts. The FSO is pivotal to the successful execution of classified contracts.

In larger cleared contractor organizations the FSO is most likely a full time commitment held by a department manager or higher level employee. This FSO is supported by a staff of security specialists who may manage classified contract administration, safeguarding classified documents, process classified information on information systems, security clearances and other disciplines. The FSO oversees the entire security program as executed by the competent staff. In a best case scenario, they will report to the senior officer of the organization.

In small business the FSO may be the owner, chief officer, vice president or other senior leader picking up an additional responsibility. This is more of a situation of selecting the most knowledgeable, capable and competent cleared employee. However, the FSOs are already very busy trying to meet cost, scheduling and performance objectives. They may be able to implement and direct a security program to protect classified information, but not the day to day job functions that can pull them away from critical tasks. Jobs such as document control, visit authorization requests, security clearance requests and etc can be delegated to other competent, organized and more flexible employees.

As the small enterprise grows, more and more experienced FSOs are beginning to understand a growing company's needs and have returned to college finish their education. Colleges and universities are now offering a variety of security and management degrees perfect for meeting the growing FSO education requirements. Professional organizations also offer security certifications. Consequently, the pool of experienced and educated FSOs is growing. Cleared defense contractor executives should clearly consider the FSO job description and list the exact qualifications desired before posting the position as a job announcement.

FSOs should understand more than just the technical aspects of administering a security program. Understanding how to mark, safeguard and disseminate classified information is important. However, the FSO should reach beyond the description of implementing a security program to safeguard classified material. The position also requires assessing risks to the classified material, interpreting safeguarding requirements, communicating and incorporating a culture of compliance within the organization, and projecting the impact of classified contracts on the enterprise. To do this, the FSO should possess the vision and skills to see where the security program needs to go, how to get there and encourage a security vision from the senior executive level downward. Without the proper influence, the FSO is may not be able to run a program to protect classified material. Effective tools include:

- Corporate Culture
- Metrics
- Convergence
- Planning for Growth

Corporate Culture

How do effective FSOs and security managers develop a culture of compliance with regulations and security programs? Quoting regulations only exasperates cleared employees and the very act does little to foster a climate of cooperation. However, developing relationships based on a good understanding of business, the company mission and influence goes a long way toward implement the successful security program.

The corporate culture of successful organizations is published organization wide and employees are well versed. Each employee should understand how they fit into the company mission and the importance of their contribution toward the enterprise's success. Though employees and business units have separate functions, they work toward the common goal of producing a product or service. Though each office has a different product, funding or budget item, each fulfills their obligation in a chain of responsibilities necessary to get the product to market. When a business unit breaks down or fails to fulfill its mission, other business units are affected. For example if buyers do not order from suppliers, products cannot be assembled. If the human resources department does not enforce ethics rules, morale could plummet.

In the same manner, the FSO performs a vital mission of protecting classified information. Failure to safeguard classified material could result in a defense contractor losing the facility clearance and ultimately cost current and future contracts. Just as hourly workers are continuously training on performing in compliance with safety and human resources policies, security awareness should also be part of the culture. Security as an afterthought or viewed as a "necessary evil" has contributed to a loss in influence and commitment.

Though the NISPOM applies to classified projects, FSOs would be mistaken to assume that only cleared persons and cleared programs are worthy of their attention. Such philosophy dismisses the potential of all other employees and business units to assist in protecting classified information and thus frustrates the entire security effort. FSOs that ensure only cleared employees attend security awareness training miss out on the opportunity to include many others as "force multipliers" assisting in the security effort. For example, uncleared employees can help protect classified information by learning to recognize classification markings reporting suspicious behavior or contacts.

Metrics

What is the value of security to the corporation? Security managers often work from overhead budgets. Since many security departments do not generate income, the managers have to effectively demonstrate value added programs. Security managers use metrics to effectively demonstrate how programs, security measures and functions provide a return on investment or added value.

Metrics are tools leaders use to assess the effectiveness of their programs. These metrics indicate success, failures or areas where significant improvement is needed. Metrics data is found in surveys, inspections, and reports and are used for the specific purpose of understanding how effective the program is. The other part is to understand security goals and comparing them to the results.

FSOs should make metrics development and execution a top priority. Chief security officers, chief information officers and other executive level security managers understand how to read metrics and use them to focus with pinpoint intensity on directing their programs within their companies. Security managers in lower positions can use the same skills to gain influence. Because of the nature of compliance with government regulations, the task may be easier for FSOs to accomplish.

An FSO has readily available data to determine and communicate the effectiveness of the security program. Gathering available information, creating a detailed database and performing solid analysis will help determine the program's success. Whether or not a security program is where it needs to be can be determined from information found in the following actions:

- Incidents, infractions, violations reports with compromise or suspected compromise
- Annual DSS reviews
- Annual self-inspections
- Professional and organizational certification
- Self-reporting statistics
- Security Awareness Training
- Security budget
- Contractual requirements

The above list is not all inclusive, but contains readily available information directly affected by security or influences security decisions.

Incidents, infractions, violations and reports of compromise or suspected compromise as Metrics

These reports should be made at each occurrence and analyzed regularly. Reports indicating that compromise or suspected compromise has occurred should be forwarded to DSS. Many other reports of minor consequences are not required to be sent outside of the organization, but are extremely helpful as indicators of the organization's security health.

Incidents, infractions and violations reports indicate lapses in judgment or worse, malicious behavior of those with access to classified information. An incident or infraction occurs when a cleared employee violates a NISPOM requirement, but no loss, compromise or suspected compromise occurs. For example, a cleared employee could lock all the security containers, but forget to fill out the end of the day check list. Though no classified information has been compromised, they did not follow procedures based on a requirement during the end of day checks. Unless eliminated, such bad practices can contribute to more serious violations. As an example, violations occur when someone forgets to spin the combination on a security container dial. A suspected or actual compromise occurs when the investigation determines that an unauthorized person gained access to classified information.

Only security violations resulting in loss, compromise or suspected compromise are reported to the DSS. However, even minor incidents should be investigated and documented. For example, the seemingly small infraction of forgetting to fill out the end of day security check-list could either indicate forgetfulness or a disregard of security procedures. The root cause should be investigated and the culprit warned and/or disciplined according to corporate policy.

Consider an earlier example where an FSO received notification that the administrative security container with all combinations had been left open. The FSO had been notified of an after hours security violation. She arrived on scene and interviewed the person who had called her, inventoried the contents and inspected the security container for evidence of tamper. The next day she began an investigation to determine exactly what had happened.

Results of an investigation vary depending on the situation. In the best case, the FSO conducts an investigation and determines that the security container had been left open for an hour and that nobody had access the building since. A far worse a scenario would involve conducting an inventory confirming a missing classified document. In that case an in-depth investigation to determine loss, compromise and suspected compromise would have to be conducted.

In our best case scenario, the FSO could conclude that it is a non reportable security incident. The container had been left open but no unauthorized persons had access to the container. The FSO could use the findings in the investigation to retrain the person who had not properly closed and locked the security containers. She could also use the information for security awareness and use it to train others in the organization on proper procedures. She could also store the report and add information to a database to draw on it later for comparative analysis.

But what if such incidents and infractions had never been recorded? Relaxed security procedures could result in multiple incidents leading to a complicated situation of unauthorized disclosure. In such cases the report would be forwarded to DSS. The investigation would find information revealing that such incidents had occurred frequently. The FSO may be left with concluding that the incident could have been prevented had the situation been addressed earlier. In the worst case scenario, the investigator is left to determine whether or not the relaxed security environment contributed to the security violation and suspected compromise.

Infraction, incident and violation data can be used to pinpoint security issues in specific business units or locations. For example suppose a cleared contractor has a building dedicated to research and development and another building dedicated to modeling and simulations. The simulations operations are conducted in a closed area that allows classified work to be conducted during business hours, but it must be locked away in a security container after hours. The last person leaving the computer lab is responsible for locking the vault door and setting the alarm. The research and development area is full of cleared employees who work on large vehicles. Their labs are also closed areas and they spend most of their time assembling and testing the vehicles.

The FSO in the above scenario makes a habit of evaluating compiled security incident reports regularly, perhaps every quarter. They would never let a known incident go uninvestigated regardless of severity. The written reports would document a history of employees in the research and development lab leaving classified material on the printer. The FSO pulls the collected data and notices that twice in the quarter the security container drawer had been left unlocked. The FSO continues her search into root cause and notices that this is nothing new, but incidents seemed to have occurred less frequently since she had taken the job just a year earlier.

However, the research and development lab has had far fewer incidents. The nature of their business only requires mechanical work. There is no paperwork involved other than a few classified technical manuals that they receive from the document control office and return at the end of the day. Though they have always locked the doors properly, the cleared employees have forgotten on several occasions to set the alarms. The FSO notices the pattern and discovers that though a root cause had been discovered during earlier investigations, the former FSO had not addressed. Then, armed with data, she is ready to compile the information into reports, graphs, training aids and other media to train the cleared employees and implement security policy.

Annual DSS Reviews as Metrics

DSS is responsible for determining the frequency of annual inspections. Inspections are typically conducted every 12 months for possessing and 18 months for non possessing facilities, but circumstances can require more or less frequent visits [2]. DSS inspects the facility's security program for the primary purposes of ensuring their programs provide the proper protection of classified information they are charged with protecting. Additionally, the inspection programs are designed to improve the effectiveness of the contractor's security program. At the conclusion of the inspections, the contractor is given a rating ranging from unsatisfactory to superior [3]:

- Unsatisfactory-indicates that the contractor has lost or is in the process of losing their ability to protect classified material. The GCA's are notified and the contractor is re-inspected to measure whether or not they have met requirements of corrective actions.
- Marginal-indicates that a contractor is not meeting the requirements of NISPOM and has a substandard security program. The contractor will have another review to ensure they have performed required corrective actions.
- Satisfactory-the most common rating indicates that the company is generally in compliance with the NISPOM
- Commendable-indicates that a cleared contractors runs a successful security program and enjoys the support of management.
- Superior-is awarded for consistently high security posture and minimum amount of findings or security issues. This rating is awarded to the cleared contractors demonstrating an excellent security program with complete support from management. The rating is highly coveted and can lead to the Cogswell Award normally reserved for the most competitive companies.

Prior to each inspection, the FSO and cleared contractor leadership should present DSS with a state of security briefing to introduce and go over the company security policy. Similarly, the DSS special agent may provide an out-briefing detailing the results of the inspection. This out-briefing and soon to follow documentation of the inspection provides further data toward building an excellent security program.

Annual Self-Inspections As Metrics

The self-inspections offer other exceptional opportunities for FSOs to improve the security program as well as measure improvement from the previous DSS annual audit. The self-inspection affords the opportunity to look into procedures, review documentation, and incidents, conduct classified holding inventories and are conducted midway between the annual audits and help keep the security team focused on improvement and compliance.

Additionally, the DSS website (www.dss.mil) provides a self-inspection checklist booklet that FSOs can use to conduct their self-inspections. The self-inspection and annual review results help the defense contractor view their security program with the intent of identifying good procedures to sustain and others to improve upon. They should be conducted by anyone knowledgeable of the security program. The FSO does not necessarily need to conduct the review, but should support the self-inspection fully and the findings completely. The self-inspection can also be a team effort between employees who report to the security manager. It is not only a tool for team improvement, but also benefits the inspector with experience they may not otherwise be able to gain since it covers all areas of managing classified information, facility and personnel clearances.

Professional and Organizational Certification as Metrics

Outside agency reviews are performed to certify an organization. These reviews are thorough in an effort to discover the enterprise's business functions, policies and procedures. Depending on the inspection, each outside agency is invited to bring in experts to analyze a company's performance. The inspector visits every aspect of the organization, measuring compliance, record keeping, improvements and other performance issues and makes a determination of whether or not they are worthy of the certification.

An organizational or professional certification review is a prime opportunity for an FSO to see how the organization performs outside of the NISPOM. Not only do certification reviews inspect areas of privacy or network security, but they are especially helpful in identifying record keeping and policy issues. Though the inspectors won't have access to classified information, they may have insight to processes. They can uncover areas that may need improving as well as reinforcing organization strengths. The copy of the certification audit report provides valuable information that the FSO can apply to the security program.

Security Awareness as Metrics

Attitudes toward security awareness programs can be great indicators of the FSO's program. Comments that reflect a desire for or loathing of continuing security awareness education speaks volumes. Those who are conscious of the need to protect national security assets and classified information should understand the need for training. Refresher training is a requirement identified in the executive orders, DoD and federal agency regulations including the NISPOM [4].

When the security program is well received the managers support training as well as weave the elements of the security message throughout their work areas. When the FSO posts flyers, sends emails or communicates a security message, the managers are quick to ensure their employees have access to those messages. When the FSO practices security through walking around, employees relay enthusiastic messages that indicate their understanding and contribution to protecting classified information.

Indications that the security program is not well received include resistance to training and corrective actions. Emails go unread, phone calls go unanswered, flyers and pamphlets are unused or thrown away. Other indicators include cleared employees not knowing who the FSO is or the names of other security professionals and comments about training are negative. Cleared employees complain about the requirement and view training only as a check the block activity. When the FSO conducts a walk-through of the areas, the employees avoid the visit and provide vague answers to questions about their role in the security program.

Security Budget as Metrics

Security budget support or lack of support can either demonstrate a well received or unappreciated security program. In a functional security manager role, the intuitive FSO understands business, the company mission and how the role of protecting classified material fits. The FSO can provide risk assessment and speak intelligently of the procedures, equipment and costs associated with protecting classified information. They understand how to contract security resources to install alarms, access control and other protection measures. The FSO is also able to demonstrate an ROI for expenses.

The FSO should provide the security budget after analyzing the needs and introduce it in a manner that all business units understand. For example, if part of the budget line is to provide access control for forty doors in four different buildings the cost is understandably significant. In this example, the access controls are not required by NISPOM, but would be instrumental in protecting employees, classified information and product as addressed in a risk assessment. The budget should not be the first place to identify the need. Incorporating management involvement and support throughout the risk management process puts the company in a better position to provide the funding. Additionally, a projected ROI and due diligence research should be conducted. Sample questions and answers the FSO should be prepared to address are:

What is the benefit of access control?

Access control prevents unauthorized persons from entering the premises and gives an extra layer of protection for classified and sensitive information. The FSO should also give the risk assessment findings to support the request.

What happens if we do not implement access controls?

The organization would have to commit persons to controlling the access to the company. When considering a manager's hourly rate, this could become expensive over time. The FSO could demonstrate the cost of the access controls against the time a manager takes to ensure someone is assigned to maintain visibility of the doors (Figure 12-1).

ITEM	COST	HOURS	SALARY	SALARY SAVINGS	HVAC SAVINGS
Access Control	$28,800	750	$28/hr	$21,000	$13,000

Figure 12-1 Example of Return on Security Investment- Notice the cost reduction after installing a $28,800 access control system. Prior to installing the Access Control package, doors to the building had no access control. Employees often failed to completely close the doors upon entering or exiting. The manager performed two random checks to ensure doors had been closed to prevent unauthorized visitors. The managers also had to track down visitors and vendors who had entered without going through the visitor reception desk. The FSO realized that the door magnet and swipe card available in the access control package would realize a $21,000 cost reduction in salary paid to managers. Manager checks 300 days annually. Additionally, the organization realized a $13,000 cost reduction on heating and air conditioning.

What is the return on investment for access control?

The intangible return on investment is the prevention of damage, injury, theft, and other risks inherent to unauthorized entry. More tangible is the amount of electrical energy saved while keeping the doors closed and protecting the inside climate. In one such study an FSO estimated a reduced cost of $13,000 per year on the electric bill.

The FSO's ability to project ROI should ensure that executives understand the significance of a well supported security program. The executives will trust the counsel of a well prepared FSO. Security managers who just quote regulations or use best practices without putting much thought into the costs or talking points will quickly lose credibility. For example, a defense contractor sufficiently stores information classified at the SECRET level or below in a GSA approved container. Providing an argument that the NISPOM requires an alarm or other supplemental protection is inaccurate and irresponsible. If an alarm is desired, it should be introduced as the result of a thorough risk assessment according to data provided from crime statistics, threat assessments, as identified in this section or as required by contract. Once the data is in, the FSO can address the issues.

Security's involvement in strategic planning provides an excellent platform allowing the FSO to contribute their best efforts. A company that enjoys the influence and experience of a competent FSO reflects a good security program. When the FSO is invited to participate in strategic planning the company demonstrates that senior leaders value the security program and want the FSO's input.

Contractual Requirements as Metrics

Classified work is identified on the DD Form 254 and the statement of work. The FSO should understand associated costs inherent to the classified work identified in the contract and the DD Form 254.

Suppose a government customer has identified the work required of XYZ Contractor in a DD Form 254. Accordingly, XYZ Contractor will receive, generate and store classified information. Because of the nature of the classified work involved, the classified material will be stored separately according to the classification level and whether or not the material is Foreign Government Information, NATO, COMSEC, etc. This requires additional storage space and security containers which are expensive, but necessary.

The company is in the perfect position to anticipate the costs involved early in the planning. The costs can be calculated accurately, budgeted, and the FSO can prepare early to accept the upcoming challenges. Prior to receiving a DD Form 254, the FSO can discuss with management their key role in assessing the requests for bid and proposal.

A company that does not enjoy the FSO's input may not be very well prepared for the upcoming classified contract. They could miscalculate costs and commit the company to decisions based on lack of information as they scramble to meet compliance requirements. This lack of knowledge may affect their ability to protect classified information and may cause more than just financial consequences.

Results of Metrics Data

A security manager can use such metrics or data and write a white paper, report, or provide a picture graph to employees, managers and executives for several purposes. Regardless of the report media, the objective should be to improve the state of security and communicate the results to the executives and shareholders. Cleared employees can be trained on recognizing proper procedures and preventing security violations by changing their behavior. Managers can use the information to direct changes in their employees and provide better security. Executives can use the information to identify programs or projects with probable risks and use the data for strategic planning. Finally, the shareholder; tax payers, board of director members, customers, and employees have a good understanding of their return on investment.

Convergence

Involve other departments outside of security to improve the security program. Security measures are best implemented if part of the corporate culture and works best driven from the top down. Convergence is a term pairing information technology with physical security. Convergence can identify ways of introducing security to all organizational areas and business units.

Workplace Crime Prevention

In light of the continuous threat to employees, product and classified information, security professionals should study their craft and learn ways to counter the impact. Business intelligence continues to offer information technology to analyze and prevent the internal and external influences working to harm an enterprise. Not only do defense contractors protect classified information, but they could be continually focused on preventing theft, vandalism, workplace violence, fraud, and computer attacks. The FSO should continue to implement programs to protect classified information as well as techniques of identification, analysis, risk assessment operation security and prevention, to mitigate risks.

Many private and publicly traded companies have invested security staff and compliance officers to address privacy and protection issues. This staff focuses efforts to identify and prevent theft of information, technology and product. Some of the security staff focus on loss prevention, a discipline oriented toward identifying risky behavior, observing others, investigating theft, and finding methods of reducing risk.

Convergence has typically involved security and information technology resources, vigilant employees and closed circuit television (CCTV). This is a great deterrent and detection device for both the internal and external threat. Television cameras employ the use of tilt/pan/zoom and digital technology records the data for instant recall. This data can be reviewed to see the habits and patterns of suspect customers and employees.

Vandalism is a constant threat to facilities in various locations. Empty parking lots on the weekend or late at night can attract trespassers and vandals. Family members of employees are part of workplace violence patterns and criminal trespass activities. Though rare, these events have left a heavy toll on businesses. Depending on where a product falls in the lifecycle, research and development, work in progress, shipping or in transit, expenses will fall on the company and be passed to the customer.

Security solutions to detect and prevent these events include monitoring the workplace and removing the internal threat, building security in depth to prevent the external threat, training employees, and employing loss prevention techniques. Some additional mitigating factors include traditional security methods. When needed, additional lighting, security cameras and panic alarms do wonders to give employees a peace of mind as well as help prevent violent behavior. Knowing security is in place deters the criminal element.

Fraud Detection and the FSO

Fraud, espionage and other inconspicuous corporate crime are difficult to detect. Detection can be accidental, the result of a tip, an audit (internal, external or surprise), hotline or as referred by law enforcement. Focus and discipline could be perceived as the best means to detect fraud. As with reporting adverse behavior of cleared employees, the practice can be applied to crime. Employees could participate in verifying paperwork, checking records and reporting indicators of possible criminal behavior. Unchecked fraud could impact the defense industry as many defense contractors have less than 500 employees. Large economical losses can devastate an unwitting company and incidents of fraud can continue for long occasions before detected.

Information technology and the use of business intelligence or other software used to configure data, spreadsheets or reports can be applied to detecting and preventing corporate crime and espionage. Employee and hotline tips are most effective if used correctly. Computer links could be set up on corporate sites to allow anonymous employee reporting and phones can be programmed for anonymous tips.

Most methods of fraud or crime discovery have proven to be reactionary events. Fortunately companies have the capability to automate almost everything. Time sheets, accounting, billing, production and supply chain records are often software based. Contractors have employed access control measures such as card scanners, code readers and biometrics. This technology leaves a trail of employee activity and can used to detect suspicious behavior. Taking lessons from Chapter 8, computer keyboard activity can be limited by password protection and IS sensitive data and computer use can be restricted. Computer and related media should go through the security department before introduction or removal. This is already in place in classified closed areas, but again, convergence and successful security programs require due diligence in all enterprise areas. Aside from employee protection and assistance roles, this data can be mined to see patterns and recognize traits of abuse and fraud.

Computer Attacks and the FSO

Computer attacks are a huge risk to all businesses. The threat of hackers, malicious viruses, and those who hijack websites and hold financial transactions for ransom are just a few serious events of which the security manager must be aware. Technology can be stolen or destroyed, reputations can be ruined, and personal information can be stolen. These attacks can cripple an enterprise and could take months or years to recover. The FSO could help the IT department focus on these threats and provide tools to detect and combat existing and future threats.

Worms and viruses quickly destroy years of input. These threats appear innocently enough in the beginning and when the right time comes, they activate. They recreate themselves, and spread throughout networks. Cyber saboteurs continually snoop, trying to learn passwords to exploit for espionage, theft or their idea of fun. Hijackers enter a system and threaten to cripple financial transactions until payment is made; extortion in high-tech form.

Employee internet discipline is a vital countermeasure. Aside from being an issue of abuse and possible investigation, employee internet activity could cripple a company. An enemy doesn't have to break down your defenses to wreak havoc. Just like old vampire lore, all an employee has to do is invite them in. When employees visit unauthorized websites, download unauthorized software, transfer data from a home computer or forward corrupted email, they can cause just as much harm. Blocking websites, allowing only company designated personnel to upload software, and screening all mobile media or preventing all media and portable storage devices are all effective countermeasures the FSO can enforce.

Unprotected systems perpetuate all the above threats. Businesses that get involved either innocently as naive contributors or as the hapless victims suffer greatly financially and productively. There is another cost that could take longer to recover from. A technically illiterate or unprotected business has no excuse when dealing with customers or partners. Embarrassing things happen when a cyber crime investigation leads to a witless company that inadvertently released sensitive information.

There are many existing security methods available to help companies take the offense against such attack. As the in the above examples, this effort takes the coordination, input and involvement of all business units and departments in the organization. This cannot be given to the security department alone to handle. However such actions should be accountable to one department.

Other aggressive measures that can be taken are password protection, rules on internet use, firewalls and internet access blocking. These can be regulated with the convergence concept. Software already exists to help generate and protect passwords on network and stand alone systems. These help ensure not only that authorized users are accessing the systems, but they also provide a basis for auditing systems. Information technology can track who used which system to access which information, the user leaves an automatic electronic trail.

Companies can use firewalls to protect information from both leaving and entering the enterprise system. These firewalls help prevent hacking, hijacking and malicious viruses and should be updated often. If a structure exists, the FSO should work with IT to run an analysis to identify a threat.

Threat recognition works best when tracking such statistics as where the threat is coming from, how often the defenses are probed, what the threat is using to probe the defenses and what times of day are the threats are most active. The FSO and key managers should look at their organizations through the eyes of the perpetrator and identify what makes their business so tempting to target. Additional information concerning threat analysis and identification can be found with DSS, military counter-intelligence, FBI, law enforcement organizations and government customers.

Preparing for Growth

Business for defense contractors is growing fast. How do defense contractors structure and align to meet the growth? Additional contracts can easily require cleared facilities to have closed areas, additional classified storage, different classified media and other unique protection and storage requirements. Analysis of growth and personnel requirements can help security managers stay on top of all upcoming events.

Growth for the FSO involves not only the number of cleared employees, contract and storage requirements in a possessing facility. Meeting legitimate growth is another area where an FSO is involved in strategic planning. New contracts with varying classified work requirements, new facility or alternate locations with physical security needs and an increase in classified storage or volume are all concerns an FSO should be able to address. Such growth affects the security department and input from the FSO benefits the entire organization.

When classified contract requirements necessitate the need for additional security personnel, the FSO should be prepared to hire based on identified employee characteristics. Just as the senior executive should identify an FSO's desired traits such as growth and management potential, technical competence, and skills, the same should be taken into account while preparing to hire additional security help. Potential security professionals should not only be U.S. citizens with security clearances, but demonstrate competence in the tasks they are asked to do and a desire to perform. They should also have the ability to grasp and teach concepts of security.

If available, hiring a security specialist who has worked in the career field for other defense contractors is a good option. They already possess the skills and the hiring manager will just have to ensure they have the ability to fit in with the company. However, another option may be to hire someone who lacks the skills, but has the desire and ability to perform well with a little training. In either case, because of the complexity and differences in contracts, no two organizations work the same way. Two defense contractor companies working under NISPOM can remain in compliance while having different operating procedures. Hiring a person with a desire to learn, formal education and a perfect match for the company culture would be desirable even thought they lack technical competence. The nuances of security can be taught on the job and at formal training.

As early as possible, FSOs and security specialists should work toward establishing operating procedures and a job performance description. New employees can become successful faster with formalized training. This training should be unique to the organization and is made with milestones that eventually allow new employees to work unsupervised. The new employee can enroll in government provided on-line and residence training, lessons provided by company personnel or on the job training directly under their manager's supervision. With a good training or certification plan in place, much of the employee's success can be measured within the first 90 days.

SUMMARY

There is a large distinction between being a security technician and a professional. Security technicians work on individual tasks and are focused on task completion. Security professionals should not only be technically proficient, but should understand how security fits into the company culture. To better guide the organization's security program, the FSO should understand the organization's primary mission and how it makes money. Understanding the goals, mission and culture and how to implement the security program helps the FSO establish credibility and integrate into the company culture.

The FSO has many tools to help improve organization's security posture. These tools provide metrics that can be used to relate to executives and senior managers who understand evaluations, ratings and assessments. FSOs who translate security needs and requirements based on facts, risk management and compliance help executives make good decisions.

PROBLEMS

1. A facility security officer has many milestone tools available for finding solid facts about their security program. Name two of the tools the FSO can use to gather information about their security program's posture.

2. After conducting a preliminary investigation on a security incident, the FSO concludes that though a security violation had occurred, there was no compromise or suspected compromise. What can the FSO do with the results and discoveries made

during the investigation?

3. DSS conducts an annual security review to determine a defense contractor's ability to protect classified information. What are the four ratings a defense contractor is eligible for? Which rating makes the contractor eligible to compete for the Cogswell award and what is required of a contractor to get that rating?

REFERENCES

1. Department of Defense, DoD 5220.22-M, National Industrial Security Operating Manual, section 1-201, February 2006
2. Department of Defense, DoD 5220.22-M, National Industrial Security Operating Manual, section 1-206, February 2006
3. Defense Security Services, Industrial Security Letter 1-206, Security Review Ratings (ISL 04L-1 #8), downloaded from https://www.dss.mil/GW/ShowBinary/DSS/about_dss/press_room/2006/isl_2006_L_2_august_22_2006.pdf
4. Department of Defense, DoD 5220.22-M, National Industrial Security Operating Manual, section 3-107, February 2006

HELPFUL WEBSITES:

DSS Downloads including Self-Inspection Check List
Http://dssa.dss.mil/seta/downloads.html

CHAPTER 13 CAREER ADVANCEMENT

INTRODUCTION

The industrial security field is growing as fast as the US Government increases classified contracts. As a result, security clearance opportunities are available at both entry and advanced level positions. When a Government entity awards classified contracts, the winning defense contractor is responsible for protecting the classified information involved. The type of work specified in the DD Form 254 can help determine amount of cleared employees necessary to protect classified information and perform administrative functions. The need for educated, informed and business savvy FSOs and industrial security specialists is increasing proportionately.

Employees starting out in an entry level security position can experience a rewarding career. Performance, training and experience play major roles in career progression. Cleared employees are qualified to receive incredible security training provided free by DSS. Once established, a new employee can earn promotions within the organization or as hired by other defense contractors. Seasoned employees have received raises, promotions and significant job offers based on their education, training, and ability to implement security programs while saving valuable resources and reducing costs.

This chapter introduces the methods of how a security professional can grow in experience and excel in their profession. Discussion includes professional and institutional education, certification, organizational cost reduction and other career enhancing tasks. Those who understand how to apply their education, experience, certification and understanding of risk management stand out and are rewarded.

POTENTIAL FOR SECURITY CLEARANCE REQUIRED JOBS

There are more than 12,000 cleared Department of Defense contractor facilities. Considering that organizations can have anywhere from one to thousands of cleared employees, the amount of employees performing classified work is in the hundreds of thousands. Positions requiring security clearances include scientists, program manager and other technical experts, to janitorial and repair services. Security clearances are required to gain access to government websites or networks regardless of whether or not classified information will be accessed.

Even though a job may require a security clearance, an employee does not always need a security clearance to apply for the job. The potential employee must only be eligible for the security clearance. Many frequently asked questions in the defense contractor field are from those who want to know how to get a security clearance so that they can apply for a job. Familiar requests include: "Can I get a security clearance in case I need to apply for another job?" Some employees in the defense industry who do not have clearances often request one just in case it is needed later. However, a clearance is contract and performance related; one cannot get a clearance just to apply for a job.

A job seeker's main responsibility should be to find a match to a job they can do well and get the interview. The job description may require the ability to get a clearance, but uncleared people can and should apply. It is up to them to get an interview and win the job. If the potential employer finds a good match, then they will hire the employee and subsequently put in the clearance investigation request. The defense contractor and Federal job industry provide opportunities for both skilled and unskilled workers to apply for jobs at varying levels of experience. As technology changes and homeland security needs increase, more opportunities for cleared work may arise. Once the applicant gets hired, they can gain experience, education and certification to become a more competitive employee.

Becoming A Cleared Contractor

Security clearance jobs can be found at many websites. The jobs posted in these sites can be searched based on criteria such as: Federal agency, business name, job title, job description, location, etc. On the other hand, businesses and entrepreneurs can become a defense contractor entity by applying through www.ccr.gov. This website allows the establishment as a contractor and building of their profile. Once established, the new company can register and bid on government contracts, including those requiring classified work. However, getting a classified contract directly with the government is not easy. Many defense contractors have experienced success only after subcontracting with a prime cleared contractor.

Becoming a Cleared Security Professionals

More and more job announcements for FSOs and experienced security specialists are requiring a certification and education. Until recently, the only experience necessary was the ability to get a security clearance and a High School Diploma or GED. However, more and more announcements require formal education to include college and a preference for security certification. The defense security industry still provides a good career field to gain entry level experience and move up quickly; simultaneous education and certification will make future leaders more competitive.

The NISP provides an excellent opportunity for an employee with little experience to enter the field. For example, a veteran of the armed forces with a security clearance and some security experience may find it easy to transition to a security specialist job. Additionally, a young adult with limited work experience or skills may be able to join the security division of a large defense contractor in a security support role after getting an interim security clearance.

Often, some cleared employees transfer to full time security after discovering rewarding work as part of an additional duty. This can occur as they experience and a preference for FSO responsibilities. As the classified contract grows, their skills also increase to a point where they can make the transition to full time FSO. Security managers can also move to higher level security positions as chief security officer, corporate security officer or equivalent position as experience meets opportunity.

Large Defense Contractors and Government agencies have available entry level security jobs. The job title is often security specialist and job descriptions allow for many experiences. Some descriptions use language such as the following:

> "The candidate must be eligible for a security clearance. Job responsibilities include receiving, cataloging, storing, and mailing classified information. Maintain access control to closed areas. Provide security support for classified information processing and destruction. Initiate security clearance requests and process requests for government and contract employees conducting classified visits. Implement security measures as outlined in NISPOM."

Administrative, military, security guard, police and other past job experience may provide transferable skills to allow a person to apply for the job. Once hired, the new employee learns the technical skills, and can quickly advance applying their other experiences and education.

The job of FSO is complex and requires experience. However one can get started by learning to perform such tasks as filing receipts, wrapping packages, checking access rosters, applying information system security, or bringing classified information into an IMS and safeguarding system provide great foundations to build careers upon. Many employees attend university and other adult education opportunities while serving full time in the security field. On the other hand, some who begin in the security field learn about other defense contractor jobs and apply for other work within the organization such as contracts or program management.

Advancement

Moving up in the industrial security profession depends on opportunities within the company. Those security specialists who perform in large companies may be able to advance as leadership and other opportunities become available. In smaller companies, advancement depends on the growth of contracts or the amount of work on the few contracts the company performs on. Whether implementing security in a large or small company, the employee should be ready when an opportunity arises.

Large defense contractors performing on multiple classified contracts and programs offer various positions. In such an environment the company can have hundreds of classified contracts with statements of work, DD Forms 254 and other contractual descriptions of work to be performed. The FSO and staff support the classified work by safeguarding and facilitating the proper use of classified information. The security specialist can gain experience in many possible arenas to include maintaining security clearances, administering contract security, safeguarding classified information, enforcing access controls and other security functions while working in a sensitive compartment information facility, closed area, special access program or other environment. With multiple contracts the cleared security employee can have the opportunity to work in different disciplines if they desire and depending on the needs of the company. Alternatively, the employees can remain in their discipline indefinitely and continue to grow in specialized experience.

Some defense contractors are dependent on very few classified contracts. An industrial security professional in this environment may be able to work in all disciplines as identified above. Their few classified contracts (in some cases a single contract) may not require more than the work of one employee to develop and implement measures to safeguard classified information.

Non possessing facilities may only require administering security clearance functions. There is no requirement for storage of classified information or any classified work performed on location. Experience is limited to one security discipline. Advancement may come from the growth of the contracts or the scope of work. Alternatively, the employee could apply for work with another Defense contractor to gain other desired experience.

Streamlining work

The security staff, FSO and other parts of the enterprise not directly paid for contract by a contract is referred to as overhead. These employees charge their salaries, services and support to the company. Overhead includes other career fields such as human resources, contracts management, accounting, safety and others who do not charge their time to a contract. Overhead expenses come out of a company's budget. These positions do not earn money for the company. In fact, they spend money on salaries, supplies, equipment, software and other items necessary to support the enterprise. Industrial security specialist charging to overhead spend money and resources protecting classified information. Supplies and equipment take up valuable space, generates waste related costs and expenses when maintained unnecessarily. Personnel in the security department require salary, benefits, training and health care. FSOs should learn to prioritize security efforts and streamline performance and equipment costs.

Security Equipment

If required other expenses include construction costs for closed areas, SCIFs, vaults and areas for classified meetings. Security containers and other GSA approved security devises are expensive and must be maintained properly. FSOs and security specialists working with multiple security containers, vaults and personnel should consider how to reduce expenses while maintaining the proper level of security.

Security Services

Cleared employees are needed for the safeguarding, processing and disseminating of classified information. Conducting inquiries, staffing classified document repositories, maintaining personnel and facility clearance and changing security container combinations are part of the day to day functions of a security specialist. Other services include sending classified information by USPS or authorized overnight carrier. This could constitute a large part of the budget the FSO should be projecting. USPS Registered and other required mailing service costs add up proportionally as the volume of mail increases.

Process And Bottom Line

Since overhead does take from an organization's top line, it is important for managers to understand how best to reduce expenditures when at all possible. The FSO should understand how to reduce costs without decreasing security effectiveness. Those who have accelerated their careers have done so after being recognized for reducing costs without sacrificing national security.

Successful programs designed to engineer out waste work well with services to reduce costs, eliminate waste and perform more effectively. This requires a dynamic change in thinking led by strong leadership. The predominant thinking should not be to provide security at all costs. Consider a few tasks routinely conducted by industrial security specialists in two different disciplines. The first is in personnel security and the second is in document control. The personnel security specialist maintains records on employees who are being processed for a security clearance or who already have security clearances. Information in the file includes employment data, the SF 312 Classified Information Nondisclosure Agreement and security training records. These records are thick with information that included a copy of the SF 86 Questionnaire for National Security Positions as well as paper copies on any information about the security clearances and the cleared person.

In recent years, changes in privacy laws and the development of new security clearance on line databases have led to less hard copy a information required to be stored on site. Prior to the DoD's implementation of the JPAS, copies of security clearance status, SF 86, signature pages, and many other files had to be maintained. Paper files were dense and required room for storage.

Systems like JPAS automated the personnel security system. The national database proved a reliable method for keeping up with and tracking the security clearances and status. Records are updated on line and most transactions can take place without the exchange of paperwork and the online systems eliminated the need for bulky personnel files. Other personnel actions such as submitting and receiving visit requests were also executed with more confidentiality as personal information is better protected on the secure server, and without wasteful paperwork.

Within the last few years, the Department of Defense also put out new requirements that SF 86 forms would not be maintained on persons who already had a security clearance. In this system, the FSO receives the SF 86 electronically and reviews it. If accurate and complete they submit it to the DSS through JPAS. FSOs are authorized to print a copy to keep on file through the investigation stage. However, once approved, the records must be destroyed.

Some FSOs were reluctant to make the required changes. However, the issue of privacy is paramount to the U.S. Government and there is a huge training program underway to protect personal identifiable information. DSS began inspecting compliance with the record maintenance during the contractors' annual reviews. Slower moving FSOs had to adjust quickly. The FSOs who could envision the changes adapted quickly, using initiative to bring their companies into compliance sooner based on a well developed and comprehensive time line. Additionally, the reduction in paper copies of the SF 86 freed valuable storage space.

The proactive FSOs embraced the changes in the personnel security requirements. As DSS prepared to implement the system, these managers quickly realized that they could begin streamlining their systems. While some FSOs continued to purchase additional lateral cabinets and other office furniture to store the growing personnel files, others were purged their files of redundant copies and freeing up valuable employee time and company funds.

Cost reductions at all levels add up. Cutting costs while maintaining NISPOM requirements gets a person noticed. Simple initiatives can produce immediate results. Consider the task of wrapping classified material and preparing it for shipment. This is routine and such a part of business that huge budgets are allotted to mailing classified material. FSOs ensure that removing classified material is a matter of national security and not one of convenience. Enforcing such discipline can reduce costs significantly, by preventing the unnecessary dissemination and related costs. Many meetings or conferences could occur without the introduction of classified information. If needed, there may be more secure ways of transmitting other than using mail or a courier service.

Where mailing is absolutely necessary, there are measures the FSO can take to reduce costs. Packages are expensive to mail and are often charged by weight. The type and amount of wrapping material significantly impacts the price of mailing the item. A trained person can wrap a package far cheaper than a novice. The difference in weight can add up quickly depending on the volume of items to be sent. Process can be improved by providing written instructions, policy or classes on how to prepare classified information for dissemination. This investment in personnel not only improves the security of the item, but can help streamline the process, shorten preparation time and reduce costs.

Reducing Costs

Consider an FSO's leadership dilemma in the next example. During his first few months at XYZ Contractor, his security employees expressed opinions that engineers working on classified projects needed extra reminders of classification levels. To compensate, the security employees applied additional classification markings beyond the required markings already provided on the top and bottom of the front and back cover of classified documents.

The FSO understood that Federal regulations required applying risk management to reduce wasteful and redundant operations. He reviewed the NISPOM and document marking references to ensure he understood the requirements. He also re-read the DD Forms 254 and related SCGs for all classified contracts to identify any unique marking or storage requirements. He used his IMS inventory software to pull up information about how many classified documents the company received and generated. He also pulled past purchasing requests for security supplies.

His research revealed that the company purchased over $3,000 worth of unnecessary label making supplies annually. Additionally, the document custodian's process bottleneck occurred during the application of markings. Whether receiving documents from outside of the organization or as newly created, his staff added the unnecessary additional markings even though they were already properly marked. The additional markings cluttered the document, covered valuable information and provided unnecessary redundant work and ineffective security measures. Often, the engineers waited far too long to access the classified material as it went through the preparation process.

After careful evaluation and retraining his employees, the FSO ended the practice of additional markings. He led the employees to improve security and reduce the hourly and material costs associated with over marking the documents. He also demonstrated his fiscal responsibility in a detailed budget amendment showing a significant cost reduction.

Data Mining

FSOs can also reduce costs during classified document storage and inventory. Knowing what type of classified information is stored and how it is stored can lead to effective product management. For a possessing facility, a new classified contract can lead to more classified information and storage requirements. The FSO would need to know what type of storage would be necessary. For example, an increase in classified information on DVDs or CDs requires different storage shelving than that of paper documents. Two hundred DVDs can be stored in a smaller area than as many 150 page documents. A competent IMS database or software can help an FSO identify these types of trends. The FSO can research such information by pulling up records of the number and type of documents received, stored, and disseminated or destroyed.

Additionally, good software can work with barcodes and scanners. When the FSO logs in classified information, they can also input bar code information. When the FSO stores, issues, destroys or disseminates classified information, they can scan the barcode. The information is then entered into the IMS and the classified information status is updated. Such scanning identifies documents by bar code, document number, and other vital information.

Barcode inventory is used regularly in retail and other inventory applications. Manual inventory is costly. However, when inventory is conducted with simultaneous daily operations, it can be time saving and purposeful. When used properly, barcode inventory can allow the custodians to free valuable time, save the company overtime and other expenses, and maintain the same or better level of security and required inventory events.

FSOs can recognize wasteful movement and processes in their security departments. They can draw on security experiences and transferable skills from other jobs to make positive changes and reduce expenses. FSOs should effectively lead and train employees in such changes in processes and demonstrate cost reduction to management. Defense contractors and Federal agencies regularly reward employees who take the initiative to identify wasteful processes and recommend solutions. Additionally, figuring the security return on investment (ROI) adds to the cost reductions.

Consider the installation of access control such as card readers. Though not required, they may be necessary to prevent unauthorized persons from entering a facility. An FSO should be able to demonstrate reduced costs through compared heating and cooling bills before and after the installation of access controls systems. For example, suppose a cleared contractor has three warehouses with ten doors each that remain open at all times. Unauthorized persons have entered on several occasions and employees have practiced little discipline in keeping the doors closed. The new FSO performs a risk and cost analysis pointing to a need for an access control system.

The FSO should provide a sound business plan to demonstrate to shareholders the benefits of a more secure work environment. In the past, management has attempted to maintain closed doors by recommending that supervisors check the doors several times daily. The FSO schedules time with his immediate vice president to inspect the procedure. Soon the vice-president notices the lack of discipline, possible liability with unauthorized visitors and waste of process with frequents supervisor door checks. Shortly thereafter, management authorizes the installation of the access control system. The FSO keeps management informed of results and how installation contributed to reducing costs. By keeping the doors closed, the access control system cost was made up from saving in air conditioning costs over the period of a year (Figure 13-1).

ITEM	COST	HOURS	SALARY	SALARY SAVINGS	HVAC SAVINGS
Access Control	$28,800	750	28	$21,000	$13,000
High Security Locks	$4,200	5	28	$140	
Crash Bars	$500	NA	NA	$0	
Door locks	$2,000	NA	NA	$0	
2 Cameras	$1,345	5	28	$140	

Figure 13-1 Example of Return on Security Investment- Notice the cost reduction after installing a $28,800 access control system. Prior to installing the Access Control package, doors to the building had no access control. Employees often failed to completely close the doors upon entering or exiting. The manager performed two random checks to ensure doors had been closed to prevent unauthorized visitors. The managers also had to track down visitors and vendors who had entered without going through the visitor reception desk. The FSO realized that the door magnet and swipe card available in the access control package would realize a $21,000 cost reduction in salary paid to managers. Manager checks 300 days annually.

INDUSTRY SPONSORED CERTIFICATION

Certification says a lot about a professional. This individual has dedicated personal time and has committed to intensive study to improve their skills on the required topics. Supervisors and managers may set a goal for employees to reach a level of experience or even challenge them to seek a certification. Employees who have achieved a professional certification have experienced preference in hiring, retention and promotion. Though a certification does not guarantee an employee such benefits, it does demonstrate a few important qualities to their management. Primarily, those certified convey a commitment to the profession, investment in the enterprise, and a high level of experience and knowledge.

Organizations that hire employees with certifications or encourage employees to become certified, benefit from the experience. In many cases, employers pay for the exams and other fees related to the certification requirements. They recognize the dedication their employees demonstrate, experience gained, and the marketability of the certified. Other benefits to the company include bragging rights and certifications can be included in company profiles. When applicable, defense contractors can mention employee certifications when listing capabilities and responding to requests for bids. For example, they can mention that the FSO "is board certified to protect classified information" and list the certification and source. Those who solicit bids also recognize certifications to include prime contractors and Federal agencies. Certifications are also good credentials for vendors who install security systems, guards, document destruction or provide other security services.

As leaders, FSOs can help security employees understand how to create incredible security programs. Focusing on training, interaction with other cleared employees, self-improvement and institutional education should be part of professional development. FSOs who write security evaluations for direct reports have an excellent opportunity to help them establish goals to become better at their jobs, more impacting in their careers and hopefully, groomed to become FSOs themselves. Challenging employees and team members to achieve personal and professional goals breeds success.

Industrial Security Professional Certification (ISP)

FSOs could set the ISP Certification as a goal and encourage staff employees to achieve. The employee gains from such education and a prestigious career milestone. The organization also benefits from what the security employee learns and applies on the job. When employees study for the ISP Certification, they learn: how to read and apply the

NISPOM, the importance of forming professional relationships with cleared employees, how the cleared contractor and the DSS representatives interact, and much more.

A leader also creates pride in the organization and employee by making them more competitive in their career and providing basis for professional pride. The path to the ISP Certification goals should not be taken alone. When employees are challenged with the goal, the manager can help by providing or allowing education as found on the DSS, professional organization or vendor websites. Studies on NISPOM topics are available on the internet as well as on site. If an FSO has a staff, they can consider helping them start a study group.

If the cleared contractor facility has a security staff, the FSO can provide an opportunity to cross train. Security employees who work personnel security issues could work with document control and other security disciplines to cross train as well as give practical experience for the exam. FSOs could also direct their security employees from one discipline to inspect another during the annual self inspection.

Another idea is for the FSO to create an internal job certification program. This helps integrate new employees into their jobs. A self-certification program would train an employee on performing individual tasks. The employee works under a mentor who verifies and documents the training. This training covers how the cleared contractor facility security employees practice document control, manage personnel security, provide classified contract support and etc. The goal is to have the new employee working unsupervised within 90 days. This program can be extended to cross training employees who concentrate only on one task. This will help them become more experienced and more prepared for the exam.

Employees may not feel comfortable asking for training, setting prestigious goals, or asking for funding for professional organizations or certifications. However, a supervisor who is aware of such opportunities can encourage the employee to become engaged.

The DSS also understands the importance of individuals who achieve the ISP Certification as well as the organizations that hire them. The FSO can display the certificate and refer to it during the annual inspection as continued training. DSS also recognizes that the achievement goes above and beyond NISPOM requirements.

The ISP Certification is sponsored by the NCMS (Society of Industrial Security Professionals) [1]. Though NCMS membership is made up of several thousand security specialists and FSOs, the ISP certification is open to non-members and includes cleared security disciplines such as: personnel security, guards, document control, contracts management and all other disciplines.

The certification is not only for those with security titles, but also for those who perform security functions while working with classified information and material. For example, a company president who also serves as FSO, an engineer, project manager, clerk, cleared security service provider, military service member, Federal employee or anyone else who can demonstrate that they protect classified information in the performance of their job. The ISP Certification is increasing in demand and gaining momentum. You can find out more about NCMS and ISP Certification through their website www.classmgmt.com or by searching "industrial security professional certification" or "ISP Certification" in your favorite search engine.

Other certification

There are many sources available for certification applicable to both the defense contractor and government security professionals. Some have more weight than others, but all require good preparation time. The certifications mentioned below are but a few of the most popular. All of them cannot be listed here and the intent is not to recognize one above the other. For convenience, we are listing four certification sources familiar to those who are experienced in the industrial security field.

Some other pertinent security certifications are provided through the American Society of Industrial Security (ASIS) International. This organization is made up of more than 35,000 security practitioners, suppliers and service providers throughout the world. The scope of coverage is larger and less industry specific. As a professional organization, ASIS enjoys a membership consisting of law-enforcement, military, government, defense industry, loss prevention, and other professionals. To meet the demand for a professional presence, ASIS sponsors three certifications meeting differing needs in the security industry. The Certified Protection Professional (CPP), Certified Professional Investigator (CPI) and Physical Security Professional (PSP) each provide professionalism and opportunities to excel in broad disciplines.

Certified Protection Professional

The CPP certification is for those who have a broad range of security experience to meet complex security issues [2]. This is certainly a leader's certification for FSOs, chief security officers, information system security officers, and higher level security managers. Holders of the CPP certification understand the threats that face the workplace, employees, product and the public. The CPP designation distinguishes the approximately 10,000 certified professionals from their peers. This has a significant application in the defense industry as industrial security professionals, security specialists and FSOs demonstrate their knowledge of physical security, personnel security, business management, security principles, information security, emergency procedures, investigations and legal aspects. Those with the CPP certification may have the edge on promotions, leadership positions and hiring opportunities. Additionally, some key job announcements list the CPP certification as a favorable qualification.

Certified Professional Investigator

The CPI certification is for those who have experience with case handling, witness statement collecting, interviews and other investigative skills [2]. This is a board certified investigator's certification with application in pharmaceutical, gaming, loss prevention, and law enforcement industries. It may even be a pertinent credential for those who investigate events of loss, compromise or suspecting compromise of classified information. Holders of the CPI certification convey to management competency in their fields and the ability to get the source of a problem. Consider the tremendous loss companies face annually with theft of technology, identification and proprietary information. Those who hire investigators want the most capable. The CPI certification demonstrates the capability. As with the CPP those who have the CPI may enjoy an edge on promotions, leadership positions and hiring opportunities.

Physical Security Professional

The PSP certification is for those who have experience with physical security, risk assessment, threat analysis, and implementation of security measures [2]. This is a board certified certification and the holder is capable of performing risk analysis and implementing security measures to meet identified threats. In other words, they identify risks and threats, design systems to counter the threats and implement the systems to reduce the risks. This field has significant application for organic security personnel and vendors as well. The credibility the holder enjoys may make them a top choice for those who make hiring and contracting decisions. The risk analysis skills are very necessary in protecting the company, product, employees and visitors. Risk analysis also helps reduce cost while heightening security based on priority of work. As with the CPP and CPI certifications, those who have the PSP may enjoy an edge on promotions, leadership positions and hiring opportunities.

Certified Information Systems Security Professional

The Certified Information Systems Security Professional (CISSP) is sponsored by International Information Systems Security Certification Consortium or ISC2 [3]. For those working as an Information System Security Manager, Information System Security Officer, Chief Information Officer or other mid to senior level management positions in information security should consider the CISSP. The CISSP measures competency and experience in 10 key areas: Access Control, Application Security, Business Continuity and Disaster Recovery Planning, Cryptography, Information Security and Risk Management, Legal, Regulations, Compliance and Investigations, Operations Security, Physical (Environmental) Security, Security Architecture and Design and Telecommunications and Network Security.

OPSEC Professionals Society

For those who are interested in operations security (OPSEC), the OPSEC Professionals Society (OPS) offers the OPSEC Certified Professional (OCP) certification [4]. The OCP is for those who are actively engaged in identifying vulnerabilities of sensitive government activities and denying an adversary's ability to collect information on the activities. In addition to the five years of experience, the candidate for the OCP should have a four year degree and at least 48 hours of formal OPSEC training. The applicant submits a 10 page paper on the topic of OPSEC using one or more of the five OPSEC processes (identification of critical information; analysis of threats; analysis of vulnerabilities; assessment of risks; and the application of appropriate countermeasures). For those with less experience, the OPSEC Professionals Society offers the OPSEC Associate Professional Certification (OAP). The OAP candidate should be an OPS member in good standing with at least two years of experience with OPSEC and complete at least 20 hours of OPSEC training.

SUMMARY

There are many opportunities to learn and grow in the industrial security professional field. This profession allows a person to join in an entry level position and move up based upon experience, education and ability to implement a superior security program while remaining compliant and minding costs. The FSO or industrial security specialist can build credibility and influence necessary to lead a security organization. The important concept is to apply technical ability and transition from an administrator to a sought out leader.

RESOURCES

1. Industrial Security Professional (ISP) Certification Program Requirements and Application, NCMS (Society of Industrial Security Professionals, http://www.ncms-isp.org/documents/ brochure.pdf, downloaded May 2009

2. Professional Certifications in Security, Applicant's Handbook, http://www.asisonline.org/certification/handbook.pdf, downloaded Jan 2010 CISSP For Professionals,

3. The International Information Systems Security Certification Consortium, Inc., (ISC)², http://www.isc2.org/uploadedFiles/ Credentials_and_Certifcation/CISSP/CISSP_for%20Professionals.pdf, downloaded May 2009

4. OPSEC Certified Professional, OPSEC Society, http://www.opsecsociety.org/certification_OCP_Section_I.htm, downloaded May 2009

HELPFUL WEBSITES

Certification
Http://www.asisonline.org
Http://www.ncms-isp.org
Http://www.isc2.org/
Http://www.opsecsociety.org
Http://www.redbikepublishing.com
Clearance jobs
Http://www.usajobs.com
Http://www.clearancejobs.com
Forming a defense contractor company
Http://www.ccr.gov
Industrial Security Education
Http://www.dss.mil http://www.redbikepublishing.com

APPENDIX A
How to prepare for a Defense Security Services (DSS) Inspection

DSS performs annual reviews to ensure cleared contractors are protecting classified information according to the national industrial security program Operating Manual. DSS conducts the reviews every 12 months for possessing facilities and every 18 months for non-possessing facilities. However, other factors could affect the frequency. DSS will send a notice prior to inspection. Initial notification could be by phone, mail or email and followed up in writing.

The inspection should be an exercise of what DSS, the FSO and cleared employees already understand about the security program. The relationship will be a reflection of what the FSO has established with employees and DSS as identified in this book. Such relationships create an environment where all elements take ownership of the program and DSS representative is aware of program effectiveness throughout the year. The inspection should be a wrap-up of what everyone already understands about the program. In a best case scenario, there should be no long hours focused on passing the inspection. In other words, the inspection should be just another great security day.

Prior to the inspection, DSS should send a request for information. Requested information includes information about the facility and personnel security clearances. The questionnaire is detailed and will take some time to gather the requested information. Most information can be researched using the Joint Personnel Adjudication System database. For example, be prepared to disclose number of cleared employees by clearance level, number of classified documents on site by classification, organizational changes that affect the facility clearance level and etc.

Depending on which parts of NISPOM apply to your company, prepare the following for presentation (see the NISPOM questionnaire covered in Chapter 2. Some FSOs create a folder for the DSS representative to help the inspection flow smoothly. The folders include useful information about the security program to help the FSO answer questions and demonstrate program effectiveness. Though DSS has not yet released inspection criteria, the DSS Self Inspection Handbook available at http://dssa.dss.mil/seta/documents/self_inspect_handbook_nisp_08.pdf is a good resource to base DSS reviews on. Items to consider include, but are not limited to the following:

1. Original and current facility security clearance documentation
- Sponsorship Letter
- DSS FL 381-R Cleared Facility Letter-Provided by DSS acknowledging organization as cleared facility
- DD FORM 441- Department of Defense Security Agreement
- STANDARD FORM 328 Certificate Pertaining to Foreign Interests
- Key Management Personnel List
2. Personnel security clearance information
- PCL Information (JPAS Printout)
- Personnel clearance information
- Current Outgoing Classified Visit Request Authorizations
- Consultants
- Number of Non-US Citizens
3. Copies of DSS and self inspection results. Address any issues or findings.
- Last year's DSS Inspection
- Self-Inspection
- Implementations made after inspections
4. Provide list of all DD Form 254 Department of Defense Contract Security Classification Specifications

This will remind the DSS representative of the security requirements and how your organization is poised to meet and exceed those requirements. Your risk assessment matrix should also be included to demonstrate security focus as related to current threats,

NISPOM and DD Form 254 requirements.

- Contracts Information
- DD Form 254 Information
- Current Classified Contracts List (DD 254s)
- Prime and Subcontractors

5. Security Incidents/Violations

- Preliminary investigations
- Mismarked documents
- Unauthorized disclosure

6. Reports to DSS

- Adverse Information
- Suspicious Contacts Report
- List suspicious contacts reported to DSS

7. Demonstrate Security Program Awareness

8. Proof of (documentation and proof of attendance):

- Initial security briefings
- Annual Security Awareness Training
- COMSEC, NATO, and other access briefings
- Location and type of posters
- Handouts available
- Automated or other email notices
- Security training websites for employees
- Certifications of training for FSO and security specialists
- Upcoming training dates

9. Locations of where classified information is stored)Security Containers and Closed areas)

- Location
- Type
- Record of combination changes

10. Classified processing

- Copies of certifications and accreditations
- List of IS
- Copy of SSP

11. Paper trail/receipts of classified documents received, copied, transmitted, downgraded, declassified and destroyed.

12. International Operations

- List of Export Licenses
- Technology Control Plan
- Defensive Security Briefings

While preparing for the inspection, send reminders to all employees to help them recall the security program, the name of the FSO and key terms they need to know. Cleared employees may be interviewed as part of the review. They should understand and be able to answer questions concerning foreign travel, required briefings, reports, access, need to know and the ever popular adverse information.

On the review day, prepare a warm reception for the DSS Special Agent. Prepare a briefing and ensure senior managers and Key Management Personnel attend. This will give a good impression of company involvement.

APPENDIX B
Definitions

Access-The ability and opportunity to gain knowledge of classified information.

Adverse Information-Any information that adversely reflects on the integrity or character of a cleared employee, that suggests that his or her ability to safeguard classified information may be impaired, or that his or her access to classified information clearly may not be in the interest of national security.

Authorized Person-A person who has a need-to-know for classified information in the performance of official duties and who has been granted a PCL at the required level.

Classified Contract-Any contract requiring access to classified information by a contractor or his or her employees in the performance of the contract. (A contract may be a classified contract even though the contract document is not classified.) The requirements prescribed for a "classified contract" also are applicable to all phases of pre-contract activity, including solicitations (bids, quotations, and proposals), pre-contract negotiations, post-contract activity, or other GCA program or project which requires access to classified information by a contractor.

Classified Information-Official information that has been determined, pursuant to reference (b) or any predecessor order, to require protection against unauthorized disclosure in the interest of national security and which has been so designated.

Classified Visit-A visit during which a visitor will require, or is expected to require, access to classified information.

Cleared Commercial Carrier-A carrier authorized by law, regulatory body, or regulation to transport SECRET material and has been granted a SECRET facility clearance.

Cleared Employees-All contractor employees granted PCLs and all employees being processed for PCLs.

Closed Area-An area that meets the requirements of NISPOM for safeguarding classified material that, because of its size, nature, or operational necessity, cannot be adequately protected by the normal safeguards or stored during nonworking hours in approved containers.

Cognizant Security Agency (CSA)-Agencies of the Executive Branch that have been authorized by reference (a) to establish an industrial security program to safeguard classified information under the jurisdiction of those agencies when disclosed or released to U.S. Industry. These agencies are: The Department of Defense, DOE, CIA, and NRC.

Cognizant Security Office (CSO)-The organizational entity delegated by the Head of a CSA to administer industrial security on behalf of the CSA.

Compromise-An unauthorized disclosure of classified information.

CONFIDENTIAL-The classification level applied to information, the unauthorized disclosure of which reasonable could be expected to cause damage to the national security that the original classification authority is able to identify or describe.

Constant Surveillance Service-A transportation protective service provided by a commercial carrier qualified by SDDC to transport CONFIDENTIAL shipments. The service requires constant surveillance of the shipment at all times by a qualified carrier representative; however, an FCL is not required for the carrier. The carrier providing the service must maintain a signature and tally record for the shipment.

Contractor-Any industrial, educational, commercial, or other entity that has been granted an FCL by a CSA.

Courier-A cleared employee, designated by the con-tractor, whose principal duty is to transmit classified material to its destination. The classified material remains in the personal possession of the courier except for authorized overnight storage.

Declassification-The determination that classified information no longer requires, in the interest of national security, any degree of protection against unauthorized disclosure, together with removal or cancellation of the classification designation.

Derivative Classification-The incorporating, paraphrasing, restating, or generating in new form information that is already classified, and marking the newly developed material consistent with the classification markings that apply to the source information. Derivative classification includes the classification of information based on classification guidance.

Escort-A cleared person, designated by the contractor, who accompanies a shipment of classified material to its destination. The classified material does not remain in the personal possession of the escort but the conveyance in which the material is transported remains under the constant observation and control of the escort.

Facility (Security) Clearance (FCL)-An administrative determination that, from a security viewpoint, a company is eligible for access to classified information of a certain category (and all lower categories).

Foreign Government Information (FGI)-Information that is:
- Provided to the U.S. by a foreign government or governments, an international organization of governments, or any element thereof with the expectation, expressed or implied, that the information, the source of the information, or both, are to be held in confidence; or
- Produced by the U.S. pursuant to, or as a result of, a joint arrangement with a foreign government or governments, an international organization of governments, or any element thereof, requiring that the information, the arrangement, or both are to be held in confidence.

Freight Forwarder- Any agent or facility designated to receive, process, and transship U.S. material to foreign recipients. In the context of this manual, an agent or facility cleared specifically to perform these functions for the transfer of U.S. classified material to foreign recipients.

Government Contracting Activity (GCA)-An element of an agency designated by the agency head and delegated broad authority regarding acquisition functions.

Handcarrier-A cleared employee, designated by the contractor, who occasionally handcarries classified material to its destination in connection with a classified visit or meeting. The classified material remains in the personal possession of the handcarrier except for authorized overnight storage.

Industrial Security-That portion of information security concerned with the protection of classified information in the custody of U.S. industry.

Information System (IS)-An assembly of computer hardware, software, and firmware configured for the purpose of automating the functions of calculating, computing, sequencing, storing, retrieving, displaying, communicating, or otherwise manipulating data, information and textual material.

Limited Access Authorization (LAA)-Security access authorization to CONFIDENTIAL or SECRET information granted to non-U.S. citizens requiring such limited access in the course of their regular duties.

Material-Any product or substance on or in which information is embodied.

Multiple Facility Organization (MFO)-A legal entity (single proprietorship, partnership, association, trust, or corporation) composed of two or more contractors.

Need to Know-A determination made by an authorized holder of classified information that a prospective recipient has a requirement for access to, knowledge, or possession of the classified information to perform tasks or services essential to the fulfillment of a classified contract or program.

Original Classification Authority-Government Officials who have been designated in writing to make an initial determination that information requires, in the interest of national security, protection against unauthorized disclosure, together with a classification designation signifying the level of protection required.

Personnel (Security) Clearance (PCL)-An administrative determination that an individual is eligible, from a security point of view, for access to classified information of the same or lower category as the level of the personnel clearance being granted.

Prime Contractor-The contractor who receives a prime contract from a GCA.

Protective Security Service-A transportation protective service provided by a cleared commercial carrier qualified by the SDDC to transport SECRET shipments.

Restricted Area-A controlled access area established to safeguard classified material, that because of its size or nature, cannot be adequately protected during working hours by the usual safeguards, but that is capable of being stored during non-working hours in an approved repository or secured by other methods approved by the CSA.

SECRET-The classification level applied to information, the unauthorized disclosure of which reasonably could be expected to cause serious damage to the national security that the original classification authority is able to identify or describe.

Security Classification Guide-A document issued by an authorized original classifier that identifies the elements of information regarding a specific subject that must be classified and prescribes the level and duration of classification and appropriate declassification instructions. (Classification guides are provided to contractors by the Contract Security Classification Specification.)

Security in Depth-A determination made by the CSA that a contractor's security program consists of layered and complementary security controls sufficient to deter and detect unauthorized entry and movement within the facility.

Security Violation-Failure to comply with the policy and procedures established by this Manual that reasonably could result in the loss or compromise of classified information.

Standard Practice Procedures (SPP)-A document prepared by a contractor that implements the applicable requirements of this manual for the contractor's operations and involvement with classified information at the contractor's facility.

Subcontract-Any contract entered into by a contractor to furnish supplies or services for performance of a prime contract or a subcontract. For purposes of this Manual a subcontract is any contract, subcontract, purchase order, lease agreement, service agreement, request for quotation (RFQ), request for proposal (RFP), invitation for bid (IFB), or other agreement or procurement action between contractors that requires or will require access to classified information to fulfill the performance requirements of a prime contract.

Subcontractor-A supplier, distributor, vendor, or firm that furnishes supplies or services to or for a prime contractor or another subcontractor, who enters into a contract with a prime contractor. For purposes of this Manual, each subcontractor shall be considered as a prime contractor in relation to its subcontractors.

TOP SECRET-The classification level applied to information, the unauthorized disclosure of which reasonable could be expected to cause exceptionally grave damage to the national security that the original classification authority is able to identify or describe.

Unauthorized Person-A person not authorized to have access to specific classified information in accordance with the requirements of this Manual.

US Person-Any form of business enterprise or entity organized, chartered or incorporated under the laws of the United States or its territories and any person who is a citizen or national of the United States.

APPENDIX C

BL Bill of Lading
CAGE Commercial and Government Entity
CIA Central Intelligence Agency
CM Configuration Management
COMSEC Communications Security
CSA Cognizant Security Agency
CSO Cognizant Security Office
DAA Designated Accrediting/Approving Authority
DGR Designated Government Representative
DNI Director of National Intelligence
DoD Department of Defense
DoE Department of Energy
DSS Defense Security Service
EAA Export Administration Act
FBI Federal Bureau of Investigation
FCL Facility (Security) Clearance
FGI Foreign Government Information
FOCI Foreign Ownership, Control or Influence
FSO Facility Security Officer
GCA Government Contracting Activity
GSA General Services Administration
IS Information System
ISOO Information Security Oversight Office
ISSM Information System Security Manager
ISSO Information System Security Officer
ITAR International Traffic in Arms Regulations
LAA Limited Access Authorization

MFO Multiple Facility Organization

NACLC National Agency Check with Local Agency Check and Credit Check

NISP National Industrial Security Program

NISPOM National Industrial Security Program Operating Manual

NSA National Security Agency

OADR Originating Agency's Determination Required

PCL Personnel (Security) Clearance

RFP Request for Proposal

RFQ Request for Quotation

SCI Sensitive Compartmented Information

SCIF Sensitive Compartmented Information Facility

SSBI Single Scope Background Investigation

SSP Systems Security Plan

TCO Technology Control Officer

TCP Technology Control Plan

TP Transportation Plan

INDEX

A

access 19, 24, 26, 28, 31, 32, 36, 38, 40, 41, 42, 48, 50, 53, 54, 59, 60, 64, 65, 66, 67, 68, 74, 84, 85, 86, 87, 88, 89, 90, 91, 92, 93, 94, 96, 99, 102, 103, 113, 114, 118, 127, 139, 140, 144, 145, 150, 151, 152, 154, 155, 156, 157, 158, 160, 163, 166, 167, 168, 169, 170, 171, 172, 173, 174, 175, 176, 177, 178, 179, 180, 181, 183, 184, 185, 192, 193, 197, 207, 211, 215, 217, 218, 219, 220, 221, 222, 223, 225, 231, 232, 233, 235, 244, 247, 248, 251, 255, 258, 259, 261, 263, 272, 276, 277, 278, 282, 284, 290, 292, 293, 298, 299, 300

Access 38, 48, 58, 65, 91, 92, 102, 152, 157, 162, 176, 179, 180, 213, 231, 247, 259, 277, 278, 300, 305, 313, 316, 320

access control 50, 91, 150, 151, 156, 160, 167, 168, 171, 177, 179, 180, 184, 247, 248, 251, 277, 278, 282, 292, 299, 300

Access Control 176, 278, 300, 305

accountability 21, 22, 27, 29, 47, 55, 90, 99, 101, 102, 106, 107, 108, 110, 115, 128, 141, 143, 145, 156, 167, 172, 177, 181, 182, 191, 192, 193, 202, 208, 210, 217, 218, 224, 225, 253, 256

accreditation 165, 166, 167, 182

adverse information 72, 159, 216, 220, 230, 237

Adverse Information 216, 230, 311, 313

Annual refresher training 223

Audit Capability 176

authentication 163, 168, 169, 171, 172, 174, 175, 177, 178, 180, 184, 185

Authorization Letter, 209

Authorized Person 313

Availability 166

C

CAGE 61, 62, 84, 100, 193, 319

CCL 244

Central Adjudication Facility 65

Certificate Pertaining to Foreign Interests 60, 61, 62, 64, 217 certification 165

Certification 166

Certified Information Systems Security Professional 305

Certified Professional Investigator 304

Certified Protection Professional 304

Challenges to Classification 37

CIA 314, 319

CISSP 305, 307

classification markings 24, 27, 36, 38

classified 19, 20, 21, 22, 23, 24, 25, 26, 27, 28, 29, 30, 31, 32, 33, 34, 35, 36, 37, 38, 39, 40, 41

Classified information 20, 27, 29, 36, 39

Classified Information 38, 48, 49, 51, 53, 58, 65, 100, 101, 102, 107, 118, 139, 144, 157, 162, 192, 203, 213, 222, 249, 295, 313

Classified Information Nondisclosure Agreement 222, 295

Classified Information Non Disclosure Agreement 38

Classified Visit 310, 313

Classified Visits 257

Cleaning 94, 169, 170

Cleared Commercial Carrier 313

Cleared Commercial Carriers 201

cleared employee 39, 43, 51, 67, 68, 70, 72, 90, 115, 119, 120, 140, 150, 151, 153, 157, 159, 160, 163, 165, 173, 175, 184, 185, 196, 204, 208, 215, 219, 220, 222, 223, 224, 229, 230, 231, 234, 236, 248, 254, 266, 271

Cleared Employees 101, 314

cleared facilities 63, 139, 168, 191, 204, 205, 224, 265, 284

Closed Area 314

Closed areas 151, 152, 218

CM 174, 175, 319

Cognizant Security Agencies 20

Cognizant Security Agency 8, 314, 319

Cognizant Security Office 9, 56, 314, 319

Cognizant Security Offices 20

combination 47, 153, 154, 155, 156, 160, 173, 222, 235, 271

Commerce Control List 244

Commercial and Government Entity 61, 84

Commercial Carriers 201, 203

Compilation 37

Component Marking 121, 122

compromise 21, 22, 28, 31, 34, 52, 67, 70, 87, 95, 100, 103, 106, 107, 111, 113, 117, 119, 120, 127, 142, 143, 144, 150, 155, 156, 165, 167, 168, 177, 181, 182, 196, 197, 206, 207, 210, 216, 228, 234, 235, 236, 255, 257, 271, 272, 273, 286, 304

Compromise 31, 41, 314

COMSEC 48, 57, 81, 86, 89, 90, 92, 94, 96, 179, 199, 218, 224, 279, 311, 319

CONFIDENTIAL 27, 28, 29, 34, 38, 41

Confidentiality 166, 176

Configuration management 174, 175

Constant Surveillance Service 198, 203, 314

Continuous Evaluation Process 72

Contractor 9, 59, 61, 81, 82, 83, 84, 85, 88, 90, 91, 92, 100, 110, 114, 124, 140, 170, 209, 231, 249, 258, 259, 279, 290, 297, 314, 316

Courier 48, 86, 95, 100, 191, 198, 199, 204, 213, 314

CPI 304, 305

CPP 304, 305

CSA 8, 20, 21, 64, 92, 152, 219, 314, 317, 319

CSO 9, 20, 21, 84, 314, 319

D

DAA 319

Data Transmission 176, 178

DCS 199

DD Form 254 36, 49, 63, 77, 78, 79, 80, 81, 82, 83, 84, 85, 86, 87, 90, 91, 92, 93, 94, 95, 96, 97, 98, 126, 127, 157, 196, 218, 220, 252, 279, 84

DD Form 441. *See* Facility Security Clearance

Declassification 115, 314

declassify 35

defense contractor 19, 20, 30, 37, 39, 40, 43, 44, 51, 60, 70, 74, 80, 88, 99, 108, 158, 159, 160, 163, 164, 199, 205, 221, 223, 231, 237, 239, 243, 250, 251, 252, 253, 256, 258, 260, 265, 268, 269, 275, 279, 285, 287, 289, 290, 291, 292, 303, 307

Defense Contractor. *See* Facility Security Clearance

Defense Courier Service 95, 100, 198, 199, 213

Defense Industrial Security Clearance Office 65, 75

Defense Security Services 20

defensive security briefing 158, 248

Department of Defense 20, 21

Department of Defense Security Agreement 60, 62, 63, 64

Derivative Classification 38, 315

Derivative Marking 121, 124

Designated Government Representative 253

destruction 27, 39, 99, 111, 118, 128, 145, 146, 174, 181, 210, 211, 217, 229, 292, 301

DGR 253, 319

Director of National Intelligence 20, 25

DISCO. *See* Facility Security Clearance

DNI 25, 91, 92, 319

DoD 4, 21, 41, 58, 62, 63, 75, 76, 97, 112, 137, 138, 161, 162, 186, 187, 188,
198, 200, 212, 213, 238, 262, 276, 287, 295, 319

DoE 92, 319

DSS 20, 21, 22, 25, 30, 43, 47, 50, 55, 59, 61, 62, 63, 64, 65, 66, 67, 69, 75,
76, 79, 80, 81, 84, 86, 87, 90, 91, 92, 94, 95, 98, 100, 101, 106, 107,
109, 119, 151, 155, 157, 158, 162, 163, 164, 165, 167, 168, 169, 174,
193, 196, 202, 203, 205, 210, 211, 216, 217, 218, 219, 223, 224, 228,
229, 230, 234, 236, 238, 239, 250, 251, 252, 253, 254, 255, 256, 257,
259, 271, 272, 274, 275, 284, 287, 289, 296, 302, 309, 310, 311, 319

E

EAA 319

EAR 240, 241, 244, 263

Electronic Questionnaires for Investigations Processing 66

emergency kit bags 144, 145

EO 12356 24

EO 13526 27, 28, 29, 34, 35

e-QIP 66, 68

Escort 315

Executive Order 12829 21, 23, 39, 41

Executive Order 13526 27, 39, 41, 42

exit briefing 220

Export Administration Regulation 240

Express Mail 108, 198, 200

F

Facility Security Officer 20, 21

FBI 32, 67, 76, 158, 165, 219, 228, 229, 319

FCL 8, 9, 22, 43, 59, 60, 61, 62, 64, 65, 74, 75, 82, 217, 265, 314, 315, 319

Federal Bureau of Investigation 32, 67, 162, 228

FGI 31, 110, 256, 257, 260, 315, 319

FOCI 56, 61, 64, 217, 319. *See also* Facility Security Clearance

Foreign Government Information 31, 92, 255, 279, 315, 319

Foreign Ownership Control or Influence 61

FOR OFFICIAL USE ONLY 92

Freight Forwarder 315

FSO 20, 21, 22, 23, 25, 36, 40, 43, 44, 45, 46, 47, 48, 49, 50, 51, 52, 53, 54,
55, 56, 57, 58, 62, 63, 65, 66, 67, 68, 75, 77, 78, 79, 80, 81, 85, 89, 90,
91, 92, 94, 96, 99, 100, 101, 102, 103, 105, 106, 107, 109, 110, 111,
113, 128, 139, 140, 141, 144, 150, 151, 152, 154, 155, 156, 157, 158,

159, 160, 163, 165, 168, 193, 194, 195, 196, 200, 202, 203, 204, 206, 208, 209, 210, 211, 215, 216, 217, 218, 219, 220, 222, 223, 225, 227, 228, 232, 233, 234, 235, 236, 237, 254, 255, 256, 259, 260, 265, 266, 267, 268, 269, 270, 272, 273, 275, 276, 277, 278, 279, 280, 282, 283, 284, 285, 286, 287, 291, 292, 293, 294, 295, 296, 297, 298, 299, 300, 301, 302, 303, 306, 309, 310, 311, 319

G

GCA 9, 43, 60, 61, 63, 64, 65, 77, 80, 81, 84, 85, 86, 87, 88, 91, 92, 93, 94, 95, 96, 131, 133, 192, 198, 201, 203, 204, 205, 210, 239, 250, 252, 253, 254, 255, 257, 260, 274, 313, 315, 316, 319.
General Services Administration 198
general user 168
Government Contracting Activity 8, 30, 60, 77, 89, 198, 315, 319
GSA 50, 51, 52, 80, 105, 110, 119, 147, 151, 152, 153, 179, 202, 279, 294, 319
GSA Approved Overnight Delivery Service 202

H

Handcarrier 315

I

identification 61, 87, 95, 107, 108, 113, 121, 127, 128, 140, 166, 171, 172, 174, 177, 178, 179, 180, 183, 204, 208, 210, 236, 281, 284, 304, 306
Identification Marking 121
IMS 108, 109, 146, 191, 192, 193, 196, 210, 218, 292, 297, 298
Industrial Security 6, 8, 9, 20, 21, 24, 41, 42, 47, 58, 65, 75, 76, 97, 100, 112, 137, 138, 159, 161, 162, 176, 186, 187, 188, 193, 212, 213, 238, 250, 262, 287, 301, 303, 307, 316, 320, 331
Industrial Security Facility Database 100, 193
Industrial Security Letters 47
Industrial Security Professional Certification 301
information management system 107, 113, 139, 256
information management system (IMS) 107, 113
Information Security Oversight Office 24, 26
Information System 163, 168, 305, 316, 319
information systems 163, 165, 167, 168, 179, 184, 185
Information System Security Manager 163, 305
Information System Security Officer 168, 305
Inner Layer 194
Integrity 166
international export 240

International Traffic in Arms Regulation 240
Investigating Security Violations 234
IS 163, 164, 165, 166, 167, 168, 169, 170, 171, 172, 173, 174, 175, 177, 178, 180, 181, 182, 183, 184, 185, 282
IS certification 166, 167
ISFD 100, 193, 196, 202
ISOO 24, 37, 127, 319
ISP 301, 302, 303, 307
ISSM 163, 164, 165, 167, 168, 170, 172, 173, 174, 177, 178, 182, 183, 184, 185, 319
ISSO 168, 170, 172, 174, 177, 178, 182, 183, 184, 319
ITAR 158, 162, 240, 241, 243, 245, 246, 247, 249, 258, 263, 320, 331

J

Joint Personnel Adjudication System 65
JPAS 65, 66, 67, 68, 69, 91, 101, 140, 223, 231, 295, 296. *See also* Facility Security Clearance

K

key 45, 51, 56, 60, 61, 80, 156, 168, 232, 243, 259, 279, 284, 304, 305
Key Management Personnel 60, 61

L

LAA 247, 316, 320
Limited Access Authorization 231, 247, 316, 320
loss 21, 22, 34, 45, 53, 100, 106, 107, 113, 119, 120, 143, 156, 165, 185, 197, 200, 206, 216, 220, 232, 234, 235, 236, 269, 271, 272, 281, 303, 304

M

magnet 278, 300
Metrics 269, 270, 271, 274, 275, 276, 277, 279, 280
MFO 316, 320

N

NACLC 66, 68, 90, 320
National Agency Check with Local Agency Check and Credit Check 66
National Industrial Security Program 20, 21, 24, 25, 40, 41, 42
National Industrial Security Program Operating Manual 21, 25, 41
National Industrial Security Program Policy Advisory Committee 24
national security 20, 21, 22, 23, 25, 27, 28, 29, 30, 31, 32, 33, 34, 35, 37, 39
National Security Council 24

need to know 38, 40, 63, 65, 86, 91, 109, 111, 115, 118, 119, 127, 139, 140, 150, 151, 153, 155, 157, 172, 175, 176, 177, 179, 180, 181, 182, 183, 184, 185, 192, 204, 229, 247, 251, 298

Need to Know 1, 3, 4, 316

NISP 20, 21, 23, 24, 25, 26, 27, 29, 30, 35, 39, 40, 56, 62, 65, 157, 175, 219, 223, 291, 320

NISPOM 9, 21, 22, 25, 27, 37, 39, 40, 41, 43, 44, 46, 47, 50, 51, 54, 55, 56, 57, 58, 60, 62, 63, 68, 77, 79, 80, 85, 86, 92, 95, 99, 102, 103, 107, 126, 128, 141, 142, 143, 144, 146, 147, 152, 153, 155, 157, 158, 159, 162, 172, 175, 177, 179, 189, 191, 192, 194, 200, 201, 210, 215, 216, 217, 219, 233, 246, 247, 249, 253, 258, 265, 269, 271, 274, 276, 277, 279, 285, 292, 296, 297, 302, 310, 311, 314, 320, 331

NISPPAC 24, 25

Non-possessing 81, 140, 141

NSA 89, 94, 140, 179, 198, 199, 211, 320

NSC 24

O

OADR 35, 135, 320

OCA 19, 21, 28, 29, 30, 33, 34, 35, 36, 38, 39, 41, 115, 117, 121, 122, 127

OCP 306, 307

ODAA 165, 167, 185, 189

Office of Designated Approval Authority 165, 189

OPSEC 32, 86, 94, 95, 306, 307

OPSEC Certified Professional 306, 307

Original Classification Authority 21, 29, 316

Outer Layer 195

Overall Marking 121

Oversight 24, 26, 62, 127, 159, 212

P

Page Marking 121, 122

PCL 22, 44, 59, 65, 67, 74, 310, 313, 316, 320

Personnel (Security) Clearance 316, 320

Personnel Security Clearance 22

Physical Security Professional 304, 305

Portion Marking 121, 122

Possessing facilities 88, 141, 191

Postal Service 100, 191, 198, 200, 201, 204

PR 67, 68, 72

Prime Contractor 9, 59, 82, 84, 316

privileged user 168

Protection Level 175, 176, 185
Protection Profile Table 176
Protective Security Service 201, 316
PSP 304, 305

Q

Questionnaire for National Security Positions 65, 295

R

Rail 206
receipt 91, 99, 104, 105, 106, 107, 108, 109, 110, 111, 113, 128, 193, 195,
196, 197, 199, 202, 203, 205, 211, 217, 232, 254, 255
reporting 24, 37, 44, 45, 47, 56, 72, 107, 132, 158, 159, 178, 181, 182, 199,
215, 216, 220, 223, 228, 234, 266, 270, 271, 282
Resource Control 176, 181
restricted area 150, 160, 217
Restricted Area 317
RFP 77, 317, 320
RFQ 77, 317, 320
risk assessment. *See* Facility Security Clearance
Risk Assessment 50

S

Sanitization 170
SCG 34, 36, 37, 63, 78, 79, 81, 87, 93, 95, 108, 114, 127, 129, 132, 157, 218
SCI 25, 66, 91, 92, 96, 179, 320
SCIF 50, 92, 320. *See also* Facility Security Clearance
SECRET 8, 9, 27, 28, 29, 30, 34, 37, 40, 41, 48, 50, 51, 66, 68, 81, 82, 85, 88,
90, 94, 99, 104, 106, 107, 108, 110, 114, 115, 116, 117, 118, 121, 122,
123, 124, 125, 126, 128, 129, 131, 132, 133, 135, 136, 144, 145, 146,
147, 151, 152, 157, 165, 170, 173, 175, 184, 185, 191, 192, 194, 196,
198, 199, 200, 201, 202, 211, 212, 222, 249, 254, 257, 279, 314, 316,
317, 318
security awareness training 20, 23, 45, 54, 158, 221, 228, 270
security classification guide 34, 36, 38
Security Classification Guide 36, 78, 135, 317
Security Containers 152
Security Documentation 176, 182
Security in Depth 317
security plan 45, 47, 63, 167, 173
Security Testing 183, 184
Security Violation 317

Sensitive Compartmented Information Facility 50, 91
Separation of Functions 176
Session Controls 176, 181
SF 86 66, 67, 68, 72, 295, 296
SF 312 38, 159, 220, 223, 231, 237, 238, 295
spillage 165, 167, 175
SSBI 66, 68, 90, 320
SSP 173, 182, 184, 185, 311, 320
Standard Form 86. *See* Facility Security Clearance
Standard Practice Procedures 317
Subcontract 317
Subcontractor 317
Subject and Title Marking 121
System Assurance 176, 183
System Recovery 176, 183
system security plan 173

T

TCO 240, 320
TCP 251, 259, 320
threat awareness briefing 158
TOP SECRET 8, 27, 28, 29, 34, 48, 50, 66, 68, 81, 82, 85, 88, 90, 99, 104,
    107, 110, 115, 118, 121, 122, 123, 124, 128, 131, 144, 145, 146, 147,
    151, 152, 165, 175, 184, 185, 191, 192, 194, 198, 199, 200, 202, 211,
    222, 257, 318
TP 320
training 19, 20, 22, 23, 24, 28, 29, 33, 40, 45, 54, 56, 81, 90, 106, 107, 116,
    120, 123, 125, 126, 127, 130, 131, 132, 133, 134, 157, 158, 159, 160,
    162, 165, 167, 168, 204, 215, 216, 217, 218, 219, 221, 222, 223, 224,
    225, 226, 228, 231, 232, 235, 237, 238, 240, 245, 246, 269, 270, 273,
    276, 281, 285, 286, 289, 294, 295, 296, 301, 302, 306
transmission 39, 100, 102, 103, 128, 146, 177, 180, 192, 196, 199, 211, 212
Transportation Plan 320
TS 66, 123, 124

U

unauthorized access 53, 103, 151, 157, 166, 174, 178, 179, 211, 217, 231,
    232, 255
unauthorized disclosure 20, 21, 25, 27, 28, 29, 33, 38, 39, 40, 44, 61, 63, 64,
    100, 102, 103, 105, 107, 113, 119, 127, 129, 139, 144, 165, 166, 194,
    217, 218, 219, 221, 228, 240, 247, 248, 257, 272
Unauthorized Person 318

uncleared facilities. *See* Facility Security Clearance
Uncleared Facilities 59
United States Munitions List 241
US citizen 43
USML 243, 244
US Person 246, 318
USPS 109, 198, 200, 202, 203, 204, 212, 294

V

violation 85, 103, 105, 141, 153, 222, 228, 230, 234, 235, 236, 248, 272, 273, 286

W

Working Papers 146

ABOUT RED BIKE PUBLISHING

Our company is registered as a government contractor company with the CCR and VetBiz (DUNS 826859691). Specifically we are a service disabled veteran owned small business. Red Bike Publishing provides high quality books and include the following which can be found at www.redbikepublishing.com and Amazon.com:

NATIONAL SECURITY TOPICS

1. DoD Security Clearances and Contracts Guidebook ISBN 978-1-936800-80-3 and ISBN 978-1-936800-99-5
2. Insider's Guide to Security Clearances ISBN: 9781936800988
3. ISP Certification-The Industrial Security Professional Exam Manual ISBN: 9780981620602
4. National Industrial Security Program Operating Manual (NISPOM) ISBN: 978098162060857
5. International Traffic in Arms Regulation (ITAR) ISBN: 97809816288

Training Topics-Available at www.redbikepublishing.com

1. NISOM Training
2. Derivative Classifier Training
3. ISP Certification Study Tips

PUBLISHING

Get Rich in a Niche-The Insider's Guide to Self-Publishing in a Specialized Industry ISBN: 978-1-936800-04-9

OTHER TOPICS/NOVELS

1. Rainy Street Stories-Reflections on Secret Wars, Espionage and Terrorism ISBN: 978-1-936800-10-0
2. Commitment-A Novel ASIN: B0057U3GLS

ARMY TOPICS

1. Ranger Handbook SH 21-76 ISBN-13: 978-1936800087
2. US Army Physical Readiness Training TC 3.22-20 ISBN:97809816240
3. US Army Physical Fitness Training FM 21-20 ISBN:97809816240
4. US Army Leadership FM 6-22 ISBN: 978-0981620671
5. US Army Drill and Ceremonies FM 3-21.5 ISBN: 978-1936800025

CPSIA information can be obtained
at www.ICGtesting.com
Printed in the USA
BVHW041143220920
589371BV00014B/368